GEORGIAN
BRIGHTON

The view looking down from the east side of the Old Steine, roughly where St James's Street is now, shows Russell House and the bathing machines in the mid-1760s, together with the *Castle Inn* and the site to the north on which the Royal Pavilion was developed. From 'A Perspective View of Brighthelmston and of the Sea Coast as far as the Isle of Wight' by Jas. Lambert.

GEORGIAN BRIGHTON

Sue Berry

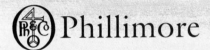

Phillimore

2005

Published by
PHILLIMORE & CO. LTD
Shopwyke Manor Barn, Chichester, West Sussex, England

ISBN 1 86077 342 7

Printed and bound in Great Britain by
CAMBRIDGE PRINTING

Contents

List of Illustrations

Acknowledgements

When a town's historic resources have been treated with such scant regard by the various layers of local government as Brighton's were for many years, a tragic consequence is the loss not only of public administrative documents but also local business records, letters and deeds. One result of this lack of an archive has been a tendency to dismiss the early history of Brighton and the buildings which survive as a testimony to it as unimportant. The lack of a collections policy allied with effective cataloguing of what has been rescued has only recently been remedied by the appointment of an archives officer attached to the East Sussex Record Office and paid for by the residents of the City of Brighton and Hove.

Authors always depend upon the goodwill and time of others. I would particularly like to thank Helen Glass, June Knight, Jan Lank, Ron Martin and Henry Smith for their help and enthusiasm. Pauline Colwell, Jennifer Nash and Anne Hart of the Search Room at East Sussex Record Office were especially helpful with finding documentary references. Many members of Adult Education classes run at the Friends Centre in Brighton asked questions that helped me to think about what the scope of this book should be. Jim Johnston and Alec Sidney inspired my interest in the history of landscapes and how people shape them. My husband Pat deserves my deepest appreciation of his support and faith in this project as papers and pictures moved from house to house. Simon Thraves of Phillimore has done his best to turn a renegade academic into a clear writer. Any failure to make this a readable book that contributes to our understanding of an utterly fascinating topic – the regeneration of a declining seaside town by the arrival of wealthy tourists – is mine.

Introduction

Between 1740 and 1780 Brighton was transformed from a decayed seafaring town into a prosperous seaside resort. By the time that George, Prince of Wales (the eldest son of George III) made his first visit in 1783 Brighton was already an important place to visit. By 1800 the resort was Britain's largest and most fashionable seaside watering place, a position which has been maintained into the 21st century.

The key period for the emergence of Georgian seaside resorts is between about 1730 and 1780 when Brighton's main competitors, Margate, Scarborough and Weymouth, were all developing at roughly the same pace as Brighton, with Hastings lagging a little behind them. After 1780 Brighton outpaced her competitors and had the full panoply of resort facilities. Between 1780 and 1820 the most important theme in Brighton's story is the building of new suburbs to accommodate the influx of visitors and the people that were needed to supply the specialist resort and normal urban facilities. These two themes are key to our understanding of Brighton during this period and both influence the way in which the town grew.

This is a study of the people and myriad of mainly small-scale projects which transformed a poverty stricken coastal town into a lively and famous Georgian resort. By 1820 the lifestyle and the scale of the architecture were both on the threshold of an enormous change. Brighton lost the intimacy of the small and densely populated Georgian resort. The new lifestyle was symbolised by the construction of Brunswick Town and Kemp Town, which were attached like a pair of wings to either end of the Georgian town in the early 1820s and drew the wealthiest visitors away from the earlier and smaller scale Georgian centre, and is another story.

Brighton: Fishing Town to
Declining Town c.1580-1740

Brighton was one of the many small ports along the south coast of England that flourished during the 16th and much of the 17th centuries and then declined. The development of Brighton's fishing and coastal carrying trade is worth exploring briefly, for the town's earlier history influenced the location of the first facilities for tourists. Its earlier history as a trading community also helped to ensure that Brighton had links which assisted the development of tourism.

By 1580 Brighton was a small fishing town consisting of three principal outer streets and one inner street called Middle Street. Most of the inner part of the town consisted of an open space called Hempshares in which Black Lion, Market and Ship Streets developed. A market place stood on the cliff top and just on its northern side were clusters of buildings which marked the beginnings of Ship and Black Lion Streets, both of which were named after inns. Paths led down the cliffs to the broad beach. On the beach stood a collection of about ninety 'shops' (tall, narrow wooden buildings for storing fishing nets), deezes (wooden buildings in which fish were smoked), capstans (which were used to haul boats out of the English Channel onto the beach) and a few cottages.[1]

The town was surrounded by its own farmland which occupied the rest of the parish. Only a small number of townsfolk worked on the 1,300 acres, of which about a third was arable, the remainder being mostly sheep pasture. By the late 16th century the number of landowners and farmers was declining quite quickly, a change that was common to most of the downland communities.[2]

Immigration to Brighton

During the 16th century Sussex shared with other parts of England the problem of rising unemployment as the country's population increased faster than prospects of employment. Simultaneously the demand for labour in some parts of the county declined; for example, agricultural practices on the downland areas of Sussex were becoming less labour intensive. Close control of many rural communities by landowners and by farmers meant that many of the unemployed had to seek housing and employment wherever this power was not exerted. By the 1580s, because of lack of employment in the region surrounding the town, Brighton's population rose. The opportunities offered by the expanding fishing industry (upon which the town depended) and the prospect of finding accommodation both attracted immigrants. In spite of attempts by some of the absentee landowners, there was no control over letting and the development of housing. The fishing industry provided employment

1   *A perspective view of Brighthelmston and of the Sea Coast as far as the Isle of Wight.* Jas. Lambert pinxt/P. Canot sculpt. Copper engraving by 1765. The earliest engraved view of the resort. The second edition was published in Edward's topographical *Surveys through Surrey Sussex and Kent* (1817) and was folded to fit into a folio sized book.

for a substantial part of the year and it could be supplemented by other work such as the coastal trade.[3]

The Fishing Industry

Consumption of fish increased in western Europe in the 16th century and, as a result, both the Scarborough cod and Yarmouth herring industries expanded, attracting fishing fleets from the coasts of Sussex and Kent. Vessels were financed by using ship shares in multiples of 32nds, a method widely used in western Europe. The money for purchasing shares was probably raised from the profits of previous voyages or by loans (in the form of bonds) and mortgages on property. People with shares in the boats and in the nets being used on them received part of the profits when they were distributed at the end of a voyage. Details of the local arrangements were described in the Customal of 1580, which laid down how taxes were paid and the town was to be run.[4]

Initially fishermen from Brighton fished for both cod and for herring in the North Sea. The fishing seasons were called 'fares' and in the mid-1500s the Scarborough Fare for cod was at its most popular with the fishermen from Brighton. Yet some thirty years later Scarborough Fare had declined in popularity, the town's fishing cycle being dominated by Yarmouth Fare for herring. This took place between September and November. The growth of the fleet for Yarmouth Fare was rapid. In 1559 only seven boats went to Yarmouth but in the 1570s there were about twenty, each having a crew of about ten. The fleet then grew more slowly, reaching a peak of about fifty boats in the 1650s with a total of about 500 men and boys. The fishermen sold their fish to the merchants of Yarmouth for curing. Relations with the merchants were not always amicable, Brighton's fishermen opposing attempts by Yarmouth to extend control of the industry.[5]

During the 1660s the rapid decline of Brighton's role in the herring industry began. The profitability of long-distance fishing was undermined by falling prices

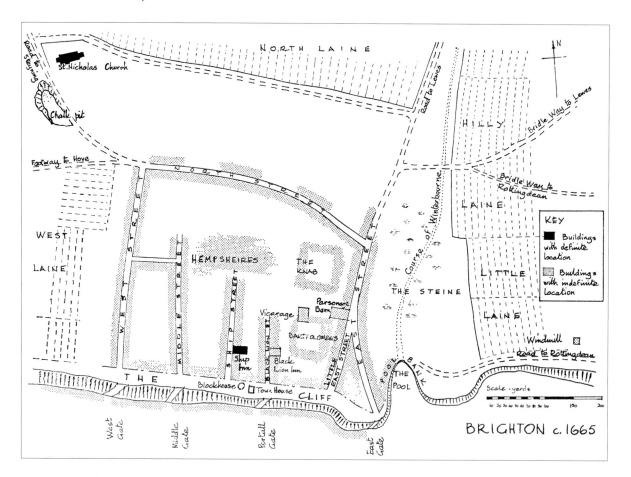

The map image contains the following labels:

NORTH LAINE

St. Nicholas Church

Chalk pit

Footway to Hove

WEST LAINE

NORTH STREET

HEMPSHEIRES

THE KNAB

EAST STREET

Vicerage

Parsonage Barn

BARTHOLOMEWS

Ship Inn

Black Lion Inn

SHIP STREET

MIDDLE STREET

WEST STREET

Blockhouse

Town House

THE CLIFF

West Gate

Middle Gate

Portall Gate

East Gate

Course of Winterbourne

HILLY

Bridle Way to Lewes

Road to Lewes

Bridle Way to Rottingdean

LAINE

LITTLE

THE STEINE

LAINE

POOL BANK

THE POOL

Windmill

Road to Rottingdean

Scale - yards

10 20 30 40 50 60 70 80 90 100   150   200

KEY

■ Buildings with definite location

▨ Buildings with indefinite location

BRIGHTON c. 1665

2 Brighton in about 1660. Sketch map by Ron Martin based on research using contemporary archives.

for the catch from the Yarmouth merchants. Fleets from the south coast were faced with the additional problem of attacks by French and Dutch privateers. During the reign of Charles I and the Commonwealth the town petitioned the government for naval protection for its fishing fleet. The Commonwealth recognised the national importance of the town's fishing and trading activities, because of the number of skilled sailors who were valuable for the manning of naval ships, but the privateers overwhelmed small naval vessels, one with about thirty sailors aboard being overpowered by a French vessel with 180 sailors. The English sailors were taken to France and then released from Dieppe. Naval escorts of one or two boats were regularly arranged, the vessels remaining with the fleet in the North Sea and then escorting them back, but after 1660 naval support seems to have ended.[6]

By the late 1650s the beaches at Brighton were suffering from serious erosion and boats were moved to new moorings in the estuary of the River Adur at Shoreham. Erosion of the beach must always have been a problem but it accelerated from about 1630. Between about 1630 and 1665 the manor of Brighton-Lewes (which held the right to grant space on the beach) lost 22 tenements (tenement meaning plot of land), including buildings and stakeplaces (where the boats rested and the capstans stood), and granted 59 plots from the manor's waste, mainly on the town's south-eastern side, as compensation. The total number of tenements on the beach was 144 in 1665. Erosion must have accelerated in the late 1600s for in 1703 only three tenements are recorded.[7] During the 1680s only 30 boats went to Yarmouth and the size of the fleet then fell quickly, the last tiny fleet of four vessels sailing to Yarmouth in 1697.[8] The other fares were local ones but they were never very significant, partly because of the lack of accessible markets. The nearest town was Lewes, eight miles away, and the rural population in the downland villages was too scattered to make the sale of fish economic.

By the early 1600s the fishermen were using the profits from fishing to buy coal from Newcastle to sell along the south coast, thus extending the period when their boats were in use and improving their profitability. They also continued the long established tradition of coastal and cross-Channel trading. In 1569 Thomas Bishop petitioned the government for compensation for goods which were taken from him in France. In the early 1600s Brighton's boats were carrying goods for the naval victuallers, transporting gunpowder to Portsmouth and taking Portland stone to London for Inigo Jones' work on the old St Paul's Cathedral.[9]

Seafaring

As the herring trade declined the town tried to increase its role in coastal trading. In order to compete with other ports that were moving into this trade in the late 1600s Brighton's mariners needed to buy larger cargo boats. These only needed small crews and so, by the end of the century, although Brighton had the biggest cargo fleet on the south coast, it could not absorb the local labour force and unemployment rose.

The fleet carried mainly coal and corn but also a miscellany of goods such as salt, grindstones and barley. The port books which survive from the 1660s reveal that trade had a seasonal pattern, coal being carried from mid-March to late August and corn from December to June. The peak of the coal carrying trade was reached about 1716 and from then decline was rapid because of competition from ports along the east coast such as Scarborough, which could afford even bigger boats. As unemployment increased the workforce drifted away from Brighton, some moving to London to join vessels operating from there and others joining the Royal Navy.[10]

The town's trading vessels played a significant role in the gathering of naval intelligence in the 17th century. Even when England was at war with France, vessels from Brighton went about their business with the French. Correspondents at ports where the Brighton boats put in on their way back from France sent information to London. As well as garnering news of French ships, the government also learnt from this system the position of ships belonging to the Navy.[11]

Unfortunately, privateers were as much a problem for the town's trading activities as they were for its fishing. Complaints, principally about privateers, and requests for escorts were taken seriously during the Commonwealth, although normally action does not seem to have been taken until vessels loaded with grain went into a port en route, such as Newhaven or Rye, and then refused to sail without escort. Cargo boats crossing the Channel were less easy to protect, but they too tried to travel in the company of other boats. In 1677 a ketch from Brighton, which was returning from Holland loaded with spices and other goods, was boarded off Ushant even though it was travelling with others. Two vessels described as 'men of war' from Algiers put 'six Turks' on the ketch, but later a French man-of-war intercepted it.

The men from Brighton told the French what had happened and said they had been mistreated by the Turks. After they sailed into La Rochelle the Englishmen were set free to return to Brighton but the French kept the boat.[12]

The inhabitants of Brighton regarded vessels driven upon the shore as another source of income and rapidly removed anything from wrecks which they regarded as useful, even though wrecks were legally the property of the state. In 1630, by the time a representative had got to Brighton from Lewes, a vessel had been pulled apart and, with the exception of the guns, the goods had been distributed amongst the townsfolk. Only the government of the Commonwealth period managed to retrieve most of the content of boats, and their method was to pay those who cooperated for their efforts. Ambrose and Henry Smith were told in 1652 that they would be paid for retrieving marble from a wrecked Dutch boat.[13]

It is probable that the government kept a careful eye on the Brighton area after 1651. Local Royalist sympathy appears to have been one reason why Colonel Gunter came to Brighton to arrange the escape of Prince Charles (eventually Charles II) after the Battle of Worcester, attempts to do so having failed in ports farther west. In 1659 Colonel Fagge and the other militia commissioners of the county were told to keep an eye on the area because Colonel Culpepper of Kent was seen in the town and he was suspected of a Royalist plot with others in the Brighton area.[14]

The Navy Commissioners also had occasional problems with pilfering. In 1667 someone must have informed against George Hodder and Richard Marchant who were found to have in their houses sails which had been stolen from the *Royal Sovereign*, a naval vessel at Portsmouth. Brighton had a reputation for such activities and the Navy Commissioners were advised to keep someone there as a deterrent.[15]

Urban Development

The varied fortunes of the town's maritime economy were reflected in its urban development. Between 1550 and 1640, as the fishing and cargo carrying trade expanded, the population increased from about 1,000 to 4,000 and the demand for houses led to infilling within the existing streets. Building began to encroach on to the Hempshares, and Ship Street, Black Lion Street, the Knabb and Little East Street developed slowly. The town's business centre was the market place on the cliff top between Black Lion and Ship Streets. On the south side of the market square stood the town hall, which was removed by erosion in about 1720. On the north side of the market place, facing the town hall, stood some service buildings which included a butcher, a slaughter house, a lime house, a herring house and five inns, the *Old* and the *New Ship*, the *Dolphin*, the *Castle* (East Street) and the *Blue Anchor*.

The town's only defence against invaders was the blockhouse, a circular building about 18 feet high and 50 feet in diameter, with walls about seven feet thick, which stood on the cliff top near the town hall with the town clock on its roof. The top floor of the block house was a magazine and the bottom a dungeon. The gun garden on the south side of the block house had room for four cannon, and building in the line of fire was officially prohibited – although at least one person did so.

Access to the beach below the cliffs was by paths. On the cliff top there may have been gates as the tops of the paths were referred to as 'gates' or 'gaps'. These would prevent small children and pigs wandering down to the beach. The only clear

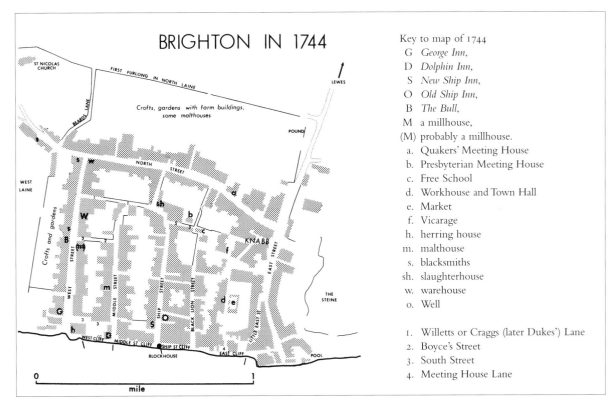

BRIGHTON IN 1744

Key to map of 1744

G *George Inn*,
D *Dolphin Inn*,
S *New Ship Inn*,
O *Old Ship Inn*,
B *The Bull*,
M a millhouse,
(M) probably a millhouse.

a. Quakers' Meeting House
b. Presbyterian Meeting House
c. Free School
d. Workhouse and Town Hall
e. Market
f. Vicarage
h. herring house
m. malthouse
s. blacksmiths
sh. slaughterhouse
w. warehouse
o. Well

1. Willetts or Craggs (later Dukes') Lane
2. Boyce's Street
3. South Street
4. Meeting House Lane

evidence of a substantial gate refers to the portal or East Street gate which faced towards the Pool Valley. Due to the erosion of the seafront, by 1727 the market place had been removed to Black Lion Street where, in that year, a new town hall with a work house was built.[16] The relocation of the market place resulted in the opening of the *Thatched House Inn* in Black Lion Street. Other occupations which required specific buildings or equipment in the town included ropemaking (the ropewalk was on the cliff top), tanning, smithing, lime making (a quarry was south-west of St Nicholas Church) and milling. In the early 1700s there was a shop selling textiles called the warehouse and amongst the tradesmen were cordwainers, haberdashers, tailors and bakers. Some of the retailers and craftsmen had dual occupations. This strongly suggests that they could not make a living in this declining community by depending upon just one.[17]

The system of urban landholding enabled development to take place quickly as the demand for accommodation increased. Most of the land was held by copyholders, who were able to extend, infill, subdivide and sublet their properties in response to the rising demand for housing, although they had to pay the freeholder (the lord of the manor) for permission.[18] In 1580 the lords of the manors who had land in Brighton expressed their concern in the Customal about the way in which townsfolk were providing extra accommodation. They thought that the number of people requiring support from the parish would increase.

Early manorial records are too slight, but by the 1660s there is enough evidence to prove that urban copyholders were very responsive to changes in the town's

3 Brighton in 1740, based on research using freehold and manorial records.

fortunes. Coincidental with the loss of the undercliff was the decline in property dealing within the town recorded in the manorial records. The number of land transactions declined during the late 17th and early 18th centuries. The higher level of activity from the late 1740s reflects an increase in speculative investment and lending money on mortgages. Immigrants arrived and bought land too, helping to push up turnover and prices.[19] The estimates of population imply that the number of residents continues to decline, but the conservative multiplier of 4.5 people per household has been used, which does not take account of the common practice of subletting rooms to families, nor does it allow for lodgers and servants. None of the buildings from this period survives in Brighton and the documentary evidence is fragmentary. It seems likely that the houses were timber-framed, the timber probably purchased from the Weald of Sussex. The locality's main building materials were chalk (which was too soft for exterior work), flint from the fields, shingle from the beaches and brickearth for brickmaking. Some imported materials were used, including pantiles from Holland.

Religion and Education

Until the 17th century, the parish church of St Nicolas, which stood alone to the north-west of the town on a low hill, was the only religious building serving the community. By 1660 a nonconformist school was established, followed in 1683 by the Presbyterian chapel (which still stands in Union Street). By 1701 the Quakers had a meeting house and burial ground in North Street (the predecessor of the present one in Ship Street). In the early 18th century a Church of England school, supported by the SPCK, taught navigation. Until 1726 the school stood in Black Lion Street.[21]

Brighton's Population c.1565-1821

Date	Information	Total Population
1565	200 Households	950
1580	102 rated landsmen	1450
c.1630	Nearly 600 families	2800
1657	About 4000 souls	4000
1676	2000 of communicant age	3340
1724	500 houses	2375
1744	454 houses	2380
1747	410 houses	2150
1753	407 houses	2140
1761	400 families and 35 people in the poor house	2035
1770	598 houses	3140
1786	3620	3620
1794	1233 houses	5669
1801	census	7339
1811	census	12012
1821	census	24429

Sources for table in order of use.
PRO SP12/39/11; Brighton Customs 1580; Cox, T., *Magna Britannia et Hibernia* V (1730), 510; Welch, C.E., 'Commonwealth Union of Benefices in Sussex', *SNQ* 15 (1959), 116; Cooper, J.H., 'A religious census of Sussex in 1676', *SAC* 45 (1903), 144; WSRO EP1/26/3, Bishop Bower's Visitation; Bishop, J.G., *A peep into the past; Brighton in Olden Times* 1744-1761 (Brighton, 1895), 21; Relhan, A., *A Short History of Brighton* (1761) reprinted by Michell, J.C. in 1829; [Dunvan, P.], *A short history of Lewes and Brighthelmston* (Lewes, 1795), 490, 553; Barron, W.A., 'Gleanings from Sussex Archives', *Sussex County Magazine* 26 (1952), 606; *British Parliamentary Papers* 1801-2 census.

Local Government

Little about local government before 1580 has been found. A vestry was responsible for the upkeep of the church and the court leet dealt with minor offences. The town did not have a Justice of the Peace in residence, the nearest being at Patcham, a village a few miles to the north. Quarter Sessions were held at Lewes. Matters affecting the land were referred to the manor courts which appear to have been primarily concerned with boundaries and division of property in the few instances where they had a role.

In 1580 the Customal specified how the town was to be governed and how the rate charges should be apportioned between the two dominant sectors of the community at that date, the farmers and the fishermen. The churchwardens were to represent the two interests, the vicar and the constable and the 'chief of the town' choosing them. The 'chief of the town' appear to have been the same 12 inhabitants who were appointed to assist the constable and to keep order within specific sectors of Brighton. The Constable and the Twelve (as they were called) were to be responsible to the View of Frankpledge, the highest court in the Barony of Lewes, to which the manor of Brighton-Lewes belonged. By 1613 members of the Twelve were serving on the View of Frankpledge, presumably because they were attracted by the status which they thought the role gave them.[22] The Customs were revised in 1619 and the last mention of the Twelve is in 1641, which suggests that the arrangements seem to have fallen into disuse. By 1690 the vestry consisted of the constable, three churchwardens, four headboroughs and four overseers of the poor and they ran the administration of the parish until 1773.[23]

5 *View of Brighthelmstone in Sussex* from *Walpole's New and Complete British Traveller.* Copper, 1784. This gives an impression of the seafront before the development of the sea defences but after the loss of the wide beach on which small seafaring boats could be kept.

Decline c.1660-1740

The erosion of the town's beach resulted in the loss of the blockhouse and other buildings which stood on the cliff top and the town sought to prevent any further losses. Concern about the cost of sea defences resulted in a petition to the Justices for assistance in 1676, but this may not have been the first application. In 1690 the town successfully claimed that it could not support its own poor and the Justices, in Quarter Sessions, responded by rating five neighbouring parishes for the town's relief. By 1703 the money was not being paid. Four of the parishes which had been rated, plus another, were instructed to pay, but three of them successfully avoided payment by proving that they were under pressure from their own poor. Brighton's problems were compounded by a period of stormy weather that so concerned a member of the vestry that they recorded two incidents in the minute book. In 1703 houses were damaged, two windmills were blown over, lead on the church roof was turned up and several ships which belonged to the town were wrecked. In 1705 the tempest was considered to be as bad as the 1703 storm. It, too, began after midnight and lasted about eight hours. Not only were healthy trees blown over, houses damaged and lead on the church roof turned up, but ships belonging to the town but moored at Portsmouth were blown onshore and damaged and men and vessels were lost.[24]

Brighton continued to ask the local Justices of the Peace for help. From 1704-5 another eight parishes were rated and five more were added in 1706, but again the problem of maintaining their own poor was used as a reason for exemption. In 1708 the Justices levied a single 1½d. rate on the eastern rapes of Sussex. Instead of several hundred pounds being paid to the parish officers, a Justice was made responsible for the money that was collected. In the 1740s about three-quarters of householders were exempted from paying rates which indicates the economic difficulties and the pressure upon ratepayers.[25]

One of the most dramatic signs of the town's decline was its loss of population, although the estimates in the table (p.9) probably over-emphasise the peaks and troughs. It is more likely that the town's population reached a peak of about 3,500 by the mid-1600s which was maintained for some years before decline began. The baptismal data from the parish register suggests that a trough was reached in the 1730s and that by the 1750s recovery was under way, but the register is inaccurate, some baptisms, marriages and burials being unrecorded. Yet there is enough evidence to show that the town's economic decline affected its demographic profile. The community aged because young people and families with children emigrated to look for work and so the birth rate fell. The number of baptisms listed in the Anglican register during the 1680s was 82 a year. It fell to 55 during the 1690s and the totals for both the Anglican and the Presbyterian registers in the decades between 1700 and 1730 were 60, 59 and 63.[26]

From the 1650s the record of probate (wills, inventories and administrations) suggests that the town's occupational structure narrowed. Compared with the smaller but longer established coastal towns such as Hastings, or inland market towns like Steyning, late 17th-century Brighton had a limited range of trades.[27] As the number of fishermen declined and the numbers of mariners increased, the demand for services fell away. When the town was dominated by fishing it undertook boat repairs and building and supplied goods for the boats such as ropes. Most of the boats on which the mariners were employed were kept and maintained elsewhere. The rope maker was probably kept in business by the needs of the farmers, the local carrier and inshore fishermen rather than by the coastal boats, which were registered as from Brighton but were too big to beach safely for maintenance.

By the 1730s Brighton was desperately in need of employment for the ageing population. The lack of sea defences meant that the coast was eroding, but that also enabled bathing machines to be hauled down the crumbling cliffs to the beach. The combination of access to the sea, cheap accommodation and proximity to London compared with most other declining ports helps to explain Brighton's emergence as a seaside resort, but nothing would have happened without the emergence of the fashion for sea bathing amongst people who could afford it.

2
Why did Seaside Resorts Emerge?

The enormous increase in national wealth during the 18th century funded not only grand country houses but also an urban revolution. Towns became more prosperous, many were better run and the number of people who chose to live in them rose because town life offered something that the countryside could not. Without these major social and economic changes, seaside resorts could not have happened and Brighton may have continued to decline.

Wealth and Urban Development

Georgian England was increasingly a nation of town dwellers. The widening range of employment and, for those who could afford them, leisure facilities acted as magnets for country people of all backgrounds. The urban population of Britain nearly trebled between the late 1600s and 1801, when 42 per cent of the nation's rising population lived in towns. Britain became the most urbanised nation in Europe. In addition to the migration to towns, by 1800 more people had lived in them for short periods than was the case in 1700. Commerce, industry and services all expanded rapidly in urban areas between 1650 and 1750, so boosting the market for leisure activities. Internal and overseas trade is thought to have trebled in value and much of the employment associated with it was in towns, especially ports.[1] This economic activity stimulated significant improvements in road and water transport which greatly facilitated the growth of resorts.[2]

London was not only the nation's political centre but also its largest manufacturing and processing centre. The increase in the number of large towns helped to reduce London's impact but the capital's population still grew substantially, from about 575,000 in 1700 to around 900,000 in 1800 and 1.25 million in 1821. The enormous variety of goods that were imported and the innovation of its inhabitants ensured that it continued to dominate the production and provision of sophisticated consumer goods. It was a very good market for the seaside resorts that developed in Sussex and along the coastline of north and north-east Kent. As transport systems improved, access became so convenient that these coastlines were ideally suited for short trips to the seaside by visitors to the capital wanting a change of scene and a break from the noise and congestion of the densely packed city.[3]

Successful towns developed a civic culture, a fashion for public display and a taste for commercial entertainment, many of the ideas being pioneered in London. They became social and consumer centres offering luxury shops and services. The most successful, such as York, were some distance from London and became magnets

for people who wished to enjoy such a lifestyle and so their populations expanded. The demand for public facilities and better run towns meant that smaller towns declined, for they could not support the range of public improvements, such as street lighting, that were expected. Successful resorts had therefore to compete not only with London but also with provincial towns, and achieve the size to ensure that enough facilities could be supported to match or surpass their competitors.[4] It was the spa resorts such as Bath, Epsom and Tunbridge Wells which managed to identify the major urban amenities needed in a resort town and to set the standards that successful seaside resorts then emulated.[5]

6   *Bathing Machines* by T. Rowlandson from *An excursion to Brighthelmstone* by H. Wigstead and T. Rowlandson, 1790.

The season at a resort was fitted into a lifestyle that for wealthy people became ever more urban, even if for some a country estate was still an aspiration. In spite of the money that was spent on country houses, especially in the earlier part of the 18th century, fewer landowners remained on their estates during the winter. They spent more time in the nearest county town or regional centre and in London, where access to Parliament, government posts and the increasingly sophisticated trading opportunities were important sources of income.[6] Spas were visited in the late summer and the autumn, and in due course the seaside resort competed for the same time slots. Both the spa and the seaside resort became popular places for women to live.[7]

The Acceptance of Standardised Terraces

The success of spa resorts was also partly due to the acceptance of standardised terraced housing based upon simplified concepts of classical architecture. In the late 17th century terraces, crescents and squares such as St James's Square and Bloomsbury Square, were successfully established in London as an alternative to detached town houses for the wealthy. Terraced housing, as illustrated by the effective development of the Georgian suburbs of Bath, had several advantages for resorts. The homogeneity of façade provided a suitable setting for the resorts' important integrative social role. Terraces were relatively cheap and quick to build compared with detached or semi-detached houses. The rate of building was sensitive to fluctuations in demand, which was important because a resort needed to respond quickly once there was a demand for more or better accommodation. Houses could be built at high densities if suitable sites were expensive, perhaps because of the local topography or a shortage of land, and high densities enabled visitors to live close to the facilities of the resort which were the key to the lifestyle of visitors during the Georgian period.[8]

The Influence of the Spa Resort

For centuries, spas had been used for medicinal purposes but most visits to them were very short and purely to drink and, where facilities allowed, to bathe in the waters. Most were saline springs, and some had other chemicals within the water such as iron. After the link between health and leisure was made, the spa resort town emerged as a popular place to visit. The medical treatment gave visitors a reason for spending time there and the leisure facilities enabled them and their families or friends to pass in comfort, health permitting. The spas were also called watering places, or places of resort for taking the waters, hence spa resorts.

The concentration of urban leisure facilities provided by the resorts was attractive to increasing numbers of rich townsfolk from the commercial, professional and industrial sectors who had the time and the money to spend on leisure, as well as a minority of very wealthy people who had bought or inherited land. For the facilities to be profitable they needed to attract a lot of visitors, and lodgings and lodging houses were built. Only the spa resorts with the best access to large numbers of wealthy people could develop as towns. The same applied to seaside resorts.

Bath, Epsom and Tunbridge Wells emerged as spa resorts in the late 1600s, Bath was a declining market and industrial town, Epsom a market town and Tunbridge Wells a new town. Whilst Bath had wealthy visitors from the West Country as well as from London, Epsom and Tunbridge Wells met the needs of wealthy people who lived south-east of London and of Londoners themselves. The majority of spas depended on regional markets and some, such as Epsom, only flourished for a short period, a later characteristic of Georgian seaside resorts.

The success of Bath in particular lured investors into the health and leisure towns. Between the mid-1660s and 1750 the population of Bath grew from 1,500 to 6,000 but the population was swelled by visitors during the season and so investment in accommodation was attractive. Other spa resort towns still developing even as seaside resorts emerged included Cheltenham, Harrogate and Malvern.

The integration of drinking and bathing in the spa waters with an organised leisure routine built around activities such as assemblies and cards was supervised from 1700 by a Master of Ceremonies (MC), who published notices of public events and helped to introduce people (if suitably rewarded with a bribe). Easily

7 *Heat* by Gillray,
engraving 1810.

understood regulations for public behaviour were published by the MC so that
everyone understood not only what amusement was available but how to behave
in public places. Spa and seaside resorts were among the places at which standards
of public conduct in towns were developed.

The Coast as a Picturesque Place to Visit

By the 1750s the seaside was becoming fashionable not only for the novelty of
sea bathing but also because of the interest in picturesque and sublime landscapes.
The rise of Brighton shows that threats of possible invasion did not prevent the
rapid growth of resorts once the fashion became established. The attraction of
the seascape is also reflected in the development of seaside villas. Some such as
Kingsgate on the Isle of Thanet and Steephill on the Isle of Wight were built
before 1780.[9]

The English Love of Consumer Fashions

The seaside resort appealed to the English love of novel fashions and preoccupation
with health which was indulged by trying out medicines that were not too testing.
The increasing interest in owning clothes that suited the occasion contributed to
the development of seaside outfits for women. Souvenirs of the seaside included
shell-covered cases and other mementos, such as Tunbridge Ware (a form of
wooden box with an image of the resort on the top), which were copied from

the spas. The antics of the visitors to resorts became popular with cartoonists and satirical writers.[10]

The Emergence of the First Seaside Resorts c.1730-1760

Sea bathing by a few people could not support a seaside resort. Although wealthy visitors were seabathing for health and pleasure all around the coast from the 1710s, at Whitby in 1718, and at Bootle and at Liverpool in 1721, there was not enough demand for facilities to be developed. The first resort where sea bathing took place may have been Scarborough. Dr Wittie of Scarborough advocated sea bathing as well as taking spa waters in the late 1660s and by the early 1730s it had been integrated into the spa routine at this popular resort on the east Yorkshire coast. The spa pump room was at the base of the cliff, a short distance to the south of the town and easily accessible at low tide across a large sandy bay. Bathing machines were apparently developed at Scarborough: one is shown in a print published in 1735, and in a print dated 1744 there is a cluster of machines in the water and on the beach. These cumbersome horse-drawn changing huts were safest upon gently shelving beaches and so the bay at Scarborough was ideal. The bathing machine's popularity ensured that seaside sites with difficult access to the sea could not be developed as resorts.[11]

From the 1730s sea bathing for health and for pleasure was increasingly widespread. Some visitors, such as William Clarke, the rector of Buxted in Sussex, who stayed in Brighton (his nearest coastal town) in 1736, still wanted a simple seaside holiday, but increasing numbers sought more diversions. In response to demand the first purely seaside facilities were built at Margate on the north Kent coast in 1735. An enterprising local carpenter advertised his seawater bath and 'convenient lodgings to be lett', which suggests that some people were already aware of the potential of formal seaside resort development.[12]

Because of the expectations of the majority of the clientèle, most of whom were already accustomed to the embellishments of spa resorts, only a few of the seaside places which were frequented by 1760 emerged from the initial phase of exploration as fully fledged seaside resorts by 1780. The number of visitors was insufficient for all to flourish.

The First Seaside Resorts

The first resorts were a quintet of old but declining coastal towns: Brighton, Hastings, Margate, Scarborough and Weymouth. Whilst bathing machines were simple to make and so quite widely available once someone had thought of them, the costs of running seawater baths imposed some limitations upon the choice of sites for resorts. Seawater baths (for those who wanted a more private and gentle approach to bathing than braving the sea) needed slight inclines without which the very simple pumps that were first used could not operate. If, as at Margate, they were built jutting into the sea, then a sheltered spot was even more essential. Entrepreneurs who sought to profit from the fashion for sea bathing recognised that they could copy most of the spa resort's facilities, the sea replacing the spa as the focus of activities. But only small towns could be transformed in line with the new fashion quickly for they already had the basic facilities for visitors such as inns and spare houses to let. Jane Austen captures this essential point well in her unfinished novel *Sanditon*.

Four more factors particularly influenced the location and timing of the emergence of the first successful seaside resorts. First, catchment. Brighton, Hastings, Margate, Scarborough and Weymouth, all of which were established as resorts by 1780, benefited from accessibility to large towns and to spas. They were all located in the prosperous, relatively densely populated regions of England. Scarborough, whose resort role from the 1770s was more dependent upon the sea than on the spa, served the north, particularly the agriculturally prosperous north-east with its wealthy towns and gentry. Not until after 1780, when rising prosperity became more widely diffused socially and spatially, could other seaside settlements successfully develop a resort as a significant part of their economy.

Second, access. Resorts needed adequate road or water communications with their catchment area. The significant role of the regional clientèle in supporting a resort, particularly during its early years, meant that good links with the respective county capitals, other prosperous towns and spa resorts were important. Entrepreneurs at Brighton, Hastings, Margate, Scarborough and Weymouth were also concerned about access to London as the country's most important social

8 Circassian Ladies Corset and Seaside Bathing Dress, invented and to be had exclusively from Mrs Bell No.26 Charlotte Street, Bedford Square [London]. From an unidentified book of fashion plates. Shows hooded bathing machines in the background c.1800.

centre. By the mid-18th century knowing the latest fashions was the key to being a successful leisure town, and access to information from London played a major role in keeping up to date.

Third, the state of the economies of the coastal towns which might become resorts. All were small coastal towns without vigorous economies which might divert capital and compete for land and labour and so make the establishment of the resort relatively unimportant. These slack economies resulted in surplus accommodation which provided space for the first flow of visitors, while sufficient capital was available to provide the basic facilities – bathing machines, a library and a rudimentary assembly room. Trade links with nearby towns gave access to more capital should it be required. Although bigger coastal towns such as Liverpool, Portsmouth and Southampton attracted sea bathing and some speculation in the related facilities, it failed to compete with their established functions for investment and for suitable sites.

The rapid development of the five specialist resort towns also helped to extinguish competition. Even after 1780, when the number of resorts began to increase slowly, small towns or large villages were usually more successful than ventures which involved only one or two people in a small settlement without surplus accommodation and capital. The total cost to a developer if all the facilities, including accommodation, had to be built and communications improved was high. Sir Richard Hotham's unsuccessful development of Hothampton (Bognor Regis) in the 1780s and the tale of the failing resort which is the subject of Jane Austen's *Sanditon* illustrate the risks. Because the risks associated with expenditure on the new facilities was spread amongst more people in a town and the facilities could be provided more quickly, there was a greater possibility of success.

The fourth and final factor was recommendation through local contacts. As the detailed study of Brighton's early development demonstrates, a strong local network of visitors who were prepared to recommend a resort was vitally important, far more than the recommendation from one of the many doctors who jostled for business or than visits from a member of the royal family.

Phases of Development as an Early Resort

All five pioneer seaside resorts passed through four stages of development which can also be seen in the history of their successors in Britain and in the development of resorts anywhere else in the world. All five passed through subsequent phases, too, but these were after 1820.

The first phase was one of exploration, when visitors experimented with sea bathing but were insufficient to make an impact on the town's economy for they used some rented accommodation and local shops and markets. The second phase, of tentative resort development with little investment other than in bathing machines and the renting of rooms for libraries and shops, passed by very quickly, and by 1760 four of the five towns had entered upon the third stage of development, Hastings lagging a little behind. During the third stage the resort function dominated the economy and additional land was needed to build housing and services for both the increasing residential and seasonal populations. Most development took place within the boundaries of the towns and resulted in the loss of older buildings and infilling. The fourth stage was reached when demand was no longer met by the old town and development spread to surrounding farmland. Investment came from a wide range of sources, not only local people but others in the region, and from the nearest large town. The new buildings consisted mainly of new lodging houses to let, the most expensive of which faced the main social area or the sea, preferably both. Brighton, Margate, Scarborough and Weymouth reached this phase before 1780 and Hastings a little later.

By 1780 Brighton had worked through the phases described above and had done so more rapidly than any other resort. Brighton's development will now be considered in the wider context of the rise of seaside and spa resorts whenever that is appropriate.

3
Resort Facilities

From 1750 Brighton's resort facilities developed more rapidly than those at Margate and Weymouth, even though investment in developments in the latter resorts began sooner. Brighton's progress is particularly striking because of the town's poverty. Whilst the town was visited for leisure and therapeutic seabathing by 1736, there is no evidence that any resort facilities were built before 1750. The town's transformation into a resort can be divided into two phases, *c.*1750-1780 and 1781-1820.

In the first phase all of the leisure facilities that would have been expected at a resort were developed. Most stood on the eastern side of Brighton's old town centre facing the Steine but the old town was redeveloped to accommodate some of the new facilities, especially lodging houses. By 1780 the daily resort routine was established and it remained unchanged until the 1820s.

The rate at which leisure facilities were built in Brighton between 1750 and 1780 is particularly striking because of the town's earlier impoverishment, its small population and the lack of a wealthy resident population to support them. The new facilities depended heavily on securing enough seasonal visitors willing to spend money and Brighton managed to attract them. In 1770 Margate's resort provision still rivalled Brighton's, but during the next decade the range of facilities in the Sussex resort developed at a speed which Margate failed to match and this in turn ensured that in 1780 Brighton was Britain's major seaside resort.

During the second phase, from 1781 to 1820, Brighton's population increased more rapidly than either Margate's or Weymouth's, and there were more wealthy residents, some of whom had retired to the town. The major theme of this phase was the rapid outward growth as lodging houses, residential housing and service buildings were constructed on farmland. The old town bounded by East, North and West Streets became the business and resort centre for the new suburbs. Between 1811 and 1821 Brighton had the fastest growth rate for any town in Britain as both the population and the number of houses doubled.[1]

Phase One: 1750 to 1780
Investment in Facilities

Today statistics can be produced to show the importance of a particular function to a town. For a resort they may include calculations of the number of visitors, their average length of stay, spending patterns, employment generated by them, the

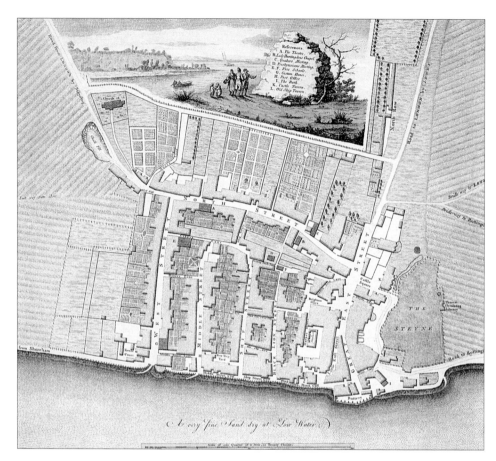

9   Brighthelmstone
surveyed by Yeakell
and Gardner,
Chichester; engrav'd
by Whitchurch. Rich'd
Thomas bookseller,
Brighthelmston, 1 June
1779.

number of beds available, and the popularity of facilities as shown by the number of
users. Such data is not available for Brighton during this period. The main evidence
for the rate at which the town developed as a resort is the speed with which
facilities were established, for they needed a clientèle in order to flourish. By 1780
the town was popular enough to support the full range which would have been
expected by then.

The Importance of the Steine

Brighton's development could not have happened without the Steine. Every seaside
settlement which aspired to become a resort knew how crucial a promenade was,
preferably one with sea views and some shelter. When visitors were first attracted
to Brighton the resort lacked a promenade along the seafront. Erosion was such a
problem that not even a road along the cliff tops existed, and the problem was not
resolved until after 1820.[2] Vehicles went up and down the narrow streets in the town
centre to reach houses along the cliff top. All prosperous and fashionable towns had
a promenade by 1750, some recycling stretches of town wall to provide one, and
so a suitable site had to be found. A sheltered location preferably with sea views
made more sense for Brighton than a length of seafront, for the season began in
the late summer and ran into the autumn. As the autumn season lengthened such a

1. The Church
2. Mr Scrase's
3. Duke of Marlborough's
4. Mr Philcox's
5. Mr Willard's
6. The Castle Tavern
7. The Ball Room
8. The Orchestra
9. Thomas's Circulating Library
10. Hollingbury Castle
11. Lewes Hill
12. North Row

10 Perspective View of the Steine at Brighthelmstone, taken from the South End. J. Donowel architect del. Peter Mazell sculp. March 1778 copper plate. The key provided by Donowell is beneath the picture.

gathering ground was even more essential. To the east of the town lay a large open area called the Steine, which gave the fledgling resort a protected promenade for visitors and an open and public setting for the tourism businesses that needed to make visitors aware of them.

Sheltered by the town from the prevailing south-westerly winds, the Steine was easily reached from the lodgings, inns, lodging houses and private houses that developed within the town and it provided easy access to the bathing machines which could be seen at its southern end. The low-lying open space was also large enough for both businesses and large houses to be accommodated, so giving walkers access to the sea and a selection of places to visit or to stand and view. Of the houses built during this period, Marlborough House still looks as it did after being altered by Robert Adam between 1786 and 1787 for 'Single Speech' Hamilton.[3]

In spite of the popularity of the site for development, the pastoral Steine depicted in the prints by Lambert and by Donowell in 1764 and 1778 is quite accurate, even if surprising to a modern resident or visitor to the town. After 1780 the development of housing to the east of the Steine began to give it the appearance of an enclosed town recreation ground.

11 The Steyne at Brighton copper engraving from *Guide to all the Watering and Seabathing Places*, 1803. This shows the changes since 1778 such as the Royal Pavilion and the second Marlborough House and North (also Marlborough) Row.

Development along the south-west and western side of the Steine began in 1752-3, when Dr Richard Russell of Lewes built a substantial detached house for his consulting rooms and Samuel Shergold, an innkeeper from Lewes, purchased a large house built in the 1740s by Nathaniel Brooker as a gentleman's residence with views of the Steine. Shergold converted the house into the *Castle Inn* and then expanded it as demand for facilities increased.[4] Russell House, built on the cliff top in a fashionable architectural style, was also visible down the Steine and East Street partly because of its large size, but it had the advantage of some shelter from the prevailing winds. From there Russell could supervise his patients, who could easily get to the beach from beside the house. Russell House remained a local landmark long after Russell's death in 1759 for it was not demolished until 1826, when the *Royal Albion Hotel* was built.

Bathing Machines, Medical Men and Spas

Seaside resorts offered a novelty that no spa could, the bathing machine. The tradition of bathing at a spa rather than swimming enabled doctors and others involved in promoting the seaside to persuade most visitors to use these contraptions and not to bathe or swim without them. They became significant employers of labour, for the machines needed supervision in the form of bathing ladies and men and children to manage the horses and to run errands. Doctors were great advocates of their use but no evidence has been found that they also owned machines. Advice as to how to bathe, what if anything to add to the seawater that was drunk as a medicine, and sales of books about the uses of seawater all helped to make the more fashionable and well connected doctors wealthier.

The lack of effective sea defences from the Steine to West Street gave Brighton a low, picturesque, crumbling cliff line. Access to the beach was by slopes cut or worn into the cliff face. The easiest access for bathing machines was at the bottom of the Steine and by 1753 these were run by the bathing men and women who charged for their services and for the use of the machine in which to change. These 'dippers' submerged bathers in the sea, since the majority did not expect to swim and may not have known how. The number of immersions would be recommended by a doctor who might also precribe how much sea water should be drunk and with what.

The machines were hauled by horses that stood about in the open. On very hot days those standing on the beach sometimes died. Bathing machines were a novelty to some visitors in the 1780s and so guide books offered explanations as to how they worked:

> By means of a hook ladder the bather ascends the machine, which is formed of wood and raised in high wheels; he is drawn to a proper distance from the shore and then plunges into the sea, the guides attending on each side to assist him in recovering the machine which being accomplished, he is drawn back to shore. The guides are strong, active and careful, and in every respect adapted to their employment.[5]

The bathing machines were a famous feature of the town, although not everyone approved of the lack of canvas canopy to hide the bather. They were regarded as safer than bathing, or dipping, without the help of the redoubtable bathing ladies and men. Tales of people who died because they failed to be careful were used to remind people of the importance of supervised bathing. One report alleged that when a man hung over a groyne to scoop some seawater a gale of wind blew his greatcoat over his head and he was swept away and drowned.

12 View of the Duke of Cumberland's House on the Steine at Brighthelmstone. Hon. James Luttrell del. W. Watts sculp. Copper engraving reproduced in the *European Magazine* in August 1786. This is Russell House, built 1753 and demolished 1826.

13   *The Castle Hotel.* Copper engraving in C. Wright, *Brighton Ambulator*, 1818.

Doctors

The majority of the treatments prescribed were similar to those at the spas but 'dipping' in the sea in the early morning (whilst, it was said, the pores on the body were closed) was the main difference. Seawater treatments were otherwise little different, for spas had saline water and some had additional chemicals such as iron at Tunbridge Wells and at Wick in Hove. Most patients were advised to drink seawater, sometimes with additives which might seem odd to modern taste, such as ground up 'seacoal', coal which had been washed up on the beach. Some patients were advised not to bathe if the doctor considered it unsuitable, but, to ensure that few potential patients were turned away, the spa and baths at Hove were regarded as very efficacious alternatives to the sea.

A few doctors with good social contacts profited from the early days of sea bathing when, owing to its novelty, there seemed to be a greater preparedness to take medical advice. Dr Richard Russell was not the only doctor who practised in Brighton during the 1750s, and on his death in 1759 there was brisk competition for his practice, which suggests that it was very profitable. All patients paid for their treatment. Russell was well connected and was consulted by members of the Pelham family of eastern Sussex.[6] His interest in sea water as a health treatment began when he saw that people who lived along the coast used it to treat stomach diseases. He added this knowledge to his interest in the treatment of secretions from the glands and developed a regime for seawater bathing and drinking. An expert publicist, he followed the fashion amongst doctors of writing about their work. In 1750 and in 1752 he published in Latin and then in English *A dissertation concerning the use of sea water in the diseases of the glands*. In his book about his work he noted that during the 1740s patients were being sent to Brighton by London doctors as well as by himself.

Dr Poole of Lewes was one of the better known local physicians who came to Brighton for the season and advertised in the local paper. On Russell's death he sought the support of local worthies against the better known Dr Schoenberg (also locally spelt Schomberg), the son of the Dr Schoenberg of London whose portrait, by Lawrence, hangs in the National Gallery.[7] In 1762 Poole bought a town house overlooking the Steine, on the eastern side of East Street.[8] He did so well that in 1766 he reshaped the house, taking great care to make it look fashionable. Amongst his purchases was turf for his new garden.[9]

From the 1760s increasing numbers of well-known London doctors visited Brighton for the season in order to treat patients and others hoped to make their fortunes from seawater treatments. Several, such as Doctors Lucas Pepys and Anthony Relhan, owned houses close to the fashionable *Castle Inn*. Lucas Pepys was married to Lady Rothes and their house to the west of the inn was grand enough to have a very large garden which is clearly marked on the Yeakell and Gardner map of Brighton in 1779. That became the Promenade Gardens in the 1790s and then part of the western gardens of the Royal Pavilion. Anthony Relhan married the widow of Sir William Hart and the owner of a house in East Street.[10] In 1761, Relhan published the first guide to Brighton, which rejoiced in the title of, *A Short History of Brighthelmston with remarks on its Air and Analysis of its Waters particularly of an uncommon mineral one, long discovered though but lately used by Anthony Relhan, M.D. Fellow of the Royal College of Physicians in Ireland*.

By 1794 there appears to have been so much competition for business that at least one doctor who lived in Brighton was prepared to go to Lewes without charging for the trip. Books about the value of sea bathing continued to be published by doctors through the period, many locally.[11] Such was the rivalry between them that when Dr Kentish of Brighton was refused entry to the College of Physicians, membership of which gave doctors greater standing, he tried to take legal action against Doctor Reynolds whom he blamed for it. In 1821 an observer described Brighton as having as thriving a 'medical tribe' as Bath and Clifton and noted that the group included undertakers.[12]

Medicinal Baths

In 1768 Dr Awsiter published a book about the medicinal uses of seawater and opened Brighton's first baths the following year. The site he chose lay to the south-west of the Steine and was close to the most popular area for seabathing. The simple classically styled building stood on the edge of Pool Valley, where the cliff on which the old town stood slopes down into the mouth of the Pool. Pipes could quite easily be laid up the gentle slope to pump sea water to the baths. In order to emphasise the value of the baths for fashionable visitors, and his associations with them, he persuaded Lady Hart and Miss Harriot Cecil to lay the first stone.[13] Awsiter's Baths lacked competition until the 1780s. A scheme to build a second bathing house in 1771 failed to gain support.[14] In 1787 Mahomed built his Indian Shampooing Baths just at the sea end of Little East Street and close to Awsiter's. The Prince of Wales patronised them in their early days, offering publicity which Mohamed was quick to use in his advertising.[15]

Chalybeate Spring

Most doctors recommended the use of the chalybeate spring at Wick when they thought it was appropriate. The spring (which still exists in St Anne's Wells Gardens, Hove) had attracted visitors before Brighton became a resort.[16] In the 1760s it was given a well house by the Scutt family who owned the site and at some stage landscaped it with fir trees.[17] There was a charge to use the spa and family season

14 *The Baths at Brighton.* Engraved by S. Rawle from drawing by J. Nixon, 1803.

tickets were advertised. By 1794 the trees had grown enough to shelter the spa from the sea winds that whipped up the ridge on which it stood and Mr Scutt's house was thought to be worth looking at.[18]

The Development of Leisure Facilities

Resorts had to have leisure facilities, for most visitors regarded the need to bathe in the sea for their health as an excuse to use them. Their correspondence suggests that the majority did not bathe regularly and only a few considered a daily bathe essential. The investment in leisure facilities and housing suggests that once sea bathing became established the growth in visitor numbers may have been considerable.

Assembly Rooms

By 1750 all prosperous towns had assembly rooms for social events and so Brighton could not afford to be without one. When in 1754 Samuel Shergold opened Brighton's first Assembly Rooms at the *Castle Inn* and began to hold assemblies during 'the season', he took a huge risk for this was still a poor small town and he was dependent on visitors. Assembly rooms cost between £2,000 and £5,000 to build in the 1750s and 1760s. The Bristol rooms were built in 1754-5 and cost £3,500 for a coffee room, a tavern and a lobby on the ground floor, with the Assembly Room on the first floor.[19] The layout at Bristol was similar to the *Castle Inn*'s first rooms, although the sizes of the respective buildings are not known.

Having been an innkeeper in Lewes, Shergold recognised the need for his new Assembly Room to be fashionable. He commissioned Crunden, a leading interior

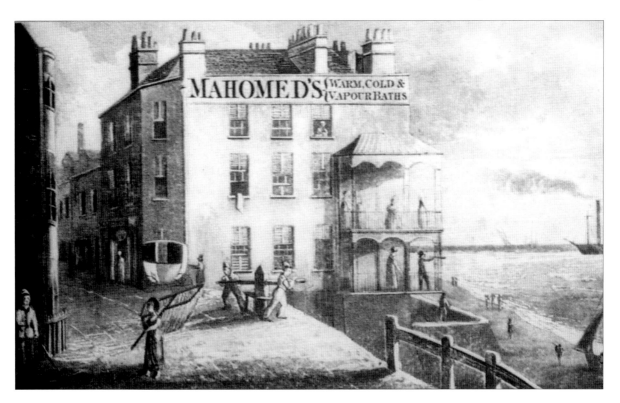

designer, to decorate the rooms, which were capable of accommodating 450 people for a dance.[20] With this large extension on its north side, the *Castle* dominated the landscape of the Steine and the social activities of the town until about 1820, when it became unfashionable. The Assembly Rooms were soon used for a range of events, masterminded by Shergold and his successors. Some were sponsored by wealthy local people or by visitors and were intended to entertain residents as well as visitors. In 1758, 200 people celebrated the taking of Cape Breton at an assembly at the *Castle Inn*, the ball ending at 11p.m. Then the dragoons paraded on the Steine, where beside a bonfire 'the populace' drank three hogsheads of ale to celebrate the event and watched as the cannon were fired.

The *Castle*'s Assembly Rooms were the only ones in town until 1761 when John Hicks of the *Old Ship Inn* (which then stood close to the town's crumbling seafront) opened his new rooms. Hicks employed Goulden to decorate the new rooms and to redecorate the card and other rooms.[21] To pay for the work John Hicks mortgaged his inn to local gentry. His investment prompted Dr Awsiter to write to the *Gentleman's Magazine* in 1761 and claim that not only had the town a 'bold and clean shore' but also two Assembly Rooms, 'one almost the best in England except York'. From 1761 advertisements show that the two innkeepers co-operated and held assemblies alternately, and by 1780 the routine had settled to a ball on Mondays at the *Castle* and one on Thursdays at the *Old Ship*. Card evenings were held on Wednesdays and Fridays at the *Castle* and on Tuesdays and Saturdays at the *Old Ship*.

15 *Mahomed's Baths, East Cliff.* Drawn by Cordwell published by R. Sickelmore in *History of Brighton*, 1823.

16 *The Pump House.* By W.N. [Nibbs?] *c.*1820. This pumped water into the Baths but was demolished in 1829.

Shergold decided to refashion and to redecorate his Assembly Rooms in the late 1770s when they were twenty years old. He borrowed money by raising mortgages on the inn and by entering into partnership. The mortgagees were Lewes businessmen and local gentry, so Shergold probably raised the money to build the first assembly rooms in the same way.[22] Crunden's revamping provided an Assembly Room 80 feet long and 40 feet wide with recesses at each end decorated with pillars. The walls were painted and also decorated with pilasters and the ceiling 'curved'. The ancillary rooms that Crunden decorated were also large. The tea room was 56 feet long and 30 feet wide and the card room 40 feet by 28 feet.[23]

Both Shergold and Hicks owned their inns and so could plough back profits into improvements and use the inns as security for loans.[24] The inns became valuable assets to the town for they also paid a lot of tax. In 1780 the *Castle* was valued at £70 10s. and paid the highest amount of Land Tax levied on a single building. Shergold also paid Land Tax on other buildings that he used for his business. In 1780 the *Old Ship* was valued at £49 and was the town's second most valuable building.

The inns were the largest visitor facilities in the town and their scale and complexity is apparent from sale documents. In 1800 the *Old Ship* had 70 beds, stabling for 100 horses, an Assembly Room, coffee and billiard rooms and wine vaults. The owners of the *Castle Inn* always had shares in other leisure and transport activities in the resort but the extent of the family assets is not clearly documented until 1807. Then a sale of a quarter share in the *Castle* included not only the inn but a large coach house on the south-west end of New Road, wine vaults, one-nineteenth share of a hot and cold baths and three of the 18 shares in the Race Stand.

The *Castle* was closed when the Prince of Wales became the owner and decided to demolish it and convert the Assembly Room into his private chapel, which was formally opened in 1822. Meanwhile a new hotel was opened on the Steine to replace it. The *Royal York Hotel* was developed on the site of 'The Manor House', the name given to the home of Richard Scrase, who owned half of the manor of Brighton. The house is marked on Yeakell and Gardner's map of 1779. The site was let to Dr Hall in about 1800 and more buildings were added to it, the group becoming known as Steine Place. In 1819 two of the houses were converted into a hotel by Dr Hall and, with the permission of the Duke of York, it became the *Royal York Hotel* in September 1819. The grand façade that was given to the north front has the date of the opening of the building at the top. This became a very popular hotel for wealthy visitors and had a view up the Steine to the Pavilion and the Downs to the north of the town.[25]

Libraries

The first bookseller was E. Verral of Lewes, who in 1759 sold books in his shop in East Street during the season. By 1760 Baker, a librarian from Tunbridge Wells, had opened a library in Brighton. By the mid-1760s both of Brighton's circulating libraries were on the Steine. They are depicted in Lambert's view of 1765 (published as a print in 1766) and on Yeakell and Gardner's 1779 map.[26] The libraries were important as informal meeting places and so it made sense to open them in places where people would gather.[27] Subscribers could stroll on the Steine in order to see and to be seen by other visitors on their way to a library. Once there they would sign the visitors' book to record their subscription and announce their arrival and

Facilities at the five earliest seaside resorts, showing Brighton's lead by 1780

Facility	Brighton	Hastings	Margate	Scarborough	Weymouth
First record of visitors for seabathing	1736	1736	1736	1735	1748
Bathing machines	1754		1753	1735	1763
Seawater Baths	1769	By 1804	1760s		1748
Spa	Old established building by 1760			Old established	
Assembly Rooms	1752	1771	1750s	1725	1748 (new 1776)
Coffee House	1752			1792	
Library	1759	1780s	1766	early 1700s	1785
Theatre troupe for season	1764		1752	1730s	
Theatre	1773		1761	1777	1773
MC and organised social life	Mid-1760s		1760s	1740s	1778
Gardens or walks	1750s			1770s	
Royal Family	1765				1780 Duke of Cumberland 1784
Improvement Commissioners	1773				1776
Lodging Houses	1750s		1767 Cecil Square	1760s	1770s
Boarding Schools	1757				by 1780

address to others who might call in to read, chat, listen to music, buy fripperies or gamble.

Woodgate's (later Miss Widgett's, then Bowen's, Crawford's and Fisher's) stood near the present Royal York Buildings, close to Brighton Manor House and Russell House. It is clearly visible on Lambert's view. Baker's (later Thomas's then Dulot's, Gregory's and Donaldson's) stood on the east side of the Steine (near St James' Street). This library had a little rotunda nearby in which musicians sat and played and was the first resort building to stand outside the town. It can also be seen on Lambert's view and on the later view by Donowell. Baker's remained isolated until the early 1780s when housing was built beside it. His choice of site and the library's success suggest that visitors found it useful. Perhaps his offer to buy and to exchange books kept people interested and as early as 1761 he was advertising 200 books for sale.

Coffee Houses

By 1770 more coffee houses had appeared beside the Steine, competing with the one at the *Castle Inn*. In 1789 Mrs Kent decided to sell hers and Stiles, the Brighton auctioneers, emphasised both the beautiful prospect of the Steine and the extensive views of the sea from the four-storeyed house. Mrs Kent was one of the many men and women in Brighton who ran a shop or similar service on the ground floor of a property and let accommodation. Over the top of the coffee house she had six bedrooms to let. There was plenty of competition and, to attract more custom, John Sanders offered billiards at his coffee house on the Cliffe.

Theatres

Until 1773 a barn on the north-west corner of Castle Square was used for plays. In November 1764 the Chichester Company of Players performed the *Busybody* and *The Mock Doctor*.[28] Advertisements include the prices for a pit, a gallery and an upper gallery. The barn was still used in July 1770 when Mr Johnson opened for the season.

Theatres were speculative ventures because of the problem of getting an enterprising manager or owner-manager who could attract good players and choose the programmes to fill the house at most performances. Theatres in resorts were open for short seasons of a few months and had to make enough money to pay the employees, keep the equipment and costumes in good order, and give a profit to the owner. The buildings were usually simple on the exterior but the interiors were expensive because of the need to provide seating and all the stage machinery.

Samuel Paine, a builder, constructed Brighton's first theatre in 1772-3, on his own land in North Street. He must have had advice on theatre construction from a theatre manager. In 1774 Mr Johnson, his first manager, gave the impression to the local paper that it was he who had built it. As the landowner and a builder by trade, Paine was probably able to build quite cheaply but, even without the cost of purchasing land, theatres cost around £1,000.

By 1777 the theatre was flourishing. When it opened for the season Mr Bailey was the box keeper and treasurer, and in September a benefit performance was held for him. The season began with two plays from the Theatre Royal in London, *The Tragedy of Jane Shore* and *The Mock Doctor*, which must have been very apt for a seaside resort full of medical men! The theatre ran some novelty events, including a pony race included as a feature between plays. In early September 1777 the first play on the programme was called *The Busybody*, in which Mrs Baddeley played Miranda, and that was followed by *The Humours of Lewes Races* after a match run by two ponies; then Mrs Baddeley reappeared in *The Padlock*. In order to stage pony races the pit was partly covered at the same level as the stage, so that the ponies raced round an oval course with members of the audience still in the centre section of the pit. A print of this event taking place in the Theatre Royal in Dublin in 1779 shows three ponies racing furiously.[29]

The Brighton theatre's fortunes were very dependent on the season and on the weather. In September 1779 Mr Bailey commented that attendances had dropped because of the humid weather. By then the theatre may have needed some improvements, too, because Paine made some alterations before the 1780 season began, a season that was graced by the presence of Mr Kean, a very famous actor of the period. The players from the playhouse at Lewes offered a series of programmes in August 1780. They began with *The Busybody*, and paired that with a pantomine called *The Wizard on the Rocks or Harlequin at Brighton*.[30]

Hunting and other Blood Sports

Blood sports were a major part of the social activities of many Georgian towns and were expected in resorts. Game certificates which allowed holders to shoot game were normally obtained by people staying in the town for some time or who lived there. As the town became wealthier so the number of people who were listed in the local newspaper as holding certificates increased. Game was expensive to rear

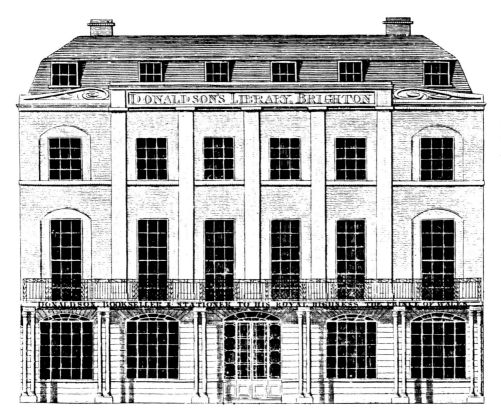

and so access to shooting was controlled. Holders of certificates had to contact local gamekeepers to get permission to enter an estate. Their names were also published.

Hunts were also run by towns during the 18th century and leisure towns such as Brighton had many visitors who would expect to hunt. The Ditchling Hounds were amongst those that early visitors could join, but from the late 1750s the town had its own hounds and dates of meets were advertised, sometimes in conjunction with hunts from another community. They appear to have chased a variety of game. In 1769 a wild fox was let loose at Hollingbury Hill for the Ditchling Hounds to chase. In 1789 they hunted a hind that was turned out of Stanmer, and in 1792 they failed to catch a hare until it reached Dulot's library on the Steine. The Prince of Wales also kept a pack of hounds at Brighton, the kennels being just north of the town.

Some visitors watched bloodsports which included bullbaiting and cockfighting arranged in the yards of the inns of Brighton and in the surrounding villages. These events were advertised in the local newpaper, the *Sussex Weekly Advertiser*, by posters and by word of mouth. Cockfighting normally cost between two and four guineas for a day and was therefore quite expensive (a year's subscription to a library cost ten guineas) and so attracted wealthy supporters such as the Earl of Sussex. Most events were held between groups of people who had travelled some distance, the gentlemen of Brighton and Henfield meeting at Preston for a cockfight in 1777.[31]

Boxing matches were organised in the same places as cockfights and bear baiting and resulted in injuries and deaths all of which were reported in the local paper. Mendoza the Jew, famous for his fights, was amongst the pugilists.

Novelty Races

Novelty races were popular entertainments, and in the 1750s and 1760s visitors travelled over the Downs to Rottingdean, to the east of Brighton, to watch racing, for prize money by men and for articles of clothing by women. By the early 1770s the same types of races were being held on the Steine, and jackass races were also arranged there.

Cricket Matches

Visits to cricket matches at Rottingdean were supplanted in the late 1750s by games on the Steine. The teams became increasingly respectable as prosperous townsfolk teamed up with visitors to play in the Brighton Club. Opposing teams came from further and further away and by 1792 Brighton was playing Middlesex. Yet again, gambling was involved and the teams played for prize money.

Phase Two: 1781–1820

The Season

By 1780 almost every facility that a visitor might have expected was available in Brighton. By the late 1780s there were enough visitors for some duplication of the existing facilities to be profitable. At the peak of the season between July and the end of October the town was so busy that the theatre could hold performances on four days a week.[32] The process of development consisted of improving and enlarging existing premises and building more of some facilities such as baths and libraries. Even in 1820 most of the visitor facilities were still concentrated in the East Street-Castle Square-Steine area.

Improving the Steine

By the mid-1770s there were arguments between investors in the tourism facilities around the Steine and the fishermen about how the Steine should be used. The tourist sector wanted it made into a formal promenade; the fishermen, who dried their nets on its southern end, did not. One of the roles of the new Town Commissioners of 1773 was to manage the Steine as a public space. By 1777 the southern part had been railed and new turf laid with footpaths crossing it.[33]

By the late 1780s the Steine was being used for a variety of activities including informal ball games as well as spectator sports. It was decided that part of the land should be palisaded and turfed for the decorous promenaders and all other activities were forbidden in this area. The Master of Ceremonies announced that running, racing, cricket, trap ball or any other game was prohibited in the palisaded areas and the prosecution of defaulters was promised. The winterbourne (chalk stream) that flooded the Steine in front of the Royal Pavilion during the latter part of the season was contained in a drain in 1793.[34]

As the seaward end of the Steine was landscaped so entertainments were pushed north of the Pavilion until 1818, when this area was also enclosed. Then The Level (now just north of St Peter's Church) was left as the last large recreational area. In 1821 a public meeting was held to agree plans for further improvements

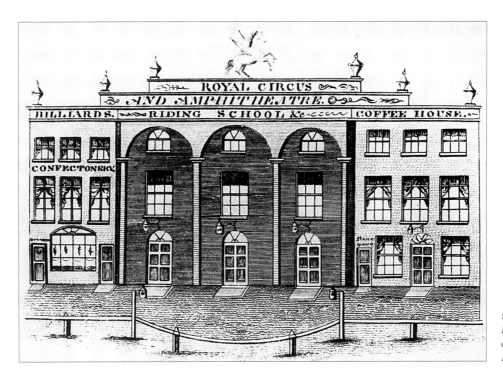

18   *The Royal Circus Riding School.* Copper engraving, C. Wright, *Brighton Ambulator*, 1818.

to the whole area. By the end of the 1820s, the whole of the Steine had been landscaped.

Promenade Gardens – a Private Subscription Garden

The first subscription garden in or close to Brighton was developed in a sheltered location which lies partly under New Road. The gardens had belonged to a town house and can be clearly seen whilst in private ownership on the map of Brighton by Yeakell and Gardner, on which the elms are marked just to the north of Castle Square.[35] Opened in 1793 by Mr Bailey, the layout of the gardens was similar to the smaller subscription gardens near town centres in Bath and wealthier provincial towns. The main feature consisted of two rows of elms with paths winding between them. Colourful flowering plants and shrubs gave form to the landscape. When the Prince of Wales purchased the land in 1802 the trees were integrated into the gardens of the Royal Pavilion.[36] The garden provided breakfasts, newspapers, music and other entertainment to those who could afford the subscription. The Prince of Wales and members of his circle of friends were amongst the visitors who attended firework displays and recitals for which well-known musicians were hired.

The Theatres after 1780

The story of theatres in Brighton after 1780 illustrates the way in which most developments from that date were largely either duplication or improvements of existing facilities. In the early 1780s Joseph Fox, who managed the theatre at Lewes, took over from Johnson at Brighton and managed both places. The programme became more adventurous and included a pantomime that finished before 10.15 p.m. 'whilst there was still moonlight to light the way home'. Fox also added opera, *The Beggar's Opera* by John Gay being first performed in Brighton in 1783. He persuaded visitors to sponsor some of the plays, Lady Shelley and the Countess of Essex both doing so, and Fox persuaded the libraries to sell tickets, but probably for a charge.

In 1787 Mr Fox petitioned Parliament for permission to erect a new theatre. There was opposition to this from Mr Attree, a solicitor who was the agent for Samuel Paine, owner of North Street Theatre. Fox also wanted permission to offer more performances each week and applied to Quarter Sessions (where magistrates licensed play houses) for authority to stage three plays a week.

Parliament gave its consent to the building of the new theatre and in 1790 construction began in Duke Street. The project appears to have been a partnership between a timber merchant, Stephen Poune (who owned the land), an auctioneer called Henry Stiles and Mr Fox. Meanwhile Fox refitted the old theatre and continued to use it. The theatre in North Street became known as the Old Theatre, and in August 1791 a benefit for Mr Paine of the 'Old Theatre' was held at the new one.

Mr Fox applied for the licence to hold plays in the Duke Street Theatre in April 1790. It became known as the New Theatre. This larger and more lavish building was described in July 1790 as 'little inferior to the Haymarket' in London. Fox continued to advertise the diverse mixture of entertainments that he had run at the old theatre, adding in 1791 the exhibition of 'The Orleans Menagerie'. Menageries of wild animals were popular during this period.

The opening of the grander Duke Street theatre forced the old one in North Street to close but the New Theatre's interior was still unfinished in 1791 when Fox died. By then it had cost at least £2,500. The new manager of both the Brighton and the Lewes theatres was Mr J. Palmer of the Haymarket theatre. He quickly employed Mr Dixon to paint both theatres and add a railing to the front of the Brighton Theatre (as it was now called) on which the Royal Arms were displayed and near which new patent lamps were attached.

Theatre managers rarely lasted long and in 1794 Mr Powell became the manager. He also made changes to the theatre which are not described as finished until 1796, when Mr Holland was completing the scenery. Meanwhile the ownership and the management changed hands again, Henry Cobb and Mr Burchall transferring the lease to J. Barnard.[37] In 1796 Barnard staged a moral play written by Richard Sickelmore, a resident of Brighton, called *The Dream: a serio-dramatic piece in two acts*. It was performed during the earlier part of the season, on 23 August, and was described by the writer as a 'tale about a son who thus early addicted himself to that insufferable habit of drinking, joined a society of strollers and declined'. Sickelmore then published the play in 1797.[38]

In 1807 the Duke Street theatre was closed by Cobb and demolished because he had built the bigger, more lavish, Theatre Royal in New Road. In 1806 Cobb had paid John Field £1,250 for two plots on the west side of New Road looking towards the Royal Pavilion and formerly part of the Royal Pavilion Estate. A condition of the sale of building plots along New Road was that the Prince of Wales should approve the design for buildings erected along it, which he did in 1807. The theatre was let by Cobb in 1807 for £850 a year for two years to John Brunton senior, who had leased the theatre in Duke Street. The building costs of the Theatre Royal are

19   *Brighton Races* by T. Rowlandson from *An excursion to Brighthelmstone* by H. Wigstead and T. Rowlandson, 1790.

20   Woodgate opened this library at the south end of the Steine in *c.*1760. Miss Widgett occupied it in 1779, Bowen succeeded her and Crawford rebuilt it in 1788. J. Heath sculpt. Copper engraving.

estimated at £6,000, which may have stretched Cobb financially.[39] In 1807 he sold half his share in the new theatre to Sir Thomas Clarges of Yorkshire.[40]

Georgian theatres were hard to run profitably, the majority having to recoup their costs during short seasons, so the high turnover of managers and owners in Brighton is not all that different from the majority of towns.[41]

The Founding of the Race Course

At first Brighton lacked a race course and visitors had to attend the races at Lewes. From August 1783 they were held on the site of the modern Race Course on a chalk promontory to the east of Brighton. The course lacked a race stand until 1788 and racing was organised from the *Castle Inn*; thereafter the new race stand became the meeting place for the planning of the races. The first race stand had its roof lead stolen at least once and in 1803 the structure was destroyed by fire and rebuilt.

To get the event going, both townspeople and Sussex landowners offered prizes in 1783. Gambling was also heavy during the three days of racing, Mr Wyndham betting 100 guineas on a horse racing for four miles. Local people of note were honoured by the naming of races after them. The Smoaker Stakes was named after one of the male dippers who tended the bathing machines. The race days were very successful and soon the number was extended to four and then five.

To mark the importance of the races, the Master of Ceremonies called the formal assemblies in race week the Race Balls. The races themselves were attended by notables such as the Duke of Cumberland, the Prince of Wales and the Duke of Richmond as well as people from a wide range of backgrounds. The Duke of Richmond continued to support Brighton even after he had laid out his own race course at Goodwood in 1800. The local newspaper soon felt obliged to warn readers who attended the races at Brighton about pickpockets attracted by the crowds. The races were used by local landowners as an excuse for inviting friends and relations to Brighton. Lord Sheffield, for example, invited Lord North, the Prime Minister.[42]

More Libraries

Both libraries beside the Steine survived until the 1820s, although more were built in the Steine, Castle Square and East Street area. From about 1780 their owners seemed to have difficulties in making them pay, which suggests that there were too many. Bowen closed his library for the winter in November 1780, and when John Gregory took over Dulot's library in January 1783 he added perfumes and other goods to the range of items for sale and made some improvements to the building. Dance music was used as an attraction by Mr Rawlings in East Street.

4
Brighton's Visitors

The Development of the 'Season'

By the mid-1750s wealthy and influential people were visiting Brighton. The Countess of Huntingdon in 1755 brought her youngest son to the town to use sea bathing to try to improve his health. Members of the Pelham family of eastern Sussex were also staying in the town by 1760 and they used Russell as their doctor.[1] Visitors such as these sought entertainment and in the later 1750s Samuel Shergold of the *Castle Inn* formally advertised the start of 'the season' in late June, which meant he was holding evening assemblies twice a week in the resort's only Assembly Rooms.[2] When the rooms at the *Old Ship* were opened the evenings were more fully occupied. As the range of activities increased in the 1760s so the appointment of a master of ceremonies became necessary. He could co-ordinate the resort's activities and integrate different groups of visitors.

Captain William Wade, the Master of Ceremonies for Bath between 1769 and 1777, was the town's first MC. He seems to have been appointed to the post in Brighton in 1769. In 1808 he was succeeded by Mr Forth.[3] Masters of Ceremonies who held posts in more than one place were not unusual, for resorts had different seasons, Beau Nash having served both Bath and Tunbridge Wells. From 1777 Wade devoted all of his time to Brighton, having resigned from the post in Bath.

The main tasks of the MC were to link the available facilities in a programme of activities and to introduce visitors to those whom they wished to meet. He was also expected to regulate social behaviour if required. In return for organising the season he received fees from the inns and other businesses who used his services and from individuals. Periodically a benefit ball would also be held to augment his income.

No detailed description of resort routine before 1800 has been found and the following account of its development with an MC officiating is based upon a variety of sources. The organisation of Georgian routine presumed that visitors would live publicly. Therefore new arrivals were expected to subscribe to several places where they could meet, such as the Assembly Rooms, a library and baths. The charges were published by the MC in consultation with the respective owners. These subscriptions were quite an expensive aspect of resort life, which helped to limit the number of visitors.[4] In 1794 the Duke of Marlborough, whose house was then to the north of the Royal Pavilion, paid five guineas towards the 'Town Plate', a horse race, subscribed to charities as wealthy visitors were expected to do, paid two guineas as his subscription to the Promenade Grove for the season, two guineas for a ball and six guineas for a public supper. Like everyone else the Duke had also to pay for his staff and the costs of running his house.

The majority of visitors rented houses and were soon integrated into the daily pattern if they chose to join in. The day began with sea bathing or a visit to the baths between 6 a.m. and 9 a.m. The bathing machines lacked awnings and bathing was a mixed, public affair; bathing clothes were not compulsory although nakedness was not always approved of. From 1800 bathing was segregated and bathers were expected to cover up. After bathing and paying the women or men who attended each machine and the boy (if one was employed to manage the horse which pulled the machine in and out of the water), the visitors then followed the day's routines.[5]

In 1782 Fanny Burney wrote of sea bathing during her fifth visit to Brighton:

> Mrs and the three Misses Thrales and myself all rose at 6 o'clock in the morning and 'by the pale blink of the moon' we went to the seaside where we had bespoke the bathing woman to be ready for us, and into the ocean we plunged. It was cold but pleasant. I have bathed so often as to loose my dread of the operation, which gives me nothing but animation and vigour.[6]

However, Dr Johnson, who was a friend of both the Thrales and of Fanny was less convinced of the value of sea bathing. He wrote from Brighton to a friend in 1776 to say that he had stayed six weeks in the town but had not tried seabathing until almost the end of his stay, and whilst he doubted its value he would continue.

Having bathed, visitors returned to their lodgings or went to the coffee rooms in the two big inns or (from about 1770) to one of the coffee houses to read the papers, talk or write letters, and eat breakfast. On some mornings the alternative from about 1770 was to go to a Public Breakfast such as the one held at the *Castle Inn* by the Duke of Cumberland in September 1771. These were arranged in both the *Old Ship* and the *Castle*. From the early 1790s they were also held in the Promenade Gardens.[7]

After breakfast some people went to church or to chapel, choosing in the later 1760s between the parish church of St Nicholas, the Countess of Huntingdon's Chapel, the Quakers' Meeting House in North Street and the Presbyterian Chapel in Ship Street. In 1793 the Chapel Royal in North Street was opened but no more religious buildings were built until 1808, although some of the existing ones were enlarged.[8]

The afternoon was filled with diverse amusements: promenading, riding on the Downs, watching cricket matches and other entertainments on the Steine, visiting shops and bookshops, reading or chatting in the libraries, viewing the camera obscura, walking in the gardens and attending public teas. Showing off equipages (horses and carriages) by driving around the edge of the Steine also became popular. In 1797 the equipage of Mr Mestayer, a ship builder, was regarded as worthy of remark as he had a four in hand with three outriders.[9] Many visitors occupied themselves with activities which they organised themselves or discovered by enquiry, such as riding to local scenic spots like Stanmer Park or the surrounding villages. From the 1780s, local guide books enthused about places which suited the fashion for the Picturesque, such as Preston Manor and the nearby woodland called the Rookery where there was a tea garden. This was already open in 1769 and must have been one of the earliest inland tea gardens that depended upon a seaside resort.

In the evening the MC integrated an increasing number of entertainments in a way which gave variety and reduced competition between the main highlights, such as the dress balls, musical performances and theatre evenings. A benefit concert for Mr Barthelemon at the *New Ship* cost 10s. 6d. to attend in 1783, the programme consisting of vocal and instrumental music. The tickets were sold by the libraries and the price would have included a handling charge for the librarian.

The sea was also used for yacht races and water parties which were watched from the shelter of the Steine. Participants included local landowners such as the Duke of Richmond. Military manoeuvres on the Steine and the Downs were popular with the visitors too, especially when the Prince of Wales was present.

The rapid development of a full range of resort facilities and the lengthening of the formal season during which they were all open reflected the town's success. In the 1760s the season began in late June and lasted only until the end of September but the MC organised a few formal assemblies up to the first week or so of December.[10] By 1779 the season started in early July and lasted until November. By 1782 it had lengthened again to end after Christmas. Gambling was a very popular pastime for all social groups in this period and *The Times* expressed concern about the extent of gambling at Brighton on several occasions, but little comment appears in the local paper or in letters written from or about Brighton.[11]

The MC continued to run events until the 1820s but the arrangement died with the passing away of Captain Eld, who had succeeded Mr Forth. Lists of people who attended his balls were published in the *Sussex Weekly Advertiser*.[12]

As the resort became established so it attracted invalids and others who came to enjoy the sea out of the season when accommodation was cheaper and quieter. This helped to keep the town's residents employed and the housing occupied.

The Visitors — Numbers

The only evidence of the number of visitors consists of estimates. Other indicators of the town's success are the increase in the number of houses and the lengthening of the season.

Original Visitors' Lists or Subscription Lists from the libraries have not survived. The earliest list is dated 1769 and arranged in alphabetical order, which suggests that it was culled from a library list at the end of the season. There are 320 visitors of whom about one in eight had a title. Some of the visitors without knighthoods or peerages were obviously related to those who did have them. Because there are no addresses and few initials, further analysis is difficult.

Members of the nobility and gentry who held land in Sussex, such as the Abergavennys of Eridge, the Egremonts of Petworth, Sir Ferdinand Poole, some members of the Sussex branch of the Pelham family and Lord Bridger can be identified. Whilst it can be assumed that Captain Lechmere was related to the Worcestershire family of Hanley Castle, and the 'Mr, Mrs and 3 Misses Foley' came from the same county, some names such as Captain Cook were ubiquitous. From about 1770 the county newspaper published visitors' lists compiled from the libraries' subscription books during the early part of the season, but with even less detail than the 1769 list described above, so this is little help in drawing an accurate portrayal of the visitors.[13]

Estimates of the Number of Visitors and the Resident Population

Year	Visitors	Resident Population
1769	Minimum 320	3,000
1783	Tolerably full	
1787	July–October library list	3,800
2,000		
1794	10,000	5,700
1811	12 or 15,000	12,000
1814	4,000 on one day on Steine	
1817-18	June–October 7,000	
	November–February 2,300 11,000	18,000
	February–June 1,700	

Sources: *Sussex Weekly Advertiser* except the following: 1811 VCH Vol.2 (1907), 203; 1814 in *The Times* 13 September 1814, p.3; 1817-18 Wright, C., *The Brighton Ambulator* (Wright, London, 1818), 102.

Special visitors, such as members of the royal family and the Russian ambassador, were always noted separately in the local newspaper and sometimes in *The Times* and other London papers. This makes the dates of their first visits quite easy to find. Members of the royal family started to visit Brighton in the 1760s – the Duke of Gloucester in 1765, and then the Duke of York in 1766. From 1771 the Duke and Duchess of Cumberland were regular and popular visitors. The Duke of Clarence brought Mrs Jordan to the town.[14] The town's popularity with his uncles might have been one reason why the Prince of Wales came in 1783, when he stayed for 11 days as a guest of the Duke of Cumberland. Grove House (later Marlborough House), which the Duke had rented, stood at the northern end of East Street facing the Steine.[15]

In 1784 and 1785 the Prince returned to Brighton. In July 1784 he occupied the detached lodging house of a wealthy landowner, Thomas Kemp, which faced the Steine and stood between Grove House and the *Castle Inn*. Mrs Fitzherbert, his companion, stayed in a lodging house at the north-western corner of East Street near Kemp's house, in a row of houses which became known as Marlborough Row. This discreet arrangement was probably repeated in 1785 when they are said to have married.[16] The Prince attracted more visitors but the claims that he either converted a fishing village into a resort by his presence or that he regenerated a decaying town, although discredited a long time ago, are still repeated.[17] The Prince was attracted by the town's reputation as a fast-growing resort and by the presence of people that he knew. Easy access to London was also important for him, and reports of his activities in the local and national press show how often he travelled up to London for short stays when in Brighton.

Local Contacts

Local contacts played a significant role in attracting visitors to Brighton. The Duke of Marlborough was a relative of Thomas Pelham of Stanmer House which stands only a few miles inland from Brighton. Members of the Pelham clan were visiting the resort before 1760 and the Duke of Marlborough first visited in 1762, probably on their recommendation. In 1771 the Duke bought from Samuel Shergold a 'capital messuage' which the former had built in 1765 to let. It became the first Marlborough House.

The Duke of Marlborough was a Spencer and related to Georgiana, Duchess of Devonshire, who visited Brighton in the late 1770s. Whilst sea bathing on the recommendation of her doctor to try to prevent further miscarriages, she met Mary Graham, with whom she became close. Charles James Fox, related by marriage to the Lennox family of Goodwood in West Sussex, was amongst the vistors that Georgiana knew.[18] She also knew the Duke of Richmond (of Goodwood) and Thomas Pelham. Both Georgiana and Bess (Foster), the 2nd Duchess of Devonshire (another visitor to the resort), were friends of the Prince of Wales.[19] Di Beauclerk, the artist, was another Spencer to visit Brighton, receiving hospitality from the Duke of Marlborough.[20]

In the 1760s several houses were bought or built by visitors to Brighton. Henry Thrale, a wealthy brewer from Southwark, bought or inherited a house on the east side of West Street in 1760, and his father Ralph seems to have had title to it when he died in that year.[21] In 1768 the Right Honorable John Shelley, Treasurer to His Majesty's Household, bought for £948 19s. a house built by Thomas Kent in 1766 on the west side of West Street.[22] Sir William and Lady Denise Hart had a house in East Street by 1766.[23]

21 Mrs Fitzherbert's House, Brighton. Izard St James's Street.

Visitors' Impressions

Visitors' impressions of the resort as it developed are important because visitors' reactions determined its success. But diaries and letters are difficult sources to use because the reasons for the author's description cannot be established. In spite of some of the comments below, the majority of the visitors must have liked Brighton as it became increasingly popular. Favourable comments by acquaintances must have been as important as the recommendations of physicians for visitors were looking for diversion and good company as well as a health cure. Publicists' descriptions of the town can be compared with the visitors' remarks. Dr Relhan claimed in 1761 in his *History*:

> the town improves daily as the inhabitants, encouraged by the late great resort of company, seem disposed to expend the whole of what they acquire in the erecting of new buildings or making the old ones convenient. Should the increase of these [improvements] in the next 7 years, be equal to what has been in the past [7 years] it is probable that there will be but few towns in England that will exceed this in commodious buildings.

As early as 1762 Mrs Green observed to Mrs Collier that, 'in the last three weeks there has been a great deal of company ... I think all public places are alike, for it is just like Bath, and you see a vast many fine folks.'[24]

By the early 1760s the town was attracting literary figures and their friends, including Charles Churchill, who wrote from Brighton to William Hogarth, the artist. It is at this point that the town's long association with artists and writers appears to have begun. Thomas Gray (then a famous poet) was another visitor and in 1764 he followed a routine that many other people must have known at that date. He rose at six to buy fish, then read the papers and walked on the beach. He breakfasted at nine and then dressed formally at ten, dined at 4 p.m. (as was customary at that time), went to the Assembly Rooms, played cards and after a light supper went to bed at 10p.m.[25]

A visitor in 1766 gave the most succinct summary, albeit in a rather negative way, of why people visited Brighton and the impact they were having on it:

> Brighton in the county of Sussex is distant from London 57 miles, is a small ill-built town, situated on the sea coast, at present greatly resorted to in the summer season, by various persons labouring under various diseases, for benefit of seabathing and drinking seawater and by the gay and polite on account of the company which frequent it in the season, unlike a few years ago no better than a mere fishing town inhabited by fishermen and sailors. It is become one of the principal places in the kingdom for the resort of the idle and dissipated as well as of the diseased and inform.[26]

Some of the visitors to Brighton were ordinary local people such as Thomas Turner, a shopkeeper of East Hoathly (to the north-east of Lewes), who was not impressed by the resort. In 1757 he persuaded his brother to bathe at Seaford instead of Brighton in case he got into 'bad company'. The pair walked to Seaford from East Hoathly and back in a day.[27]

In 1763 one newcomer, Gilly Williams, found that sea bathing agreed with him, liked the novelty of bathing and the informality, and remarked:

> It would astound you to see the mixture of sexes at this place, and with what coolness and indifference half a dozen Irishmen will bathe close to those whom we call prudes elsewhere.[28]

Inevitably there were others that found features of the town that upset them, including the uncivil behaviour of some visitors and the mere presence of others, especially if they were regarded as making the resort less socially exclusive.[29]

By the early 1770s there is less sense of novelty about visiting Brighton and the routine of an established resort is reflected in contemporary descriptions. In 1771 John Baker

> took lodgings instantly at Miss Grover in West Street at 1 guinea a week man and self. Met Mrs Charles Ashburnham, Mr Baysford and others. Subscribed to the coffee house, five shillings to the rooms, three shillings to the circulating library.

He bathed in the sea early the next day and while in Brighton went to the races at Lewes.[30]

By the late 1770s detractors no longer described the resort as primitive but instead accused it of exploiting visitors or ostracised them for their social origins and behaviour. Other resorts, including Bath, generated similar comments. Smollett's *Humphry Clinker* is one of the best satirical descriptions of Georgian resorts, Humphrey commenting somewhat acidly at times on many of them, both spa and

22 *View of Marlborough House (after refronting by Robert Adam) and Mrs Fitzherbert's House. Aquatint c.1805.*

seaside. William Cowper (poet) remarked to his friend, the Rev. Unwin, that the people of Brighton lacked 'both sobriety and wisdom' but it was possible to learn something from almost anyone of any rank by observation.[31]

Brighton attracted critical comment and satire both in written and in the form of cartoons, which were a very popular form of social comment in late Georgian England. From about 1780 the output of poems and novels about the town increased noticeably. Many were locally and privately published, providing an income for the local printers and booksellers, but a few such as a poem by Mary Lloyd were published by subscription.[32] Musical compositions became popular including *Trip to Brighton* (1791) and *Brighthelmstone Hot Bath* and celebrations of the presence of Prince George such as the *Prince of Wales in Brighton* (1796).[33]

In 1780 one author deemed Brighton:

> Only an obscure fishing village … until silken folly and bloated disease under the auspices of Doctor Russell deemed it necessary to crowd the shore and fill the inhabitants with contempt for their visitors.[34]

But in 1779 someone else published anonymously in the *Sussex Weekly Advertiser* a poem that advertised its attractions and expressed the hope that George III and his Queen might visit. Brighton sounds very much like many modern resorts:

> No favourite shore, whither health bids repair
> For a breeze or a dip can Brighton compare;
> Folks civil, neat dwellings, streets airey and clean,
> And here nature has spread her fair carpet – the Steine …
>
> Tho' in pleasing excursions, you spend the long day
> And to Lewes or Shoreham or Rottingdean Strey,
> And drink tea and Preston to vary the scene,
> At eve with new raptures you'll fly to the Steine …

The poem then goes on to point out that the Steine is a good place to meet young ladies if you are a young man.

By 1815 new ideas about landscape were influencing how Brighton was depicted. William Wilberforce wrote to Lord Teignmouth that Brighton was:

> a place at which you have been so often that I need scarely to explain why it appears to me so like Piccadilly by the seaside. I can delight in the fresh breeze and in the varied forms of the beautiful and sublime, which this single object exhibits.[35]

His comment reflects the fashion for the Picturesque, a movement that made seascapes and wild landscapes fashionable and helped seaside resorts to develop. By now the resort bustled for much of the year and amongst the attractions were the balls and suppers given by Mrs Fitzherbert which were highly regarded by those who managed to obtain an invitation. 'Walzomania' had caught on as it had at Bath and also helped to pass the time.

The town was a place to escape to and, as George Jackson said to a relative in 1812, only the quietest times of year (after Christmas and especially March to June) were cheap. Yet a carefully planned stay in the resort was less expensive than running a country estate and had fewer stresses associated with it:

This is now becoming our country house without the drawbacks of country life. Nobody breaks down our hedges, our sheep do not die of the rot, our cows do not loose their calves etc and I can follow my indoor occupations without being interupted by any visits.[36]

During the quiet spring period the townsfolk were busy building and cleaning lodging houses (especially the cesspits) and undertaking other improvements that made Brighton more attractive for its visitors in the peak period.

Few were the remarks on the times when the town failed to let all of the houses. The observation made in the *Gentleman's Magazine* in 1812 that there were many splendid and recently built houses which were empty is unusual.[37] By 1816 taste in landscape was moving away from the open areas typical of the highly managed, often treeless, sheep-farmed South Downs towards more picturesque and varied landscape such as that surrounding Hastings, although the bare cliffs and the barren downs, the donkeys pulling small carts and 'flocks of Englishmen eagerly quitting their native soil for France' did provoke some criticism.[38]

Some of the new residents and visitors were regarded as odd. The eccentricity of one was reported in the *Gentleman's Magazine*. She had moved beside the Steine and yet chosen deliberately to live in isolation in a town dedicated to socialising and leisure and she died alone and anonymously. The discovery of the body clearly concerned the magazine's correspondent.[39]

Brighton flourished because it attracted a wide range of wealthy people who had the time and money to live an expensive and public lifestyle in a resort. However, fashions change, and by 1820 Brighton was outgrowing the highly structured and public routines that seaside resorts had inherited from spas; a mark of that was the decline in the fortunes and standing of the MC. Even by 1800 there were too many visitors for the routine to work for all of those involved. Entertainment in private houses was increasingly fashionable and this needed buildings capable of holding large numbers of visitors for dinner and, in a few instances, for balls. The new era in the resort's history took a little while to manifest itself in the grand new terraced houses from the early 1820s, but Kemp Town and Brunswick Town met the needs of the new lifestyle, their development altering the way in which the older town was used by visitors.

5

The Royal Pavilion

That the arrival of George, Prince of Wales and heir to George III did not establish Brighton as a seaside resort is now clear. By 1783 the resort was well established and popular with two of his uncles, the Dukes of Cumberland and York. Although he brought new visitors, he was thought by some to attract those regarded as undesirable, such as the Lades. Much of the critical comment on him and of the Pavilion came from people who were not supporters of the Prince and his circle.[1] His real impact on Brighton is hard to evaluate because from the 1790s Brighton was used as a military base. The town also grew very rapidly in the early 19th century at about the time the Prince's visits became less frequent, which suggests that his presence may have helped but not as much as was once believed.

At first local tradesmen made a fuss of George. In the hope that it would attract more business, owners of some libraries and shops embellished their premises with the Prince of Wales's feathers as a sign of his patronage. In 1789 Dulot and Elmore celebrated his birthday by decorating their libraries and the Master of Ceremonies arranged a sailing match. Artists also valued the Prince's patronage, Edward Scott, who specialised in miniatures, being one beneficiary.[2] But as George became a regular visitor, so local interest in his activities tailed off, although the changes he made to the Royal Pavilion did attract comment.

The Royal Pavilion was George's major contribution to Brighton. Its evolution from 1786 made it a significant tourist attraction and ensured that it was a popular image for prints and comment. Between the late 1780s and the early 1820s more prints of the Pavilion were produced than of any other landscape or building in the town. By 1823 it had assumed its current appearance and most of the present grounds had been purchased, and then the Chain Pier supplanted it as the most popular image of the town.

Stages in the building of the Pavilion illustrate the problems of establishing and extending a large town house and its grounds in a prosperous, rapidly growing town where a mosaic of plots of land had to be bought. They also reveal the impact of such a development upon subsequent urban change in its immediate locality, including the location of new roads.[3] The commercial value conferred by proximity to the Pavilion inflated land prices, and this limited the amount of land which the Prince's agents were able to buy in order to provide space for their royal employer's increasingly grand buildings and gardens.

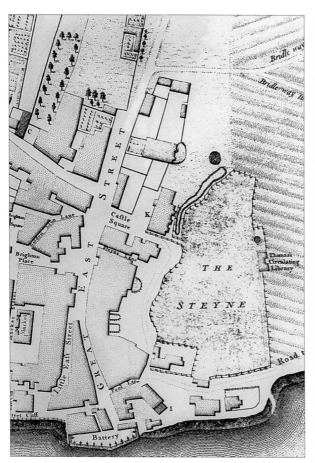
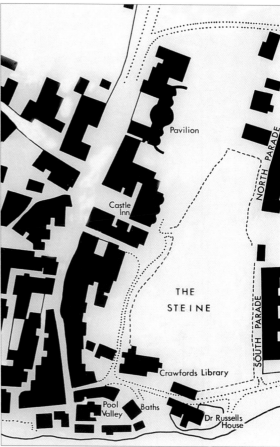

Acquiring the Site for the Pavilion

Sometime in 1785 or early in 1786 the Prince decided to have a permanent residence in Brighton. To avoid arguments with his father over the cost he asked his steward to acquire the property he had been renting. In 1786 Weltjie personally leased Kemp's lodging house with the adjacent coach house and stables for three years at £150 per annum with an option to purchase the property for £3,000. When Weltjie bought the property in 1787 he also purchased land on its south-east side, between Kemp's property and the *Castle Inn*, for £2,800 from Richard Tidy, a rich inhabitant of the town. In 1789 Weltjie purchased an icehouse in the chalk pit at the upper (western) end of North Street and in 1790 he took a long lease of land near Kemp's lodging house.[4]

Although the house overlooked the fashionable Steine and could be clearly seen from there, the site was in some respects a strange choice. In 1785 there was still a view from the eastern front of the lodging house seawards across the Steine or towards the downland. However, the agricultural land on the eastern side of the Steine was already being built on and soon after 1800 the downland view was totally lost. The Prince may not have seen that as an issue, for he enjoyed the company of people and public display and was probably more interested in the Steine and the

23   Section from Yeakell and Gardner's map of Brighton in 1779 next to a section from Budgen's map of 1788 showing the Pavilion just after Holland's work on it and the development of lodging houses that blocked the Prince's view of the sea.

people than he was in the sea view. On the west side, traffic going in and out of Brighton to London and Lewes ran along East Street past the entrance to the rear of the pavilion. To ensure some privacy on that side, land on the west side of East Street was purchased so that the Prince did not have new lodging houses looking straight at his main entrance.

As he settled into a seaside lifestyle, and his desire for space and facilities grew, purchases of land were not confined to the vicinity of East Street. George had a kennel for hounds designed by Holland and built in North Laine, north of Brighton.[5] To make more room for the Pavilion, the Prince's Dairy was relocated in 1802 to the southern end of the parish of Preston to the north of Brighton.[6]

The Development of the Royal Pavilion – Phase 1 Henry Holland c.1786-1802

From 1786 the development of the Pavilion can be divided into three phases, each dependent on the purchase of more land. In the first phase, from 1786 to 1802, building was confined to the land purchased by Weltjie in 1785-6 and the influence upon the town, either physically or visually, was comparatively slight or was overshadowed by the overall speed of the town's physical growth.

While Weltjie was buying land he also paid for the conversion of Kemp's lodging house into the Pavilion. This was partly because the Prince of Wales was so heavily in debt that his alterations to Carlton House (his London home) had to stop and other temporary economies had also to be made.[7] Henry Holland, the architect who was employed at Carlton House, designed and supervised the building of the Prince's 'Marine Pavilion'.

Kemp's lodging house was used as the southern wing of the new building, which was designed so that the state rooms faced eastwards towards the Steine and the entrance, and the two service wings faced East Street. The entrance and the drawing room had a domed roof. The bow-fronted north and south wings were symmetrical and the building was faced with mathematical tiles which are said to have come from Hampshire and are described as the colour of Bath Stone by one contemporary.[8] Holland had used tiles from Hampshire on his own house in Sloane Place, Chelsea in 1777-8 and he may have used the same supplier for the Pavilion.[9] Work began in 1786, and when the Prince inspected progress in May 1787 he expected to occupy the building within some eight weeks; the local newspaper claimed that 150 workmen were employed in order to get it finished and furnished on time.

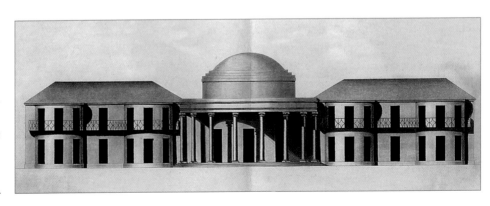

24 *Principal elevation of the Pavilion at Brighton in Sussex belonging to His Royal Highness the Prince of Wales. Henry Holland Arch't.* Richardson and Son, London, June 1796.

By 1788 over £6,000 had been spent by Holland on the Pavilion and on the construction of Weltjie's house and the Prince's Stables, both of which were built between the Pavilion and the *Castle Inn*. Holland's simple, classical design for the Prince's house and the plans for the gardens were probably based upon a book of illustrations of pavilions (or country residences) around Paris, which was published in the mid-1780s.[10] It is this building which Pasquin described as 'built principally of wood; it is a nondescript monster in building and appears like a mad-house or a house run mad as it has neither beginning, middle or end'.[11] The same satirist claimed that the land was given to the Prince by the town, 'for which he allows them £50 yearly to purchase grog and tobacco'. The Prince did donate an annual 'bounty' of £50 which was distributed to the town's poor; his example was designed to encourage other visitors and residents to do the same.

From the late 1780s the presence of the Pavilion began to affect the development of its immediate surroundings. Urban development spread along the east side of the Steine as well as eastwards along the cliff top. That views of the Pavilion attracted visitors to lodgings in its vicinity was reflected in the rents that were advertised and the rateable value of the lodging houses.

As houses were built along its fringes so the northern area of the Steine became increasingly popular for promenades and other social activities, but its use was affected by an elongated and unsightly pool of water which gathered during the autumn in front of the Pavilion and Grove House. In 1793 both the Prince and the Duke of Marlborough (who owned Grove House, just north of the Pavilion) contributed towards the cost of laying a drain along the length of the Steine down to the sea in order to improve the gardens of both properties. In return, both men were allowed to enclose some of the Steine.

25 *The Marine Pavilion belonging to His Royal Highness the Prince of Wales at Brighton.* Engraved for *The Lady's Magazine*, Copper 1799. The second Marlborough House is to the north of the Pavilion.

26   *Saloon at the Royal Pavilion*. Drawn by Rowlandson, tinted by Alken. Only print produced of the interior of Holland's Pavilion.

In 1793 the Prince's agent negotiated with Weltjie about purchasing the Pavilion Estate. Weltjie claimed that he had spent £23,249 on the purchase of land and on the building, the land costing £5,800 and Holland's work £16,200. The Prince was short of cash and the agent suggested that Weltjie should take the Prince's Okehampton Estate in part payment. Both parties agreed to employ arbitrators, who would report within a year, and to accept their decision; the two arbitrators produced different valuations in 1794. One agreed with Weltjie's valuation of the cost of the land but cut his estimate of the building costs by nearly £3,000, reducing the total to £20,992, ten per cent less than Weltjie's claim. The second estimate was based on the supposition that the 'Marine Pavilion' was suitable only for use as a royal palace. As it would not be saleable the valuation would only be based upon the value of the building materials and the land assuming that the building had been demolished. The only saleable buildings were the stables and Weltjie's house. On this basis the total value was only £15,570, which was 68 per cent of Weltjie's claim. Although in 1794 the local newspaper claimed the Prince had purchased the Pavilion, negotiations had failed. Weltjie withdrew from the arrangement because he did not want the Okehampton Estate, and he and his heirs let the estate to the Prince until it was bought in 1808.[12]

In 1794 the Prince asked Holland to provide plans for enlarging the Pavilion although encumbered with enormous debts, which included bills from Brighton tradesmen. These plans may have been commissioned while negotiations with Weltjie were being conducted. When the Prince married Princess Caroline of Brunswick in 1795, and his debts were settled, he purchased Dairy Field directly opposite the Pavilion, on the west side of East Street, to make more space. The land may have already been leased, for the Prince's Dairy was there from 1794 to 1802.[13]

No further alterations were made to the Pavilion until between 1800 and 1802, when Holland spent about £13,300 on renovation and enlargement, including extra rooms, a new entrance hall and portico, and a gallery which was decorated in the chinoiserie style. The evolution of the interior of the Royal Pavilion has been covered in detail elsewhere and will not be described here.[14] As part of the scheme Lapidge landscaped the gardens, including Dairy Field, a detached site on the west side of East Street. Such gardens were unusual in Georgian towns.[15] The work marked the end of the first stage of the Pavilion's extension.[16]

In order to enlarge the house, add extra service buildings or extend the garden, more purposeful planning and the town's cooperation were necessary, because East Street had to be closed so that land purchases on its western side could be incorporated into the Pavilion Estate.

The Royal Pavilion Phase 2 1803–1810

Buying Land for Porden's Riding Stables and the Closure of 'Upper' East Street

In the second phase, from 1803 to 1808, the grounds of the Royal Pavilion were extended to build new riding stables, now called the 'Dome'.[17] In 1802 East Street extended northwards as far as Church Street and so ran along the west side of the Pavilion. It served as the main road into the town for two of the three routes from London – via Lewes and via Clayton. These roads converged north of Brighton and joined East Street just north of the Pavilion. The road from Lewes also brought a considerable volume of traffic into East Street from Tunbridge Wells, a spa town.[18] The traffic then drove into Castle Square at the junction between North Street and East Street. There, by 1802, most of the coaching companies' offices and carriers' wagon inns were located.[19] Land which faced East or North Streets or onto Castle Square had a high commercial value because of the area's importance as a main business area. The proximity of the Pavilion encouraged the development of the fashionable Promenade Grove just west of East Street, and the aptly named Princes Place in North Street, both of which were opened in 1794. Land purchase was, therefore, going to be expensive.

The area to the west of East Street (where the Prince proposed to have his stables built) was divided into long large crofts (enclosed paddocks) stretching from the rear of buildings along the north side of North Street to Church Street. The frontages along North Street were lined with shops and houses, and stables and streets were being developed through to Church Street, where small houses, market gardens and more stabling was being built. In order to obtain enough space for the new stables, the Prince's agents had to buy entire crofts (Quakers' Croft, Promenade Grove, Furner's Gardens) as well as properties on the street frontages. Negotiations were still being concluded after the stables were built.[20]

Although the Prince was consulted about purchasing land, it is unclear who suggested that East Street should be closed to give his residence privacy on its western side and link the Palace with the new stable and grounds. The idea must have been suggested after Porden's design was approved, because in 1802 negotiations with the Town Commissioners began. The legal agreement to close

27 Pavilion at Brighton. Gardiner del. Newton sc. Copper engraving, 1801.

East Street and to provide an alternative route called New Road was enrolled at the Quarter Sessions so that it was enforceable.[21] The Prince's solicitors had few problems in arranging the closure. By way of comparison, in order to divert the main road through Arundel to London in order to extend his park, the Duke of Norfolk had the expense of obtaining a private Act of Parliament in 1803.[22]

Whilst land purchase was in progress both parties agreed the new route, and the northern part of East Street between Castle Square and Church Street was closed. The Prince agreed to give New Road to the town having laid out and surfaced it. It was opened in the spring of 1806 after soldiers were employed there. The closure of East Street enabled the Prince to contemplate more grandiose landscaping and also removed a major constraint on the subsequent redevelopment of the Pavilion, which began in 1814.[23]

Meanwhile Attree, acting as the Prince's solicitor, began the tortuous task of finding out who owned the land needed for this scheme and negotiating with them. He began to buy Promenade Grove, whose gardens were immediately to

28 *View of the Pavilion and Steyne at Brighton with the Promenade.* View by S.T. Cracklow, the figures by W.M. Craig. Etched and engraved by J. Mitan, aquatinted by J.C. Stadler, published 23 July 1806. Depicts the Prince of Wales and his equerry Major Bloomfield and many other notables taken from portraits by Dighton.

the west of the Dairy Field and had been laid out over a croft subsumed into the gardens of a large town house owned by a doctor (Sir Lucas Pepys) and his wife (the Countess of Rothes). They are visible on the map of the town by Yeakell and Gardner in 1779, where the two rows of elms are clearly marked. Lord Leslie, the heir to the Pepys family, sold the land in 1791 to John Kirby, 'high class grocer' from London. Kirby built some shops on the land beside North Street and sold more land to the Reverend Thomas Hudson for the Chapel Royal. Hudson then sold his unwanted land to two builders who built some of the shops in Princes Place. Kirby attempted to build over the rest of the garden before becoming bankrupt in 1793-4 with a lot of debt. By 1794 the elm-shaded croft had been leased by Kirby's creditors to Mr Bailey who then opened it as the Promenade Grove public subscription gardens. The Prince of Wales and aristocrats visited it for breakfasts, firework displays and music recitals until it was closed after the Prince bought it from the Pepys family and Kirby's other creditors (who included a London bank and local gentry) in 1802. The sale included some shops in Princes

Place at the entrance to Promenade Grove. All the tenants were given temporary leases until the land should be needed.[24]

Its management by trustees, none of whom were resident in Brighton, prolonged negotiations for the Quakers' Croft. They leased the three-quarters of an acre which was not a burial ground to Thomas Furner for £15 a year to use as additional land for his market gardening. His lease had to be bought by the Prince and the purchase of Furner's own gardens was concluded by January 1804.

The overall process of land purchase was protracted because Porden (the architect) and Bicknell (the Prince's chief solicitor) were anxious to save money by exchanging small plots of land not needed for the new project, such as that to the north of New Road, for property that was. They offered to erect a new building as part of the agreement if necessary.[25] An important exchange, which was necessary in order to complete the projected site for New Road, was made with Samuel Shergold's heirs. The *Castle Inn* had two separate and extensive stables, one of which stood north of the Quakers' Meeting House and blocked the projected junction between New Road (through Furner's Gardens) and North Street. It was agreed that this stable and Shergold's other stable in Church Street, which also occupied land needed for the Prince's stables, should be exchanged. In return for both plots Shergold's heirs received a large parcel of land on the north-west corner of New Road with new stables and coach-houses which were built by Porden in 1804.[26] Whereas some of the properties on the boundaries of the new grounds were purchased in order to absorb them, others, including land owned by Bradford, Sands and Brooker, were also bought in order to control land use on the estate's fringes.

29 *Corridor design for the Royal Pavilion* by H. Repton. H. Repton del. J.C. Stadler sculp. Aquatint 1808. This design was not executed.

Porden began building the stables in 1803 when, conveniently, Parliament agreed to an increase in the Prince's allowance. In 1805, when the shell of the stables was standing, the Prince commissioned new designs for the grounds and the Pavilion from Humphry Repton, the landscape gardener. By 1807 the Prince had received a copy of Repton's designs (which he produced jointly with his son, an architect), although they were not published until 1808.[27] The Prince did not use them, probably because the 'Dome' was still absorbing far more money for land and materials than anyone had estimated. The escalating costs were partly due to the complex roof design but also to the town's accelerating growth rate, which increased the cost of land, labour and building materials.

30 *Marlborough House and Marlborough Row looking from the north with the Pavilion just south of Marlborough House by H. Repton. H. epton del. J.C. Stadler sculp. Aquatint 1808. This shows the area before the demolition of this Marlborough House and the majority of the lodging houses. Repton's 'Red Book' of designs for the site from which this comes then shows his ideas for this area.*

31 *The west side of the Pavilion was designed by Holland seen from just beside Porden's new Riding Stables (now called the Dome). By H. Repton. H. Repton del. J.C. Stadler sculp. Aquatint 1808.*

32 *The Pavilion, Brighton.* Bray sculp. in Attree's *Topography of Brighton*, 1809.

Repton's ideas probably instigated the next phase of development for he recommended an enlarged 'Hindoo' Pavilion based on Cockerell's interpretation of Indian architecture at Sezincote in Gloucestershire. The Prince had visited Sezincote and knew that Repton had advised on landscaping.[28] Repton suggested that an Indian-style Pavilion would complement the Turkish style of the 'Dome' and counteract the stable's dominance of the house and grounds. His plans included converting the Pavilion's grounds into a garden which could be used all year.

By the end of 1808 the upheavals caused by the building of the 'Dome' had nearly ended. Plots of land on the west side of New Road were being disposed of to creditors or sold, for Porden was very concerned by the Prince's indebtedness. Amongst the purchasers was Henry Cobb, who built the Theatre Royal. He negotiated his purchase so adeptly that he managed to buy the land freehold instead of leasehold, as had been agreed with Porden. The latter was angered to discover that Cobb, by dealing direct with Bicknell and ignoring his previous agreement with Porden, had also extended the time over which he would pay for the land, which action made Porden's cash flow problems even worse.[29]

By the latter part of 1808 new buildings along the western side of New Road and on the western side of the 'Dome' (out of view of the Pavilion) made the dome less obtrusive from the west and north. The view of the 'Dome' from the Pavilion was still partially obscured by Marlborough Row. Its scale, and the irregular shape of the grounds, stimulated the next and final stage of redevelopment and expansion. The imbalance between the Pavilion and the new stables also provoked comments. In 1807 a regular contributor to the *Gentleman's Magazine* was complimentary about the Pavilion's design and, after commenting sourly upon the design of the nearly

completed stables, said of them, 'The whole congestion is a sort of professional frolic, running a short lived antic around the chaste and modest elevations of the Pavilion …'[30]

33 *The Pavilion at Brighton.* Drawn by J.P. Neale, engraved by Woolnoth, in Shoberl, *Beauties of England and Wales* 1813.

Plans to Extend the Pavilion Phase 3

1808-1822 – Wyatt and Nash

In the third and final stage, when the remodelling of the Pavilion was finished, extra land was purchased, which to give the grounds greater privacy resulted in the purchase and demolition of well-known landmarks, the *Castle Inn* and Marlborough House and Marlborough Row. When Nash took over the project he was determined to use every inch of land and another adjustment of roadways resulted from his scheme. In 1817 the 'waste' to the north of Marlborough House (previously Grove House) was completely assimilated into the estate and the entrance to Church Street from the Steine was moved northwards as a result.[31]

Purchasing Land

In 1810 five shops were bought in Castle Square, which backed onto the Pavilion Estate close to the Palace. The land required for the Pavilion grounds was taken and

Engraved by R. Alford, Brighton.

34   *View of the Pavilion taken from Wright's Circulating Library*, May 1818. Copper engraving, R. Alford.

the redeveloped shops were sold on. Covenants on the use of the buildings and access to a private road between them and the estate gave greater privacy. The purchase most vital for the expansion of the Pavilion was made in 1812 when Marlborough House was purchased from the Duke of Marlborough for £9,000.[32] The lords of the manor of Brighton-Lewes then confirmed the grant of a substantial area of land on its northern and eastern sides (once part of the Steine) which had been incorporated into the grounds of the house after 1780, on condition that it was not built on.[33]

In 1812 the Prince commissioned new designs for enlarging the Pavilion from James Wyatt whose only work before he was killed in a coach accident in 1813 was to link Marlborough House to the existing Pavilion as an interim measure.[34] On Wyatt's death, John Nash was appointed as the architect and he successfully submitted an 'Indian style design' which would envelop and extend Holland's classical Pavilion. Nash had once been Repton's partner and his ideas were reminiscent of the building which Repton had suggested in his unsuccessful plan of 1806.[35]

Nash's grandiose ideas prompted the final spate of purchases in this third phase of which the most important were Marlborough Row and the *Castle Inn*. Negotiations for these and the shops in Castle Square (owned by the Hall family) began in 1813 and were costly and prolonged. The first purchase of a share in the inn was made by accident. Thomas Attree noticed that Samuel Shergold Jnr was auctioning his quarter share combined with the entire title to a small piece of land adjacent to the Pavilion's southern lawn. Attree realised that if the plot were built on it would spoil the Pavilion's setting, and he resolved to buy it himself should he fail to persuade the Prince's agents to sanction the purchase in time for the auction. The property was expected to fetch £2,500. Attree claimed that he paid £2,060 but later lists of the land purchases give a figure of £1,960. The Prince's agents eventually paid Attree for the purchase and he was commissioned to buy the other shares in the *Castle Inn*.[36]

The Prince did not own all four shares in the inn until 1821 when it closed because business had declined. The congested location, competition from more modern inns, and declining interest in the assemblies, which had once been a major attraction, all conspired to end the life of this once famous hotel. The Prince's agents were probably aware of the decline in 1815 when they refused to pay £6,000 for James Shergold's half-share, which included the icehouse.

In 1822 the Assembly Room (built by Crunden in the 1760s as an extension of the inn) was converted into the Pavilion's Chapel. Alterations to the interior of the chapel included gothic embellishments, an organ and a water closet, and mathematical tiles were applied to the part of the extension that the demolition of the inn exposed. In an effort to keep down the cost of land purchases, the Prince's agents persuaded John Hall to take surplus land from the *Castle*'s grounds in part payment for his property in Castle Square. Hall agreed and leased the shops which he built on the site but constantly found excuses for failing to enforce the covenants intended to prevent windows from being inserted on the side of the building which might overlook the Pavilion and prevent noxious or noisy traders, or obstructions, near the estate's boundaries.[37]

Buying Marlborough Row

Attree found negotiations with the alert and business-like owners of Marlborough Row particularly challenging. The Prince and his agents intended to use the houses for temporary accommodation while Nash worked on the Pavilion, and then to demolish them. The nine properties had been built as lodging houses at various

35 *The south front of the Royal Pavilion J. Nash Arch't and Invent. A. Pugin del't. I. Sutherland Aquatint, c.1822.*

36   *The Pavilion Steyne Front J. Nash Arch't and Invent.* Aug. Pugin del't and T. Fidding sculp. 1824.

dates between 1784 and 1802, while the smithy at the northern end of the Row, on Church Street, was in use long before 1790. Most of the owners had other business interests in Brighton but the tenants were mainly widows who let rooms.

Attree tried to negotiate simultaneously with the respective owners of the Row to prevent prices being raised. His success cannot be assessed because of the different floor areas, ages and conditions of the properties, and valuations of contents in cases when the agreement included that element. He purchased numbers 1–8 but failed to purchase number 9 and the smithy.[38] The determination of the owner of 9 Marlborough Row to hold out for a higher price prevented the Prince from erecting a gatehouse to complement the shrubbery that had been laid out on the newly acquired land to the north of the Pavilion. While Attree was negotiating the purchases he was expected to try to ensure that payments should be spread over

some years to keep the cost of rebuilding the Pavilion more evenly distributed. To help pay for it land around the icehouse in North Street (which Weltjie had bought) was sold. That sale was helped by the development of adjacent land on which Thomas Read Kemp laid out roads.[39]

The Prince and his guests used Marlborough Row during the last stages of the redevelopment of the Pavilion. Some money was spent on repairs to the Row in 1817 and in 1818-19 internal redecoration was undertaken. Robson and Hale, the paperhangers who worked in the Pavilion, Carlton House, Hampton Court and Buckingham Palace, cleaned and repaired old papers and hung new. In Number 4 they hung a bamboo trellis design.[40] The newly decorated interiors were not in use for long, numbers 1-4 being demolished in 1820 and 5-7 in 1821, having been occupied by George IV for Christmas 1820.[41]

37 *No. 8 Marlborough Row.*

Number 8 Marlborough Row still stands beside the north gate to the Pavilion. Known as the Lord Chamberlain's House, or Guard House after its purchase, it was used by the Hertfords. When Lady Hertford fell out of favour with George, the house must have been reclaimed by the Prince. In 1819 it became the residence of Lady Conyngham, mistress of George, who created her Lady Steward. In 1830, when the Town Commissioners gave the land they did not use to widen Church Street to William IV, the northern gate was erected as intended many years before.[42] The exterior of number 8 was redesigned in 1832 in the oriental style that we see today and became the house that Sir Herbert Taylor, Private Secretary to William IV, used when he was in Brighton.[43] When the house was renovated in 2000, layers of wallpapers dating from *c.*1816-1930 were found.[44]

The lavish Palace redeveloped by Nash was a sophisticated project in many respects. From 1818 the heavy and unfit George could have saltwater pumped into a bath there, after the installation of suitable equipment and water storage.[45] A visitor said critically in 1821:

Nash has been principally employed, and he seems to have produced an Ephermeran wonder, which would not carry his fame to the next generation; large sums have doubtless been expended which may prove beneficial to those who have been employed in the undertaking; but it can never convey any lasting credit on our natural taste …[46]

By 1822 the Pavilion was finished, and in 1823 major expenditure on the estate and buildings at Brighton ended. George was now 63 and had spent most of his adult life creating and changing the Palace. He paid his last visit to the Pavilion only four years after the work was completed and died three years later. By then Windsor Castle and Carlton House were absorbing his attention. At least £250,000 was spent on Carlton House between 1820 and 1829, when it was demolished. The Pavilion might have suffered the same fate in the 1840s, but it was purchased by the town after Queen Victoria had indicated that she no longer wished to use it.[47]

Until the early 1820s the Steine survived as an established resort area because of the lack of an alternative promenade. The Pavilion screened it from the network of streets and industry developing on the old town's northern side. It acted as an eyecatcher and gave the Steine a focus which was retained even after the coast road, opened by King George IV in 1822, provided a new promenade for the rich, and linked the newer, bigger and better planned housing that was beginning to be built in Brighton's eastern and western suburbs.[48]

When George IV died in 1830 his seaside palace was in the busy centre of a bustling town, whilst fashionable visitors were mainly resident in the outer suburbs, especially Brunswick Town and Kemp Town. The King and his court were no longer located conveniently close to each other, and this may have played a role in the ultimate demise of the Pavilion as a royal palace.

6

The Influence of European Wars
on Brighton

Between 1750 and 1815 Britain frequently feared invasion. That fear was greatest in 1756-7, 1759, 1779, 1796-8, 1801 and 1804-5. The coastline of Sussex was thought to be especially vulnerable for most of it is low lying. Brighton is located in a shallow bay that was especially tempting as the gently sloping beach that attracted bathers was also very suitable as a landing place for seaborne invasions. Thus Brighton became one of the assembly areas for the soldiers needed to defend this stretch of coastline. The famous white chalk cliffs that are associated with the south-east coastline only feature in Sussex between Brighton and Eastbourne.

Yet, although England was involved in European wars in opposition to France for more than half of these 65 years between 1750 and 1815, Brighton continued to develop as a resort. The presence of the soldiers reassured and attracted visitors. They provided good business for townsfolk of all kinds, from builders to suppliers of foodstuffs to prostitutes. The visitors seem also to have had a great confidence in the ability of the Navy to keep the coast secure.

Occasionally there were panics when foreign vessels appeared. In 1759 (during the Seven Years War) a fleet of ships seen off the coast caused alarm, for it was assumed to be French. When it proved to be Dutch, that 'dissipated all fear of invasion'.

Defending Brighton c.1750

By 1750 Brighton's unused Elizabethan blockhouse was falling into the sea and, although there is a sketch of the town by Lemprière in about 1740 that seems to show a wall along the front, the town was undefended. Had there been a wall at least some reference would have appeared in the very extensive manorial records, for it would have made a handy reference point when locations of properties were being described.

None of the towns along the Sussex coast was big enough at that time to justify the costly defences built for naval bases such as Portsmouth during the Anglo-Dutch Wars (1652-1724). The government depended on the Royal Navy to deal with coastal defence. Whilst some townsfolk in Sussex complained about the loss of their trading and fishing vessels to piracy and to privateers during the periods of warfare, others invested in privateers and sought to profit. In 1758, just after the start of the Seven Years War, the *Prince Ferdinand*, a privateer from Brighton, captured a Dutch ship and towed it into Rye. Reprisals against such activities were inevitable. In 1779 Frenchmen sought a ransom for the safe return of Humphrey and William Guildford of Brighton, having boarded William and Humphrey's fishing boat.

The Seven Years War (1757-63)

When it embarked upon the Seven Years War the government constructed very basic defences along the Sussex coast. In 1759 five new batteries along the bay between Seaford and Littlehampton, including one at Brighton, were built.

The brick-built blockhouse at Brighton stood at the bottom end of East Street. The new Battery had a house for the Master Gunner and a room below the gun emplacement for the storage of ammunition. It was kitted out with 12 rather ancient guns which were said to be capable of firing 20-pound shot. Although they were reported as satisfactory when inspected in 1779 by Thomas Bloomfield (who claimed to be an artillery expert), the gunners themselves knew the guns were in a most dangerous condition.[1] The wooden carriages were rotten in places and several of the guns were so riddled with rust that only four of them were considered safe.

An unofficial recommendation was that the guns should only be used for royal salutes. Even that proved to be unwise, for in September 1782 the master gunner lost both his hands whilst reloading during a salute to the Prince of Wales' great aunt Amelia. Early in September of the following year, a cannon ignited prematurely during a salute to commemorate a visit made by the Prince of Wales. The explosion blew the gunner's body some distance onto the beach, shattering one of his arms and tearing off his hand, which was never found.

This battery also fell victim to encroachment by the sea and finally collapsed during a severe storm on 17 November 1786. Seventeen barrels of gunpowder were

stored in the magazine at the time. Even though the roof and two heavy guns, each weighing over two tons, tumbled on top of them, they did not explode.

During the Seven Years War some regular soldiers were stationed at Brighton for short periods, but most of the defence of Sussex (and Brighton) was undertaken by militia. The fear of invasion was such that the old idea of a volunteer militia was revived with the passing of the Militia Act in 1757. They were to supplement the Army by defending the nation but were not to serve abroad. From the late 1750s militia raised in Sussex trained around Brighton and their role in the defence of the town was increased during subsequent periods of war.

The American War of Independence (1778-83)

When the French supported the Americans in their fight for independence from Britain the government again became concerned about the security of the south coast. Reports in the local newspaper suggest that troops were retained in Brighton throughout the whole period of warfare. In 1778 Captain Trevor had a troop of dragoons quartered at Brighton for military training, while 300 militia were billeted in the inns.[2] The Sussex Militia also trained at Brighton in 1779, when additional companies were organised.

Local people, especially the wealthier landowners and businessmen, organised much of the local defence planning and provided a lot of the manpower. The overview of defence of the county was entrusted to the Lord Lieutenant for Sussex.

39 *The Blockhouse* 10 September 1773 Godfrey Sc. Copper and in Grose, *Antiquities of England and Wales,* 1785.

40 *Dr Syntax at a Review*. Drawn and etched by Thomas Rowlandson 1813. A sight that would have been familiar to visitors to Brighton.

In 1781 Lord Sheffield (of Sheffield Park, north of Lewes) was very unhappy about the problems of protecting the county's long coastline with his small militia force. He located his regiment in 22 different places along the 80 miles of coastline. He pointed out to Lieutenant-Colonel Gage (of Firle Place) the vulnerability of the foreshore to the west of Brighton (in the parish of Hove). There, he thought, an invading army could be landed quite easily because vessels could moor close to the shallow shelving beaches.[3]

Lord Sheffield also identified an alternative choice for invasion at another bay in Sussex, Pevensey Bay, some twenty miles to the east of Brighton, where other resorts such as Hastings were developing. He thought the hills to the north of Brighton would make a very good defence system for an advance guard against English forces from the land side, whilst the invading fleet unloaded the rest of its army.

Wealthier local people were also expected to raise money towards the cost of uniforms and did so by public subscriptions, their names being published in the newspaper in return for this patriotic action. In 1779 the Duke of Richmond (of Goodwood) subscribed £500, Lord Abergavenny (of Eridge) £100, Lord Pelham (of Stanmer) £100 and Thomas Kemp (of Coneyborough) £20, all being regular visitors to Brighton.

By 1783 a combination of pressure from local people and international events made the government even more concerned about the safety of the Sussex coast. Many countries in Europe had joined an alliance against Britain. The protection of the coastline became a higher priority and more soldiers were deployed there.[4]

Lord Fielding's Light Dragoons appeared in Brighton in April 1783 and remained until June and more soldiers were stationed along the coast until the Treaty of Versailles was signed. The government still expected the Navy to act as a shield for the coast and occasionally movements of frigates off Brighton were recorded. In 1782 *Thomas* was claimed to be on a 'secret mission'.

In the mid-1780s, after peace was declared, the Duke of Richmond and Lord Sheffield reviewed the defence of the Sussex coast. There is no evidence of investment in barracks or fortifications at Brighton but the amount of local training increased and by 1788 there were annual military manoeuvres in the area that involved both regular soldiers and the local militia. In 1788 the First Regiment of Light Dragoons was briefly based near the town, followed in 1790 by the Sussex Militia, and then in 1791 the Queen's Own Regiment of Light Dragoons and the 7th Regiment of Light Dragoons. Soldiers were occasionally caught stealing or causing affrays. Soldiers were subject to criminal law when stealing from within their own regiment, so John Starr was sent to the House of Correction for stealing clothes belonging to Joseph Cotton an officer, whilst the regiment was based in Brighton.

The French Revolutionary (1793-97) and Napoleonic Wars (1798-1802, 1804-15)

The long period of warfare against Revolutionary and Napoleonic France resulted in a considerable investment in military buildings by the government, who had also to pay both the regular soldiers and the suppliers of goods to the Army. This expenditure resulted in extra income for Brighton's residents and the presence of the Army also helped to boost the town's rapid increase in population.

The government did not deploy soldiers, militia and volunteers along the coast of the county until after war was declared between England and France in February 1793, when the defence of the lower and thus more vulnerable stretches of coast again became a priority. It still depended heavily on the Navy and the local

41 Extract from Piggott's map of 1826 showing the infantry barracks behind Marlborough Place.

paper kept people informed about the deployment of vessels. Inevitably speculation was common and some newspaper reports about the identity of passing shipping were misleading and had to be corrected in later issues.

Wealthier local landowners and townsmen again undertook the recruitment of local troops and their training and deployment.[5] They also managed contingency plans. Between 1801 and 1803 Lord Sheffield carried out a detailed survey of the vulnerable areas of the county to help manage withdrawal from the coast should it be needed. His report (which survives) included an estimate of the numbers of people, livestock and horses and carts.[6]

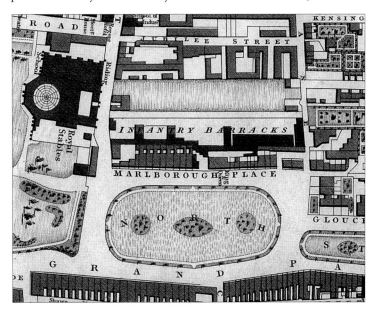

The East and the West Batteries, 1793

Of the military buildings constructed in Brighton, the East and the West Batteries of 1793 were the most impressive. The West Battery (most popular with print makers) stood just about on the site of the present *Grand Hotel* in Artillery Place. The East Battery stood at the southern end of New Steine and overlooked the site where the Chain Pier was built in the 1820s. Both batteries were designed by Captain Twiss of the Royal Engineers. He was also involved in the construction of the Martello Towers which were part of the same defence scheme for the south coast.[7]

The West Battery had a small barracks that accommodated 26 men, a house for the master gunner, a magazine and a furnace for heating the shot; it was demolished when the coastal promenade was widened in 1858. The Eastern Battery suffered from erosion and was probably useless in 1807 when its guns were moved to the West Battery. Little was left of it by 1809.

Naval Signal Stations

In spite of all the soldiers stationed along the coast, the Royal Navy was still regarded as the most important defence against invasion or raids. The Admiralty set up small manned signal stations to keep in touch with naval ships. One was built on the Downs, near the Race Course. The signal stations also kept the Army informed and when, in 1796, the master of the signal station interrogated a French frigate and failed to get a satisfactory answer, he sought to notify the master gunner at the West Battery. But by the time the guns were ready the frigate was well away.

Accommodating the Soldiers

Between 1793 and 1803 Brighton served as a major base for the deployment of regular, militia and volunteer troops. There were so many that barracks and camps were built to house them.

The regular soldiers were a paid force, most of whom could serve both at home and overseas. The majority were deployed only for short periods in Brighton and then moved on, some going abroad to fight. The exception were the Sussex Fencible Cavalry who only served at home.

The militia, a major part of the Army's manpower in 18th-century Sussex, were paid infantry soldiers recruited from the county in which they served and selected by ballot. Militia service was unpopular and men regularly deserted. It was not unusual for names of deserters to be listed in advertisements. Some of the better-off men selected by ballot paid for substitutes to serve instead. A Militia Society was set up in 1796 in Brighton to pay for additional militiamen and to raise subscriptions towards the costs. In 1796 the militia were expected to take part in the annual militia exercise at Brighton that, exceptionally, lasted 28 days. Even during periods when the threat of invasion was greatest, such as 1803, the local militia in Sussex expected to serve full-time for no longer than three weeks.

Volunteers lived at home and served part-time in the Army whilst continuing to work. Active only during periods of warfare, their equipment was provided by the government and by the wealthier local residents such as Colonel Holroyd and Captain Paine of Patcham Place. The volunteer corps of Sussex cavalry that was raised in 1794 had a considerable part of its costs met by public subscription, to which Brighton people contributed. Shergold, the innkeeper of the *Castle*, topped the list with £100, Thomas Kemp gave £50 and Thomas Scutt (of Hove) £10.

Recruiting for the Navy

At the same time as the Army was trying to recruit personnel, the Navy advertised for seamen. In 1779, when the European nations joined the American War of Independence against Britain, the Navy sought 50 able-bodied seamen and promised to pay a bounty of three guineas to those who joined. Press gangs were also used in towns such as Brighton. They were highly unpopular and local fishermen and their families did their best to avoid 'pressing', at least one fisherman maiming himself. Their presence sometimes caused riots. In 1796 the Admiralty granted local fishermen protection from impressment, probably in response to pressure from prominent local worthies, and so at the start of the French Revolutionary Wars the Navy had to change its recruiting tactics. From that point 20 guineas was offered as a bounty to those who joined from Brighton.

Barracks in and around Brighton 1793-1815

In the early 1790s the government seemed to think the defence of the coastline to the west of Brighton was particularly important and that the period during which defences would be manned might be quite lengthy. So barracks were built to house both regular soldiers (including the Sussex Fencibles) and cavalry. The militia, who were only kept together for short periods during which they practised their manoeuvres, were still expected to use tents. Local volunteer forces were equipped and remained based in their own homes.

There were few barracks anywhere in England before 1793 and none in Sussex. They were built as part of a specific defence strategy for the south coast. Whenever there was fear of invasion, for example between 1796-1800, most of the barracks in the county were occupied. They were empty between 1800 and 1803 and then redeployed after another invasion scare, when about 20,000 soldiers were spread along the 80 miles of Sussex coastline. They were regarded as expensive to run, and as soon as the government could stand down the soldiers and sell off any supplies and buildings it did so. So the contents of the cavalry and town barracks were auctioned in 1807.[8] By 1815 many of the barracks were disused and, because they were mostly timber, falling apart.[9] It is within this framework that developments in Brighton can be interpreted.

From 1793 visitors to Brighton had plenty to watch. Not only were there military manoeuvres and encampments of tents but also a considerable amount of building work. Yet few references have been found in visitors' letters or diaries, although they must have taken an interest, for in *The Times* in 1796 there was criticism of the soldiers' accommodation.[10]

In 1794 the *Sussex Weekly Advertiser* first reported that a barracks was being built near Charles Street, but that was wrong; the building was the riding school that Hughes and Co. had just completed. The newspapers commented on a shortage of materials and labour, but it was not easy to tell whether this was poor planning and stingy budgeting on the part of the Board of Ordnance, who appear to have been handling the logistics, or a genuine shortage because of the amount of building in progress in Brighton.

42 The Infantry Barracks behind Marlborough Place on a print of 1839, only one of a pair that show them clearly. *Birds Eye view of Brighton from the New Church*. Drawn, engraved and published by Ino Bruce, Brighton November 1839.

The barracks development did not proceed smoothly. In 1795 land that had been leased for a barracks was unused and advertised for leasing for other uses. In 1796 one wing was discontinued 'for lack of bricks'. Mr Tomblins, the contractor who also built a barracks at Horsham, advertised for brick moulders. By October 1796 something had to be done about winter quarters, and the East Yorkshire Regiment and part of the Artillery marched into barracks that innkeepers had fitted up in their yards. In the yard of the *Unicorn Inn* on the corner of North and Windsor Streets a small timber barracks for infantry was built beside service buildings used by the inn.

By this time cavalry barracks were standing to the north of Brighton on the west side of the main road to Lewes and in the parish of Preston. Eventually called Preston Barracks, these consisted mainly of timber buildings on brick foundations. The plan by then had been altered to make them smaller than was first thought necessary and to include an officers' quarters, a reading room and a hospital. Rarely were they fully used. In October 1796 the First Division of

Regular Horse moved out of the barracks to vacate them for new arrivals but these were not the 800-1000 men of the East Yorkshire Militia who arrived to camp nearby. The 197 men and horse of the Lancashire Fencibles were expected to occupy them.

In 1800 Preston Barracks was reviewed and was then 33 ship-lapped huts housing 215 horses, and 169 men whose wives, children and camp followers lived nearby, greatly increasing the population of the parish of Preston. That year the War Office decided to have it rebuilt as a permanent barracks. According to War Office papers, in 1802 these barracks could hold 26 officers and 679 men but 18 officers, 169 men and 215 horses actually occupied them. Having rebuilt the barracks, the War Office decommissioned the Cavalry Guard House in the town in 1802.

Most of the regular soldiers lived in the barracks that stretched from Church Street to North Street just west of (or behind) *The King and Queen* inn.[11] These shiplap-timbered buildings on brick foundations were built to accommodate 320 men but housed up to 836 infantry in 1806.[12] Most of the time the barracks was not full and the soldiers stayed short spells, one regiment replacing another. It lacked sewerage systems and running water and so the conditions must have been unpleasant. It is visible on some of the prints of Brighton and remained until 1869. Soldiers from the Church Street barracks did guard duty at the Royal Pavilion during the 1790s and 1810s and are thought to have done some building work on it and on New Road. The military hospital stood nearby, further along Church Street, and this was sold off in 1815. Other barracks were crammed into the town, often lasting only a few years, one for 132 soldiers being built at the lower end of West Street in about 1796 and sold off in 1802.[13]

Accommodating the Militia

The militia did not serve around Brighton every year and their stays were short and in tented encampments. In 1793 a large encampment stood at Wick west of Brighton. A plan of it and some other local landmarks was printed onto a fan which was probably sold as a souvenir.[14] In 1796 the Duke of Richmond ran a major camp near Preston, north of Brighton, on Mr Smithers's land. Temporary buildings that were part of the encampment were sold off when the camp was shut down. When John Batchelor demolished a building he immediately advertised the materials for sale.

Treatment of the Soldiers

Whilst the officers may have spent comfortable lives in Brighton, most of the soldiers struggled to make ends meet and, considering their poor housing and pay levels, they appear to have been remarkably well behaved. There were few complaints in the press and these were mainly about petty pilfering and minor disturbances.[15] This was an achievement in view of the large numbers of people involved. In 1793 the newspapers claimed that the Duke of Richmond had about 10,000 men in 12 regiments spread over two miles of encampment near Saddlescomb. An observer remarked to *The Times* that the force was well disciplined and not a threat to the town although its presence had increased the price of foodstuffs.[16] Some of the non-commissioned officers may have thought they would be in Brighton for some time as they joined local lodges of masons.[17]

Not all the military force was well cared for. The poverty and mismanagement of the soldiers triggered a mutiny at a camp at East Blatchington near Seaford. The punishment of the soldiers was carried out just west of Brighton. Some soldiers were flogged and two were shot. The site, at Goldstone Bottom in Hove, became a minor tourist attraction for a short period through sympathy towards the soldiers because of their treatment. The government was concerned that local people (and not only those along the Sussex coast) might have more sympathy with the revolutionaries than they did with their own government.

Some Brighton residents might have sympathised with anti-royalist sentiments; the Prince, for example, owed money to traders in the town and offered plenty of evidence of his irresponsibility. In 1794 he sent a message to Whitehawk army camp on a prominent hill top to the east of Brighton informing the officers that the French had landed. When the soldiers arrived in the town they were not recognised as British and were confronted by the townsfolk, who beat them off. A cartoon by Nixon captures the glee with which two of George's friends, Sheridan and Fox, watched the mêlée on the seafront. The cartoon, called 'Brighton in a Bustle', depicts them peering out from bathing machines.

The image that Francis Wheatley portrayed in his paintings, *Encampment at Brighton* and *Departure from Brighton*, prints of which were sold as souvenirs, or the sentiments captured in the song called not only *Brighton Camp* but also *The Girl I Left Behind Me*, do not reflect the harsh and uncomfortable world of ordinary soldiers.[18] Some wealthier, older visitors, on which the town depended, found the presence of prostitutes off-putting and blamed the presence of the soldiers for a perceived increase in their number.

Other wealthy residents seemed to recognise the value of having the Army present and many raised money to support both it and the wives and children left without menfolk as a result of warfare. Trafalgar Day was celebrated in 1805 with enthusiasm and raised money for the sick and the injured, and a grand dinner and ball were held.[19] The town also paid 12 guineas to men, who had lived in Brighton for more than 30 days, to serve the parish.

Arguably publicity in local and national newspapers about the presence of the Army was good for the town. Periodically the residents made money from supplying goods to the barracks and camps and the additional numbers also put up the costs of accommodation and provisions for the short periods when the Army was present. There is no evidence that visitors were deterred by these increases although some complained about the extra costs.[20] Had there not been defences and soldiers giving people confidence that the coast was safe to visit, Brighton (and other resorts along this stretch of coast) may have declined. As it was, Brighton's population rose by forty per cent between 1801 and 1811 and doubled between 1801 and 1821, the period spanning the latter part of the Napoleonic Wars, when other resorts in Kent and Sussex prospered.

7

Transport Networks

Brighton's development as a seaside resort was heavily dependent upon good access, which required investment in overland, coastal and cross-Channel services. The routes to London, Lewes, Chichester and Tunbridge Wells were most important for visitors and some valuable goods were brought overland from London. Sea transport was vital for the movement of most goods and especially bulk such as coal and imported timber. The cross-Channel ferry to Dieppe was an important passenger service.

Local initiative was vital to the success of transport infrastructure. Many of the people who invested in it had other links with the resort, such as a share in an inn and therefore an interest in improving access. Before the 1750s the town's poverty meant there was no point in providing frequent scheduled overland services of any kind.

The Influence of Seaborne Trade

Seaborne trade is discussed first because of its influence on the town's development as a resort. Vessels from Brighton sold coal from Newcastle in London and carried goods to the capital from along the south coast.[1] It is likely that long established trade between the two places ensured that Londoners were familiar with Brighton's name and helped it develop as a resort.

Throughout the Georgian period seaborne trade remained vital to Brighton, even during the various periods of warfare. Almost all heavy goods such as coal, timber and grain were imported by boat from other parts of the nation or from overseas. Salt was imported from Newport on the Isle of Wight and beef was exported. Oysters were also brought by sea from a local source, probably one of the nearby estuaries.[2]

By the 1780s much more cargo was unloaded at Shoreham than on the beach at Brighton and the larger boats were kept there when being sold. Some of the larger coal barges unloaded at Shoreham and bargees tied their hawsers across the old Shoreham to Brighton road at Copperas Gap. A rider who fell off his horse when it tripped over a hawser one night posted an advertisement in the paper asking bargemen not to do so. Beach delivery was recognised as a dangerous and unreliable way of delivering goods in the 1790s especially as bigger boats were built to try to reduce transport costs. It was Brighton's need for a reliable port that resulted finally in the development of Shoreham as a modern facility.

The danger of sea travel was recognised by most coastal communities and in the late 18th century local societies were formed to deal with the problem of rescuing shipwrecked people. Practical benevolence was also an opportunity to show

43 *The beach at Brighton, Sussex.* Drawn by Henry Eldridge, engraved by George Cooke, 1814. Copper engraving.

one's contribution to the community. 'The Committee for the Relief of Seamen Shipwrecked between Brighton and Beachy Head' was supported by several wealthy Brighton worthies such as John Hicks, Henry Attree and Richard Tidy. The first two donated five guineas and Tidy £1 10s. Notable landowners such as Lord Pelham of Stanmer, Lord Sheffield of Sheffield Park and Nathaniel Kemp of Ovingdean also supported the appeal. 'The Committee to Alleviate Distress of Shipwrecks' tested equipment designed by Mr Thunder to help at the scene of wrecks. It paid for three moveable crane machines to be installed at Beachy Head, Holderness and Newhaven and also to improve the ascent from Bear's Hide Gap. Local people also contributed to support this committee.

Carriers (or common stage wagons) and Dealers

Carrier services are especially hard to trace in this period. Most seem to have managed until very late in the century without advertising in the paper. Little nuggets appear when people get caught breaking the law or have an accident but most of them are after 1790. Carriers were also called common stage wagons and the earliest advertisement for one was in 1777 when a service between London and Brighton via Godstone, Lindfield and Ditchling was announced. Valuables had to be identified to the carrier. The charge was 3s. per hundredweight, and valuables 2s. 6d. a load, but plate and jewels were not accepted. Robert Davis also refused to accept responsibility for losses of more than £20 on his service between the *Talbot* in London and Middle Street in Brighton. He expected goods to be removed within 24 hours of his arrival.

Customers by the 1790s were prepared to pay for speed and the town could support a denser network of services to more destinations. A few carrier services conveyed people as well as goods. A weekly light common stage wagon which offered seats ran from the Thatched House in Black Lion Street to Bristol via Arundel, Chichester and Bath. By this time there were some partnerships, and Grenville and Martin were amongst those who used the paper to announce the end of theirs in order to be able to settle debts and bills owing to them. Some carriers such as Davis, who was part of Tubb and Davis, also ran stage coaches.

The news reports identify a few travelling dealers with wagons who may also have carried goods for delivery. In 1798 Nicolas Lynn, a higler (chicken dealer), had to publish an apology for not paying his toll at Preston. By publicly acknowledging his dishonesty in an advertisement, for which he had to pay, he avoided being prosecuted. In 1787 a dealer in earthenware known locally as 'Goods' fell out of his wagon and hurt himself. Thefts of fish by the fish carriers or rippiers who took the catches to London (mainly in panniers) resulted in advertised rewards for any information that led to convictions.

Coach Services c.1700-1780

During the early 18th century the nearest town to Brighton with regular road services to London and elsewhere was Lewes. In 1732 a coach service to Brighton was said to be available from London but it is possible that the coach went to Lewes, eight miles to the north-east, from where a private hiring could be made.[3]

By 1745 a weekly coach service from Brighton to London was advertised. However, the coach also collected and dropped off people en route, so only a few passengers may have completed each trip.[4] The journey took two days, the coach travelling via Lewes, East Grinstead, Godstone and Croydon to Southwark. That the Batchelor family of Lewes started this service, presumably by extending their established service from Lewes to London, suggests that they were aware of a new demand for what may have been sea bathing. The Bachelors had already provided the first coach service to reach London from Lewes within a day, and managed that before the roads to London were turnpiked, which supports the theory that the road system was not as poor as some writers have claimed. From 1756 J. Batchelor ran a twice-weekly coach from Brighton to London, taking a day via Lewes. This expensive service only ran between May and September, but the service that took two days continued throughout the winter.

In 1762 Bachelor's first rivals, Tubb and Brawne, began a service to London via Uckfield with their new Flying Machine 'hung on steel springs'. For 80d. each way for an inside seat, a traveller had a weight allowance for luggage of 14 pounds, extra being charged at 1d. a pound. This service left the *Golden Cross* at Charing Cross at 6 a.m. on Monday, Wednesday and Friday and took a day to reach Brighton.

Bachelor responded to Tubb and Brawne's competition by obtaining a new coach, reducing his fares, and sending his team via Chailey. His large flying chariot 'with a box' (for securing valuables) ran three days a week each way and took only two passengers unless three chose to travel together. A one-way trip took a day and cost 80d., with 14 pounds of luggage in the fare. Again extra weight cost more. Bachelor continued to run his older service via Godstone and East Grinstead to the *Talbot* and reduced the fare. He added another service from October 1762, which ran via Lewes. Tubb responded by alleging that the lower prices that Bachelor offered implied a poorer service that could not survive at those rates. Incensed, Bachelor claimed that his family's accumulated expertise in operating services, from London to Lewes and then from London to Brighton, assured passengers of a reliable service. In fact, the demand was sufficient to sustain both firms running a single coach three times a week. Bachelor also continued his original and slower thrice-weekly service, which took two days during the summer and the winter.

Davis (who also operated as a carrier) started the third coach service in 1763. He charged the same fare as his two rivals and also offered the service on three days a week, each way. He purchased a machine (as the coaches were called) from Bachelor for another service.

In 1766 Bachelor died and his business was sold to Tubb, who took Davis as his partner, replacing Brawne. Tubb and Davis maintained the daily service to London during the summer and ran a thrice-weekly service during the winter, plus a carrier's waggon, all via Lewes. The route enabled them to fill their coaches with people from the county town of East Sussex, and the roads from Lewes were better than those that ran directly north from Brighton.

Tubb and Davis dominated the Brighton coach trade until the 1780s, various rivals failing to survive. By 1773 they must have had several coaches to be able to run the services that they offered and the investment in them must have been considerable. They had built up three services that ran three days a week on three routes in the summer and twice a week during the winter. A major breakthrough came in 1774 when Tubb and Davis advertised the first daily coach service to run all year. In 1775 they ran a daily service between London and Brighton via Reigate, but the Reigate coach was not advertised from 1776 and presumably failed. Tubb and Davis returned to their more familiar routes via Lewes and then Uckfield or Chailey. In spite of the failure of the Reigate route, Hughes and Thomson of London tried to set up a rival service, which they advertised in June 1776.

In 1777 Tubb and Davis advertised daily post coaches. These travelled faster than their 'machines' via Uckfield and Chailey and cost more: 15 shillings for inside passengers (normal services were 14 shillings) and seven shillings for outside seats. The service left Brighton at 6 a.m. and arrived at the *Talbot Inn* in London for dinner. The cheaper and slower 'Machine' continued to operate twice a week between London and Brighton for the rest of the decade.

Coaching from c.1780

In 1782 Tubb and Davis offered a light post coach via Lewes and Uckfield which presumably travelled fast for it accommodated only four passengers inside and cost 17 shillings per person, four shillings and five shillings respectively more than their other two coaches. Brighton's attraction as a resort resulted in the establishment of passenger services to other towns. In 1782 a diligence began to operate three times a week to Chichester via Littlehampton, although in 1783 it ran only twice a week. The owner was Tucker of Chichester.

In 1784 there was an increase in the number of services offered to and from Brighton. This might have been associated with the arrival of the Prince of Wales, whose first visit was accompanied by a flurry of fashionable people from London curious to see the resort which now attracted not only two of the brothers of the reigning monarch but also the heir the throne.

As demand increased and roads improved so the start of the summer services was moved back; in 1784 they began in March. More services were provided, too. From

17 May 1784 Tubb and Davis ran another coach service taking a day, via Reigate and Cuckfield, but only operated it three times a week. This was their first successful venture on this route. They also ran another daily post coach and a slower and cheaper daily chaise on their Uckfield and Cuckfield routes.

Not until 1788 were Tubb and Davis challenged. By then they offered four daily services from London having experimented and found that this worked best. The most significant newcomers were Ibbeson (or Ibbetson) and Co., based at the *White Horse* in East Street. They claimed that their daily post coach departed at 6 a.m. from Brighton and arrived at the *Blue Boar* in Holborn at 3 p.m. Their slower service went three times a week and took twelve and a half hours. The firm maintained a winter service but with only one vehicle. A Mr Weston was said to operate a service to London from the 'Gunn' on the Cliff but he did not advertise, which suggests that the service did not operate for very long. A daily stagecoach service between Brighton and Lewes was started by Smart who in 1789 extended his service to London.

Tubb and Davis now operated on three routes to two inns in London (in Holborn and at Charing Cross), and maintained a daily service during the winter to both destinations. During the summer of 1788 five coaches went to London daily (four of them owned by Tubb and Davis and one by Ibbeson and Co.) and one went three times a week. Shergold, Tilt, Best and Hicks (all of whom were innkeepers) had purchased shares in the company, but by the end of 1788 Tubb had retired and Davis remained to run the business.

During the winters of the late 1780s both companies operated a daily service which required a considerable outlay for it meant that two coaches were on the road simultaneously. Large relays of horses were needed along the route for which coach operators had to find fodder and fodder costs were probably a lot higher during the winter. Some inns would act as stages for the horses but the cost and the organisation were undoubtedly major reasons for the coach service's slow growth.

The Development of New Faster Coach Routes from 1790

From 1790 the operators' routes changed, all the fast daily services travelling via Cuckfield and Reigate and the slower ones via Lewes and then Uckfield or Chailey. In 1790 another operator started a service via Cuckfield and Reigate: William Henwood of Brighton, a dealer in horses and the proprietor of the *White Horse* in East Street, formed a partnership with a London innkeeper called Scott. They offered a coach service that left Brighton at 8 a.m. and took eight hours. At this point anonymous notices in the local paper again made accusations. Perhaps, as in the early 1760s, this was a sign of strong competition for travellers. One advertisement complained about the lateness of coaches and another about loss of letters on the London to Brighton post.

In 1791 mail coaches began to operate between London and Brighton and between Brighton and Tunbridge Wells, replacing post boys on horseback. An advertisement in the *Sussex Weekly Advertiser* claimed that the trip would take eight hours and that a night coach service left at 8 p.m. The anonymous operator stated that the sum allowed by the Post Office for the operation of the coaches was only sufficient to cover the running costs of the service during the summer; in winter post boys on horseback would be used. Other evidence indicates that Henwood,

Scott and Holebrook operated these coaches. From 1792 the mail service was run by an enlarged partnership that consisted of Hicks, Tilt, Scott, Olden, Baulcomb and Henwood and was called Henwood and Co. In 1794 it issued an advertisement offering a reward for information about the practice of post boys dishonestly carrying passengers en route and pocketing the fares. In spite of such problems extra coaches were added to the Reigate service during 1794.

In that year there were still only two coach companies operating to London, Davis & Co. and Henwood & Co. Tubb had retired and Baulcomb purchased a share of Henwood. Sometimes route-swapping was agreed. Henwood and Co. took over from a rival the coach that ran to London via Lindfield. The constant change of partners revealed by the advertisements must have made things difficult for creditors of coaching companies that did not last long, such as Grenville, Law, Crossweller and Co. Some of the people named as partners in the coach trade, such as Crossweller, also drove vehicles.

Eastern and Western Coach Routes

Slowly, coach routes to the west and the east of Brighton were introduced. Tucker and Co.'s diligence to Chichester via Arundel allowed each passenger seven pounds of luggage in the fare. Rhoades and Pell had replaced Tucker and Co. by 1786 but continued the same service, three times a week. A rival company began in 1789, offering a service by mail coach via Arundel and Chichester to Portsmouth, Bath and Bristol. The service was run by a group of local innkeepers as far as Portsmouth, where another service took over. By the mid-1790s regular coaches ran to both Chichester and Eastbourne and the latter may have been weekly. In 1784 a service that was to run three days a week to Eastbourne using a diligence called the *Blue Coach* was advertised but there is no evidence that this actually happened.

The Coaching Network in 1800

In 1800 Cobby published the first detailed street directory for the town and in it he included the earliest list of coach services. It reveals changes in the permutations of partnership that ran the companies and the number of services that the town supported. Davis and Co. no longer operated but Henwood had joined Crossweller, Cuddington, Pockney and Harding at the junction of East Street with Castle Square. Their daily post coach ran via Cuckfield and Reigate to Cheapside and Piccadilly, taking nine to ten hours for the journey. Boulton, Tilt, Hicks, Baulcomb & Co. advertised two services to London from Castle Square. Although their coach office address was 1 North Street, they were at the Castle Square end. The fast coach took the same route and left at the same times as Henwood's; their second service took the route that Tubb and Davis had used for many years via Uckfield. A post coach ran overnight via Cuckfield, leaving at 10 p.m. and arriving in London at 7 a.m. The route via Chailey was no longer used by coach operators. A third service to London, operated by the owner of the *Gun* on East Cliff, went via a new route through Henfield, Horsham, Dorking, Leatherhead and Epsom, three times a week.

Coach services continued to develop during the early 19th century. One example was the post coach to Bristol via Chichester, Portsmouth and Bath. The partnerships continued to alter and the advertisements for sales and partnerships indicate how much capital was tied up and the long periods some companies survived for. In 1801 a one-twelfth share of Boulton, Tilt, Hicks and Baulcomb's was advertised for sale. The return from the trade between Christmas 1794 and Christmas 1801 was £12, 000 a year. Four of the partners were Shergold of the *Castle*, Hicks of the *Old Ship*, Richard Wood (of Reigate) and John Davis (London stage waggoner of Middle Street).⁵ In 1806 Boulton, Gourd and Co. sought to sell a share in a coach company that they claimed was 50 years old, which was possible by then even if the names of the partners had changed.

The Management of Stables

Most commercial stabling stood to the rear of the inns but there was by 1800 a considerable amount on the town's outskirts on the fringe of arable land. The scale of investment in the larger transport operations is revealed by the sale of stables run by the *Castle Inn*. At first the stables stood between the inn and the Royal Pavilion. In 1808 the owners agreed to exchange land on which most of the stabling stood for a larger plot on the north-west corner of North Street and New Road. The sheer scale of the new stables was shown in the sale particulars of 1819. The entrance was on North Street but the plot ran some 188 feet along the length of New Road. The stabling was divided into two stable yards, with 70 stalls for horses and standing for 30 carriages and a range of granaries. The plan shows horse stalls all round the outside of the two yards, themselves linked by a narrow way through the open shed for the carriages which was built east-west across the middle of the plot. There were rooms over the stalls, presumably for the stable boys. The granaries were lined with stout deal throughout and finished with tin mouldings and strong supports, one granary being 146 feet long. They were said to hold 1,000 quarters of oats. Robins the auctioneer suggested that the long frontage along New Road gave the opportunity to develop first-rate houses and shops because of the good views of the Royal Pavilion, and the elegant shops with accommodation above that stand there today are the result of this sale. Stables on this scale moved to the outskirts of town.

The Development of Coach Offices

Shortly before 1800 the close links between inns and coaching companies began to loosen as the coach operators established offices in Castle Square on the east side of the town. By then many travellers wanted access to the new suburbs to the east of the Steine, and so Castle Square became a convenient setting down place for old and both new parts of the town. It was also the most convenient turning point, North and East Streets being both narrow and busy. Some innkeepers remained in coaching partnerships, in particular the proprietors of the *Castle*, the *New Ship* and the *White Horse* (in North Street).

Coach Capacity in the Early Nineteenth Century

Although the number of coaches had increased, the evidence suggests that a lot of visitors must have used their own transport to reach Brighton. In 1800 there were three day-time coaches to London, one night-time service and one service which travelled three times a week and may have taken two days. When all were operating there were five coaches with a daily maximum passenger capacity of 30 passengers or 162 people one way in a six-day week (four inside and two people outside). In total they carried 5,184 people in a 32-week season. Estimates for the number of visitors during the season vary between 10,000 and 12,000 but they may be very optimistic.[7]

From 1800 there was a boom in the coaching business; both the number of services and partnerships increased. By 1818 there were many more services operating between Brighton and other towns in southern England, as shown in the tables in this section, and Brighton became the major route centre of Sussex. Nevertheless, the number of people conveyed to the town by coach is not as large as some contemporary guesses suggest. In 1811 one source claimed that between 50 and 60,000 people were conveyed by coach from London to Brighton in a year.[8]

The earliest full listings of coach services in the 19th century are for 1818 and 1822. Although they show growth in the number of services offered since 1800, even the services offered for 1818 and 1822 could not carry the numbers that were thought to be possible in 1811.

Coach Services from Brighton in 1818

Destination	Daily
London	13 all year
	15 in season
Hastings	2
Tunbridge Wells	1
Portsmouth	1
Worthing	20 in summer, or 18 all year

Source: C. Wright, *Brighton Ambulator* (1818), pp.166-9.

The *Ambulator* produced a list of coach services but there is no indication of how many each could carry. *Baxter's Directory* of 1822 also gives a comprehensive list of services but the same problem applies to numbers of passengers.

Coach Services from Brighton in 1822

Destination	Daily	3 times a week	summer, 2 winter
London	15	5	
Hastings	2		1
Lewes		2	
Maidstone		1	
Oxford		1	
Portsmouth		1	
Southampton		1	
Windsor		1	
Worthing	3		
Totals	21	11	1

Source: *Baxter's Brighton Directory* (Brighton: Baxter, 1822).

The advertisements for some coach services between London and Brighton in the early 1800s suggest that coaches were bigger than previously and that their maximum capacity was eight persons plus luggage, although some still carried only four. If it is generously assumed that all carriages carried eight people, then in 1818 the London services carried 120 people a day to Brighton in the peak season and 104 in the low season. If the London coaches were always full on their journey down to Brighton and operated six days a week as advertised for a season of 32 weeks, as the timetable for 1818 suggests, then their maximum capacity during the season was 23,000 and for the year 35,500 passengers. By 1822 the number of London coaches had increased to a maximum of 20 when all the daily and thrice-weekly services were operating. This gives a maximum capacity from London of 160 people a day. The total capacity from London for the season of 32 weeks was at most 26,880 and the annual total at most 43,680 passengers.

By 1822 the impact of the arrivals from the southern network of services is significant. They probably added another 100 people a day in the season but only on the days when all services were operating. Thus the possible total capacity of the coach services in the season was about 39,362 visitors, of whom about a third may have come from places other than London (390 a week compared with 1,236 a week from London). There is no way of estimating the volume of private transport but it was probably the most important means of travel for visitors from the region as well as for members of the Royal Household.

The development of coach services in southern England as shown in the table suggests improvement in roads and levels of demand for access to Brighton that made investment a risk worth taking. It would be useful to know more about these services and how successful they were, but many were operated not from Brighton but from the other ends of the route, and many of the records are either lost or still unidentified.

Turnpike Roads from 1769-1820

The need to improve roads along a more direct route to London was recognised by local people. Turnpike trusts were speculative ventures, local people paying for the Private Act of Parliament that was required to enable the trust to charge for access to the road. In return it was expected to improve the road and was allowed to recoup its costs. Trusts were permitted to erect turnpike gates and to employ tollgate keepers. Some turnpikes had a gate only at one end; others had them at both, which put up their operating costs. This extra investment was necessary when the stretch of road had several junctions on it in order to charge as many users as possible.

Turnpike Acts for the most direct roads from London to Brighton

		Roads		
1751–1760	0		1801–1810	4
1761–1770	2	Cuckfield Rd. Lewes Rd	1811–1820	2
1771–1780	2	Henfield Rd. County Oak	1821–1830	2
1781–1790	0	Newhaven Proposed	1831–1840	2
1791–1800	0			

Source: Turnpike Acts

Brighton's residents were involved in many but not all turnpike trusts. Other people who lived along the routes also saw advantages in their development.

In July 1769 there was a meeting to discuss the possibility of setting up a turnpike trust to improve the route via Cuckfield and Reigate, which was described as offering a shorter and less hilly journey to London. In December 1769 Thomas Scrase and others met to discuss a turnpike for the Lewes to Brighton Road, which was then the main road to London. This trust was based in Lewes and most of its meetings were held at the *White Hart*, an inn that still exists. It applied successfully to turnpike the road from just outside the Brighton parish boundary and the tollgate stood close to where Preston Barracks was subsequently built. The second tollgate was at Ascham, just west of Lewes.

In 1771 the Trust sought a loan of £950 against which the tolls were mortgaged. It may have used that money to invest in more roads, for by 1773 it had extended its control to include the stretch of road between Lewes and Glynde Bridge. The Trust again sought to raise funds in 1777 by mortgaging income, and installed a weighing machine to ensure that charges for wagons were correct.

The Henfield to Brighton Trust had permission to turnpike the route from Henfield to Brighton via Woodmancote, Shaw Lane, Wickwood, Poynings Common, Seddlescomb and Devils Dyke, and it advertised that route in 1771. The trustees met regularly at the *George Inn*, Henfield where they discussed not only improvements but also requests from users, such as the carters of chalk, for the toll on their loads to be reduced.

The Brighton to County Oak and Lovell Heath Turnpike controlled the first tollgate out of Brighton on the road through Preston. This became the southern end of the most popular route between London and Brighton and the southernmost tollhouse stood near the *Crown and Anchor* in Preston, which was one of the pubs where the trust sometimes met. It also met at the *Friars Oak* at Clayton.

Information about some of the other turnpikes does not very often appear in the local Brighton newspapers because they were rather too far north. The Brighton to Cuckfield road was turnpiked during the 1770s but the only notice that appeared before 1790 was about the plan to widen this road in 1779. Sometimes meetings for the establishment of new turnpikes were published but nothing further appeared. In 1792, for example, there was a proposal to turnpike the road to Newhaven via Rottingdean and Piddinghoe.

The heyday of the turnpike trusts between London and Brighton was after 1800, as shown on the table. It was in the late 1790s that leading public figures, rather than tradesmen with a direct interest in transportation, became more involved in 'talking up' investment. By then there seems also to have been more demand from London for public coach services to Brighton and a greater influx of London traders. In December 1796 James Vallance (who played a major role in Brighton's Commissioners) chaired a meeting attended by Sir Geoffrey Vassal Webster MP and Thomas Kemp MP which set up a committee with a very clear brief, to ascertain which roads could be improved to provide a shorter route to London, and for how much. Fourteen people agreed to serve on it and to report back quickly, which they did. This initiative seems to have played a role in the expansion of new turnpike routes after 1800 in which some of these people were involved.

Shoreham Toll Bridge and Harbour Improvements

Brighton people invested in other transport infrastructure. The committee for the building of Shoreham Bridge included Samuel Shergold, Thomas Kemp, Charles Scrase, Richard Tidy, Thomas Scutt, Robert Davis and John Hicks, all of whom either lived in or had land in Brighton. It received plans and estimates from Joseph Hodskinson and Thomas Marchant at a meeting on 17 July 1780 and soon organised a trust and built the bridge. Samuel Shergold and William Attree were

44 *Embarking for the Ferry* by T. Rowlandson from *An excursion to Brighthelmstone* by H. Wigstead and T. Rowlandson, 1790.

the Treasurer and Clerk to the Shoreham Toll Bridge Trustees and Shergold paid out dividends to the subscribers to this scheme.

The Brighton-Dieppe Ferry Service from 1764

The ferry service between Brighton and Dieppe may have promoted faster coach services, and also the growth of Brighton, because it was used to go to Paris. From 1764 the regular London service contributed to the establishment of a cross-Channel packet service. This might have started sooner but for the war against the French, which resulted in shipping in the Channel being threatened by privateers. Captain Killick's advertisement for his weekly ferry service to Dieppe noted that there was now a daily coach service to London during the summer and a thrice-weekly service during the winter. Later in the same year Captain Sanders advertised that the *Prince of Wales* would sail to Dieppe when desired. Both men copied the coachmen's practice of using inns as their contact and departure points.

From 1765 demand for the service was sufficient to sustain two boats regularly during the summer. The *Charlotte* had a new captain, Stephen Marchant, and Captain Killick had a brand new craft. By 1769 there were three vessels and the typical charge was 10s. per crossing for those sharing a cabin with several persons or ten guineas for the privilege of either a single cabin (which was unusual on these small boats) or the sole use of a shared cabin. Killick's competitors were the *Free Mason* and the *Industry*, whose captain, Chapman, lost a race across the Channel, against Killick for a wager, by two hours. The newspaper reports of this escapade provided excellent publicity for Killick and for the service as a whole.

The demand could not sustain three packets but two continued to offer a regular summer service, so two sailings a week were available each way. In 1775 Killick sailed the *Princess Carolina* on Saturday evenings and returned on Tuesday evenings.

Robert Sissell took the *George* to Dieppe on Tuesdays and returned on Saturdays. Killick dropped out in 1776 and was replaced by J. Buchanan, who was master of the *Eagle*. The service became another of Brighton's facilities, and when the Duke and Duchess of Cumberland went to France in 1783 they used it. In the winter the regular service stopped.

The ferry was advertised more heavily from the later 1780s and the service expanded. In 1788 there were three schooners and a cutter operating to Dieppe and none sailed until the evening stage coaches had arrived in Brighton, which indicates the importance of the coach services from London for the ferry. It ran once a day for three days a week all year. The trade was tough and the rival masters made accusations about the safety of the other's packets. In 1786 John Butler, master of the *Prince William*, refuted allegations that the packet was unseaworthy, but an advert for the sale of the *Prince William* in 1789 describes a smaller boat than Butler's which was a year old, with two staterooms and a cabin with 18 beds, and was built at Shoreham. This suggests that the original packet had, after all, been scrapped. Shoreham became the main base for boat building, the *Prince Henry* being built 'for the pacquet trade' in 1790.

The packets continued to collect and to discharge travellers from and into small boats and rafts until the early 1820s when the Chain Pier was built out into the sea below New Steine. As vessels increased in size so embarking had become more uncomfortable because of the need to anchor further off shore. The newspaper began to carry reminders to send horses and carriages well ahead of the time for sailing. To ensure that the service continued, the Chain Pier was built.

Ancillary Trades

Henwood, whose role as a major operator of stages services has been described, was also an innkeeper and regularly sold horses. He also auctioned the equipment and horses whenever a carrier or stage-coach business ceased to trade. Henwood sold off the stock of Grenville and Co. common carriers, opposite the *King and Queen* which then stood to the north of town. This sale included ten cart horses and four others. Verrall and Son ran weekly horse sales at the *Castle Tavern*. Henwood also advertised his services as a farrier at the *Half Moon* in West Street, and did not expect to be paid if he could not sort out the problem.

The amount of capital tied up in transport services is shown not only by Henwood's auctions but also by the sale of Edward Cobby's hackney carriages and chaises, most of which would have been hired out within the town. When he died in 1794 the executors had to sell 20 hackney carriages and four single-horse chaises plus harness.

A transport industry that depended heavily on horsepower required blacksmiths as well as farriers, carriage makers and other skilled people, and by the late 1770s advertisements for journeymen in these trades were becoming common. New saddlers and harness makers also came into the town from the surrounding area.

Personal Transport

Many of the visitors to Brighton travelled in their own vehicles drawn by their own horses. The horses were then stabled locally and the owners were charged for the stabling, food, exercising of the horses and storage of the vehicle. Accidents involving private coaches were recorded in the paper almost every week. In September 1789 Mr Barry and his brother Edwin were tipped out of a phaeton as it turned the sharp corner round Dulot and Owen's library. On the same date the *Sussex Weekly Advertiser* mentioned that Lord and Lady Leslie were journeying back to Brighton from Bromley in Kent when their phaeton overturned and Lady Leslie was bruised. Mr Rose and family were going up Church Street in July 1789 when their carriage overturned and broke one of Miss Rose's arms. Local people were also injured in accidents: Messrs Bradford and Furner were returning home from Lindfield in June 1789 when their carriage overturned and Mr Furner was bruised. Pedestrians were also caught up in carriages: Mrs Cooke, a fisherman's wife, was crossing East Street when she was trapped by the horse of a gentleman's carriage and cut about the face.

During the early 19th century the coaching network between Brighton and other towns in southern England developed more rapidly. By 1822 it appears to have conveyed about a quarter of the people that travelled to Brighton. Although the development of turnpikes did help services to become more reliable and faster, it was the demand for access to Brighton that determined whether or not a service or a turnpike road would be profitable. The provision of turnpikes was very fragmented and it cannot be proved that they resulted directly in the improved services. Brighton's development as a route centre from the later 1790s happened not only because of its role as a resort. Between 1790 and 1820 there was a lot of movement of soldiers and officers and those connected with the Navy along the coast.

By 1820 the beach scene was very different from that of 1740. Most of the fishing and trading vessels were now based in Shoreham, and soon after 1820 the Chain Pier was built for ferry passengers. The period had been one of very considerable changes in transport, almost all of it the responsibility of local people or those who lived within the region.

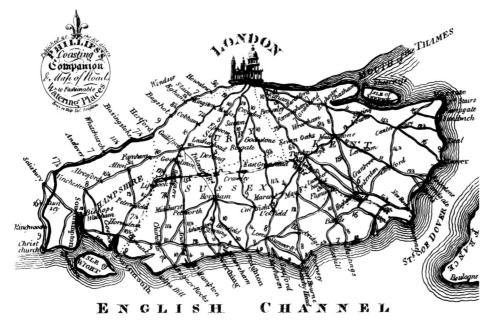

45 Map of the road network from London from Attree's *Topography*, 1809.

8

Accommodating the Visitors

Visitors stayed in five types of accommodation: inns, boarding houses (where they paid for food and lodging), lodgings (where they paid for rooms), lodging houses (whole houses which they rented), and their own seaside houses. Most sought lodging houses if they were staying for some time. The favoured alternative for single people or for short stays was lodgings. Boarding houses were not common in Brighton until after 1820. Inns were normally only used for very short stays. A few very wealthy visitors owned seaside homes in Brighton.

Inns and Hotels

Visitors to the town normally stayed at inns for short visits of only a few days or whilst seeking accommodation, because of the noise and the expense. Yet inns were vital for resorts of this period because they gave visitors a chance to decide where to rent.

There is little information about inns until 1778. At that time a rough sketch map of the town was drawn and the existing inns were marked with the number of soldiers billeted in each during a short stay in the town. This map gives a rough indication of how many people the inns were able to accommodate that year. The location of each inn shown on the sketch map has been marked on a map surveyed at about the same date by Yeakell and Gardner and published in 1779. The *Castle* and the *Old Ship* each accommodated 32 soldiers and the *Crown and Anchor* and the *New Ship* took sixteen. The remainder took either 12 or six. Soldiers were more likely to be crowded into accommodation, so the fact that only 300 men were accommodated suggests that the inns would normally have taken fewer.

The *Old* and *New Ship*, the *George* in West Street, the *Kings Head* (formerly the *Bull*, and before that the *George*), the *Gun*, the *Thatched House* and the *White Horse* were amongst the inns that existed before 1740.[1] The *Castle Inn* was the first to be opened after 1740.

From the 1750s until 1819 the *Castle* in Castle Square was the biggest. By 1807 the wealthy Shergold family owned the inn, a wine vault in Black Lion Street, a new coach house on the corner of North Street and New Road, and shares in a hot and cold baths and the race stand.[2] In 1807 the family let the *Castle* at an annual rent of £150. It was closed by the Prince of Wales and replaced in 1819 by the *Royal York Hotel* at the south end of the Steine.[3]

The *Castle* had only one rival, the *Old Ship* which still stands on Brighton seafront. The Hicks family ran this inn by 1760 and also invested in related business activities.

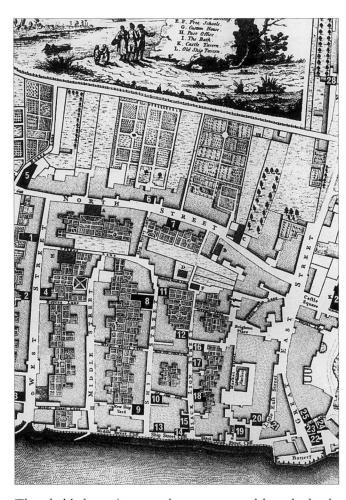

46 Pubs and inns in the late 1770s added to a map of Brighton by Yeakell and Gardner of 1779.

1. *Half Moon*
2. *Kings Head*
3. *George*
4. *Kings Arms*
5. *White Lion*
6. *Smiths Arms* [*Blacksmiths*]
7. *Coach and Horses*
8. *Seven Stars*
9. *New Ship*
10. *Old Ship*
11. *Spotted Dog*
12. *The Last*
13. *One Tun*
14. *Gun*
15. *Little Sloop*
16. *Chimney*
17. *Black Lion*
18. *Thatched House*
19. *Little Castle*
20. *Star and Garter*
21. *Dolphin*
22. *Rising Sun*
23. *White Horse*
24. *Catherine Wheel*
25. *Greyhound*
26. *Crown and Anchor*
27. *Castle*
28. *King and Queen*

They held shares in a coach company and bought land north of the town and in Ditchling for pasturing horses. They also ran a market garden to provide produce for the inn and to sell in the market. When the Hicks family withdrew from innkeeping in 1800, they let the 70-bed inn with the capacity to stable 100 horses and a coffee room and wine vault before they sold it during the early 19th century.

Inns had to be licensed and licensees would use the issue of a licence as an opportunity to thank the public for their support. Most inns were tenanted and advertisements for tenants appeared quite regularly in the local paper. The men and women who ran inns moved if they thought they saw one with better prospects and advertised that they had done so. Newspaper advertisements were also used to announce that the name of an inn had been changed. The *Last* (or *Last and Fish Cart*) in Black Lion Street was renamed the *Cricketers* before 1792 when the inn was used for an auction of blankets.

New inns and alehouses were built or converted from older properties as demand increased. By 1779 the *Crown and Anchor Hotel and Tavern* had been built about three years when it was put up for auction with the furnishings, stabling for 30 horses, a walled garden well stocked with fruit trees, and accommodation for post chaises and coach. The *New Inn* (later the *Clarence*) in North Street was built in the 1780s and

47 The *New Inn*, Brighton. Drawn and engraved by R. Alford. C. Wright, *Brighton Ambulator* (1818).

LODGINGS & APARTMENTS FOR GENTLEMEN & FAMILIES

advertised as an hotel. It was such an innovation that the local gentry discussed it in their correspondence.

When inns were rebuilt or newly built they attracted experienced innkeepers; few of the owners also managed the businesses. In 1788 Thomas Colchin moved from Danehill to the modernised *White Lion* in North Street and in 1794 to the rebuilt *Star and Garter* on the Cliff. The *Spread Eagle* in East Street was 'newly built' in 1795 and owned by Henry Skinner but occupied by Benjamin Tilstone. William Henwood moved in 1781 from the *Half Moon* to the rebuilt *White Horse* in East Street. Henwood's tenancy is surprising because in 1780 he was made a bankrupt; he was also charged along with Peregrine Phillips of conspiring with Catherine Metcalf of Rottingdean to avoid debts owed to John Isaac. During the ensuing prosecution for dishonesty Phillips attempted to dissociate himself from Henwood, but Isaac insisted that since his claim to be a portrait painter was untrue his other claims could not be believed.[4] Metcalf was described as 'of bad character' and not a resident of Rottingdean.

The demand for repairs to wagons and coaches could result in specialist services being run by the inn. By the early 1790s the *White Lion Inn* and White Lion Yard backed on to Wheelers Yard, which was entered from Air Street (at the top end of North Street). Within the yard stood stables and a wheeler's shop used by the inn. The section of land occupied by a slaughterhouse and an icehouse, neither of which was used by the inn, was sold off.[5]

As the town expanded so new inns were built on the outskirts. The *Gardeners' Arms* was built in 1790 in North Parade near the market gardens and according to Charles Shoubridge, the first occupier, 'fitted up for travellers'. The *King's Arms* was opened at the north end of Broad Street by 1814.[6]

Although innkeepers moved between inns, continuity was not unusual. When Alex Hillman of the *Greyhound* died in 1796 the family, Elizabeth his daughter and Alley his sister, took it over. Susanna Bartlett seems to have run the *White Horse* until she died in 1784, having run it previously with her husband. When Rickword gave up his tenancy of the *New Ship Inn* in Ship Street in 1791 and in the year that Susanna Lucas, the owner, died, John Baulcomb moved there and remained throughout the 1790s. The close links between innkeeping families is shown by Susanna Lucas's leaving the *New Ship* to her daughter Susanna, who was married to Alex Hicks, who was also an innkeeper.[7]

Innkeepers allowed auctions and other business activities on their premises and kept horses too, diversifying where they could. Almost all the auctions of properties and of businesses in Brighton were held at inns. Stallions for covering (or stud) were often kept in the stables of an inn during the period when their services were on offer. Henwood advertised 'The Premier' at his inn, the *Half Moon*, in 1780, charging one guinea for a mare.

Inevitably inns were targets for thieves and some thefts were mentioned in the paper. Two race horses were stolen from the stables behind the *King and Queen* in 1791 and a reward of £20 was offered for information. Money was stolen from the *Rising Sun*, the £6 11s. reported then being a large sum. Ned Terry, the ostler at the *King's Head*, was charged with illegally receiving oats and then he absconded. His dishonesty must have caused considerable losses for five guineas was offered as a reward for his arrest. Like many men described in these advertisements he was five feet six inches tall.

Sometimes innkeepers found themselves with goods and livestock that they could dispose of, and in 1794 Thomas Colchin advertised that the black pony left in his stables would be auctioned shortly unless was it removed. He would use the proceeds to recoup the cost of its keep. Publicans were sometimes caught allowing tippling when they should not. In 1805 seven were summoned before the magistrates and fined 17 shillings each for allowing tippling during the Sunday service, and 13 drinkers who were caught were also cautioned.

Horses and transport appear to have been the riskier part of the innkeepers' activities. William Henwood and Peregrine Phillips the Younger were business partners in a livery stable who were bankrupted in 1779. Mr Moffat of the *Catherine Wheel* advertised a horse and a (sedan) chair for sale. It was not unusual for innkeepers to be wine merchants, too, Thomas Tilt of the *Old Ship* being in a partnership at one point. Other innkeepers were also brewers.

Lodgings

Many Georgian townsfolk lived in lodgings.[8] Multi-occupancy was part of Georgian town life, especially within town centres. Houses in towns were often sublet either by the room or groups of rooms to tenants, who could include families. As few people owned their own transport and hired transport was very expensive, living at high densities made sense and lodgings met that need. As Brighton expanded from the mid-1770s and the new houses were let as lodging houses, so lodgings became the main form of accommodation offered by the older streets of the town.

North Street was a good example of a town centre street in which lodgings were offered. In 1800 there were 105 numbered properties in the street and 28 offered

48   *The Royal York Hotel*. Drawn and engraved by C. Wing *c*.1830.

lodgings. If the practices of families in London are typical of the resorts, and this is very likely because a lot of visitors to Brighton came from or spent time in London, then few of the people that stayed in lodgings made their own meals. Food was bought in ready cooked. Cook shops, bakers and inns supplied food and utensils and potboys delivered and collected them.

The most expensive rooms in a house divided into lodging accommodation were normally above the owner's and on the first or second floor. Higher storeys were cheaper to rent, the rooms usually being smaller and the extra stairs to climb also making them less attractive.

Lodging Houses

Lodging houses in Brighton were normally rented for between one and six months.[9] The estate agents of wealthy local families organised the renting of houses for the family during the season. The correspondence between Abraham Baley and Katherine Pelham and Lucy Clinton (née Pelham) describes the negotiations.

In 1762 Katherine Pelham, a member of a wealthy local landowning and political family, stayed in Ship Street where she rented a house with three good lodging chambers but no servants' hall from Bowell, a carpenter, for four and a half guineas a week. In 1763 Katherine was late in arranging accommodation and Abraham Baley (the Pelham's steward at Stanmer and Halland in Sussex) undertook to do his best but remarked that she would have little choice. In 1764 Baley helped Lucy Clinton to rent a house from Mr Kent with four good bedchambers. Baley thought that every bed in the house was large enough to accommodate two people. Mr Kent did not think his linen was good enough for Lady Clinton and Baley observed that Lady Pembroke and Mrs Rudge took their own linen when staying at Brighton. Kent offered to provide oats and hay for the horses but Baley claimed that had he been asked to organise the trip sooner, cheaper feed could have been secured.[10]

Most Georgian houses had their services in the basement or at the rear and their main rooms on the first and second floors, regardless of whether they were terraced or detached. In the early 1790s Mrs Leache's new terraced lodging house, No. 6 Marine Parade (just east of the Steine), stood facing the sea at the start of the Parade. A sketch plan of the interior survives and shows the layout of several floors of the five storeys with their bow windows. Typically tall and narrow, the frontage of the house was about 18 feet 6 inches and its depth about 26 feet. Owing to the lack of rear access the house had two front doors, the main one for the household and a smaller one for the services in the semi-basement.

The occupiers and their visitors entered the house by walking up a flight of steps to the main entrance into the raised ground floor. This was typically offset, in this case to the right of the bow windows, and it opened into a narrow hall. On the ground floor No.6 had two small parlour rooms, one of which was probably used for eating, and the usual arrangement of a narrow and steep staircase at the rear, lit from windows at the back of the house. The best rooms were on the first floor where the drawing room spanned the width of the house and the best bedchamber occupied the space behind it. The next floor accommodated two bedrooms, and above them the attic level had two more. Their dimensions were the same as the drawing room and the chamber below them.[11]

The raising of the ground floor by providing steps to the main door enabled the builder to light the lower ground floor. A second set of steps led down to the door to the servants' hall, which had the housekeeper's room and the kitchen branching off it. Below that level was the basement floor, with privy and adjacent well and a sink and a pump in the rear yard. Some of the terraced houses in Brighton were built with the privy and well to the rear of the lower ground floor and without a basement. Typically, Mrs Leache's house lacked a garden and the yard was small and dark. Visitors used the communal gardens in the Steine.

In the lodging houses, servants and minor members of the family lived at the top of the house and some slept in the basement or outhouses. By 1820 some lodging houses were quite elaborately decorated and well furnished. When they came to be sold, the normal practice was to sell the property fully furnished. In 1820 two furnished lodging houses were for sale on Marine Parade, 'so justly celebrated the First Parade in the World'. Both had marble chimney-pieces in their drawing rooms which measured 19.6 by 18.6 feet. They had two large parlours apiece, the doors between which could be folded back to make dining rooms 35 feet long and 14 feet wide. Both had eight bedrooms (with 13 beds in them), piped water, a butler's room, pantry, housekeeper's room, large kitchen, scullery and storeroom with back entrances to the kitchen through a yard. Both had a separate manservant's room in the yard.[12]

Boarding Houses

Only a few boarding houses were advertised in Brighton before 1820. They offered food as well as accommodation. Samuel Scase (Scrase), late of the *White Hart* in Lewes, opened a boarding house on East Cliff with fine sea views.

Private Houses

That wealthy visitors were buying houses by the 1760s has already been commented upon.[13] Local landowners found the town a convenient meeting place. The Earl of Egremont (of Petworth House) and the Duke of Richmond (of Goodwood House) bought houses in Brighton.[14] Whilst usually categorised as 'landowners', such people often had several sources of income and some held government posts. They also helped to run the county of Sussex and to raise money for good causes in the resort such as the schools and the dispensary.

Most private houses owned by visitors or by successful local people were big. In 1769 Benjamin Rothwell's former house in West Street had seven chambers, three parlours, two garrets and a 'very good kitchen, a servant's hall and three cellars, a stable for six horses and a hayloft'.

The Impact of Visitor Accommodation on the 'Old Town'

Visitors were only prepared to put up for a short while with the small houses typical of poor ports such as Brighton and soon expected modern accommodation. The oldest part of the town, bounded by the Steine to the east, the outskirts of West Street to the west and Church Street to the north, changed very rapidly in order to provide ever more accommodation within a limited space.

Between 1750 and 1780 most redevelopment took place along the west side of the Steine (facing the promenade) and along East Street. Many of these houses were then demolished for road widening in Castle Square and for the development of the Royal Pavilion. Marlborough House, Mrs Fitzherbert's House (much altered) and the Royal Pavilion are the only survivors of the private houses along this stretch of the Steine.

The degree of infilling in the old town is reflected in the changes to North Street. In 1770 North Street contained some 88 houses and a plot of land towards its southern end cost about £16. In 1787 the plot and buildings on it fetched 475 guineas. By 1794 another 60 new houses had been added within the street, making the total about 148.[15] In 1775 a large lodging house advertised in the *Sussex Weekly Advertiser*.[16] This was a fairly typical example of the accommodation aimed at wealthy visitors. The stone mentioned is probably knapped flint.

> TO BE LET, a HOUSE in NORTH STREET, Brighthelmstone; stone built; large garden with fruit trees, walled all round; summer house at the upper end, that commands a most agreeable view of the surrounding country, particularly the South Downs; six bed chambers; on the first floor, five rooms; second floor, two parlours; ground floor, hall, kitchen, pantry, detached laundry: vaults and cellaring. Said house is usually let for lodgings: and generally produces £100 per annum.

Advertisements indicate that lodging houses were normally let fully furnished. Only one inventory has been located that lists in detail the contents of a lodging house, the advertisements in the newspapers being more perfunctory. Inventories do not assess how fashionable the furnishings were nor how their condition, amount or style compared with those of ordinary houses or those where rooms were let to lodgers. This inventory is of a new lodging house built in the old town in 1779 and not one of the taller, thinner, terraced houses built on the fields from about 1780. Nevertheless it shows what the owner of a new lodging house at that date thought visitors expected.[17]

Mrs Dring's house was in North Street and may have looked very like the one that still stands in Ship Street. The valuation of £397 19s. covered everything that visitors might expect: linen for the house, including beds both fine and coarse, glass cloths and napkins but none of the personal touches that would appear in the inventory for a private house, such as pictures and personal belongings.[18] This gives the house the rather impersonal feel that tenants would probably have expected. Small items were also most easily stolen.

It is never easy to work out from an inventory the layout of a house because no plan is provided and the appraiser may not have worked through the rooms in any specific order. This may have been a three-storey town house with bedrooms on the top floor for children, guests and servants, a middle floor that was used by the heads of the household, a ground floor which included a best room to entertain guests, and the main service rooms and cellar below.

In Mrs Dring's lodging house the hall had a scotch carpet or rug in the entrance and a hanging hall lamp which was let down from the ceiling to be lit using the pulleys that supported it. Off the hall was the best parlour, which had a patent floor cloth and six mahogany chairs around one of the two dining tables. The room was warmed by a Bath stove and the sconce glass in a gilt frame would have helped to give extra light. The curtains were of Manchester Stripe, a cheap fabric, one of the sideboards was made of mahogany and the other had spider legs.[19] No decorations are listed, which may imply that the furniture was all there was in the room.

The steward's room contained mahogany furniture and almost all of the small items needed to run the household, such as 12 blue and white china teacups and saucers, eight coffee cups and a tea canister, 12 red and white teacups and saucers and a brown teapot. Whilst the 12 tablespoons and 12 teaspoons were silver, the candlesticks, coffee pot and soup ladle were silver plate.

The steward's hall, pantry and the cellar are listed together and within these rooms were 81 blue and white plates, 27 octagonal dishes, eight custard cups with covers, a Dutch tea kettle, 36 drink glasses, six beer glasses and four decanters, plus some furniture such as a deal table and two forms. In the kitchen chamber two bedsteads had half tester furnishings in blue, and the blue window curtain simply hung on a rod. Only four beach chairs and an oak chamber table were provided for this room.

The kitchen range and fender had a poker and bellows. A chopping knife and a cleaver, a basting ladle, a fish kettle, a copper furnace and cover, a rolling pin, a callender and a bottle jack are amongst the equipment provided. The deal table and dresser and the chairs made of ash were the main furnishings, a chopping block also being provided.

The dining room, two bedrooms and a dressing room occupied the first floor. Appraisers normally identified the bedrooms by the names of the rooms below so the front parlour chamber on this floor was probably over the parlour on the floor below. The dining room had a Wilton carpet and a sofa covered with canvas hidden by a loose cover made of Manchester Stripe cotton that matched the festoon window curtains. The 12 mahogany chairs and the two card tables suggest that this was more of a retreat than a dining room. A mahogany fire screen stood near the Princess metal stove. The single mirror in the room was surrounded by a carved gilt frame. The parlour chamber had dimity curtains and bed trims and two Wilton bedside carpets. The night table, chairs, chest and table were mahogany and the mirror was in a white carved frame. The room was heated with a Bath stove. In the back bedchamber the soft furnishings included red bed furniture and checked festoon window curtains, scotch bedside carpets and India mats, and a white quilt on the bed. The room had a walnut night chair, a mahogany basin stand, chest of drawers and chamber table, an oval swing glass with drawers, and a stove with a wire fender. In the dressing room were a mahogany basin stand and swing glass and table and a chair and two stools.

The house also had six rooms in the attic of which four had four-poster beds. One of the four-poster beds had worked (embroidered) bed curtains and the bedroom in which it stood had matching festooned curtains at the windows. The counterpane on the bed and the rugs were made of cotton. The mattress, bolster and pillows were filled with feathers and blankets were provided, too. The furniture included a mahogany writing desk and a mirror mounted in the same wood, and chairs of beech and of ash. The four-poster bed in the neighbouring room was trimmed with Manchester Stripe and the festoon curtains matched it. There were two 'Scotch bedside carpets'. A chest, a chair and a night table were made of mahogany but the stools were made of ash and the table of wood. This room had a fireplace with a poker beside it. The four-posters in the two other bedrooms were also trimmed with material that matched their window curtains, white linen in one and blue checked cotton in the other. The furniture was again a mixture of mahogany, beech, ash and deal with rugs on the floor. Also tucked into this floor were a 'middle back attic chamber' that was so small the bed was 'a stump bedstead', with its linen and a chair and no window, and the 'west back attic chamber', within which there were three beds and blue and red checked curtains at the windows. This room had a deal chamber table, beech chairs and walnut drawers.

In 1794 a large detached house on Brighton Place was advertised with an adjacent field, Stiles, the agent, pointing out the potential of the site for development. The 'large excellent manor house' had a detached stable block, a garden and a pleasure ground with trees and shrubs and an ice house. The owner also advertised a field that adjoined Ship Street and was separated from the house by a narrow passage under which access from the house was possible. The frontage onto Ship Street had already been developed as two lodging houses, which were also for sale. The estate was thought by Stiles to suit either a gentleman or a speculative builder because there was enough land to build a wide street from Ship Street to the Square in front of the mansion house.

Not only were houses being built to let in the old town, but also small tenements. These were constructed at very high densities and were where health problems began to appear from the 1820s as their occupancy rose. Salmon Court, Mulberry Square, Pimlico (named after Mr Pimm on whose land the development stood) and Durham and Petty France were all started during the 1780s as demand for housing increased rapidly.[20] Salmon Court and Mulberry Square were on the north side of North Street, approximately opposite the north end of Ship Street. Durham and Petty France stood at the northern end of North Street and are now under Queen's Road (the road down from Brighton Station to the town centre). Pimlico is now Tichbourne Street and Unicorn Yard was nearby. Wardens Buildings, then at the top end of North Street and not far from St Nicolas Church, is now the Arcade at the eastern end of Western Road.[21]

Location of accommodation in 1800 – old town and new suburbs

Location	Lodgings	Lodging Houses	Boarding Houses	Total advertised offering accommodation	Number of houses in area (estimated from Cobby)	Approximate proportion offering/let as accommodation
	Number %	Number %	Number %	Number %	Number %	Number %
Old Town	167	67	3	237	810	237/810
	80	32	40	56	70	29
Suburbs	41	144	4	189	294	189/294
	20	68	60	44	30	64
Totals	208	211	7	426	1104	426/1104
	100	100	100	100	100	39

Source: from *Cobby's Directory*.

The veneer of prosperity screening poverty also applied to the Steine, where houses were crammed into Steine Court, the narrow passage behind what is now the Bunne Shop in Pool Valley.[22] At the top of West Street, on the west side, Mr Brooke's house was advertised for sale in 1805 with its contents and the garden to the rear, within which stood a large building, 15 feet wide and 50 feet long, with bedrooms over it and building plots behind accessible from North Street. In due course this added to the network of small cottages behind the grander houses on the west side of West Street.[23]

By 1800 quiet locations in the old town were being noted in advertisements. Two houses to let in a small square in East Street, with easy access to the sea and to the Steine, and high walls said to protect the houses from wind and from the noise of carriages, were said to be quiet at night.

The Volume of Building for Visitors

Not until 1800 was there a detailed directory containing enough information for the impact of the demand for accommodation to be examined in depth. Cobby's *Brighthelmstone Directory* lists lodgings and lodging houses whose owners were hoping to let to visitors. It indicates not only how dependent upon tourism Brighton was by 1800 but also how quickly the old town ceased to be fashionable once the new lodging houses had been built on the fields to the east and west of the town and along the fringe of the Steine.

According to Cobby, the 141 advertised trades and professions remained concentrated in the old town but the accommodation to let was mainly located in the suburbs. By 1822 some trades, such as pubs and bakers, had started to spread to the suburbs because there was enough housing for them to be worthwhile. In 1800 there was not enough demand.

The table shows clearly the town's dependency on tourism, 40 per cent of the houses offering accommodation for visitors. Between 1750 and 1800 the proportion and number of lodging houses in the old town advertised as available for visitors seems to have risen and then declined. Between 1780 and 1800 the development of lodging houses on farmland was a necessity because the accommodation in the old town was needed not only for visitors but also for the workforce that provided facilities such as shops for visitors. Lodging houses were probably converted to lodgings because the demand was there, from visitors and also from the workforce, and thus a good income could be earned from them for most of the year. Indeed, the table above must under-record the number of houses in the old town where lodgings were available simply because they were unlikely to attract visitors and so were not advertised. Most of the small courts and alleys are missing from the list but were most likely to be multi-occupied as was customary in this period.

By 1800 lodgings were characteristic of the old town and lodging houses were typical of the new suburbs. If the available lodgings are added to the number of lodging houses to let, then almost two-thirds of the suburbs were houses wholly or partly let to visitors.

Between 1800 and 1820 the lodging house appears to have dominated development along the seafront, whilst older suburban houses and those in areas not attractive to visitors provided accommodation for local people. As the older lodging houses fell out of favour so they became lodgings and rooms were let.

The advertisers of the lodgings and lodging houses were mostly local people. Shopkeepers often used the upper parts of their houses as both family rooms and lodgings. According to Cobby's *Directory* advertisements, only four people owned or rented houses providing lodgings and lodging houses, which supports the view that the two roles were very different. Matthew Dedding let rooms in his house at 20 East Cliff and let no.19 as a lodging house; Stephen Poune and Edward Hill did the same in West and Middle Streets with adjacent houses. Nathan Smith let rooms in no.3 Artillery Place and let nos.1, 2 and 4 as lodging houses. These are the exceptions.

Buying a house to let required either plenty of cash or the ability to raise a mortgage. Given the short season, buying such places might have been quite a risky venture. The local paper constantly advertised houses that were suitable to let and Cobby lists 211 lodging houses available in 1800. Seven owners had four or more lodging houses, William Tuppen, Nicholas Johnson, Isabella Pullen and Matthew Walker, John Smith and Nathan Smith owning 33 between them. Most owners were men but 15 women including Isabella Pullen owned 26 lodging houses between them, and at least one, Isabella, acted as a developer.

Number of houses owned	Number of Owners		Total Number of Houses		
1	121	79%	121	57%	
2	21	14%	42	20%	
3	5		15	7%	
4	3	7%	12	6%	23%
5	3		15	7%	
6	1		6	3%	
Totals	154	100%	211	100%	

Source: tabulated from *Cobby's Directory*.

Owners of Lodging Houses

Judging from the addresses given in street directories and in the lists generated by local taxes, the majority of residents who profited from tourism remained largely in the old town, where their shops and other businesses were mostly located. The way in which accommodation was managed seems to have been typical of Georgian towns.

9

The Suburbs

By 1776 Brighton was unable to accommodate all the visitors that came at the peak of the season in the early autumn, and so visitors were staying in the market and county town of Lewes eight miles away.[1] The majority of fashionable visitors preferred to stay on or near the Steine where they could observe each other. Sea views were of secondary interest until the 1820s when the Steine fell out of fashion. Staying here also gave visitors easy access to sea bathing down the low lying and crumbly slope at the south end of the Steine. Brighton needed to supply more modern housing and the pressure on land in this area resulted in the development of houses along the margins of the Steine right up to Oxford Place (now just north of St Peter's Church) and then eastwards along the cliff tops. Until a seafront road was built across the front of the old town in the early 1820s, land to the west of the town had superb sea views but poor access to the facilities on the Steine and so building projects there progressed more slowly.

From the late 1770s, development depended on local builders taking the risks and judging where people might wish to live. There was no co-ordination and no town planning; no local or national government controls existed. The strongest influences on the layout of the new streets and squares were the system of ownership for the farmland and the distance of the plots from the Steine and from the coast.

Ownership of the farmland was still organised using a system that had evolved centuries ago and was very out of date by the late 1770s. The land was not enclosed into regular shaped fields; most of the arable land was still in long thin strips called 'paul pieces'. Most of the surrounding sheep pasture was held jointly (common ownership) by the owners of the arable land and was unenclosed. The survival of paul pieces dictated that terraces were built with a considerable number of houses in each in order to recoup the high costs of buying and selling land held in an archaic and unwieldy system of ownership. In spite of this major constraint, though, the volume of building was so great that in 1791 300 more beds were available than in 1790. By 1800 the suburbs had developed to the point where they housed a substantial proportion of the town's 7,300 inhabitants and most of the resort's accommodation. From then the old town specialised in shops and services and lodgings for visitors of more limited means or who were staying for only a short time.[2]

The old town's compact built-up area, with its irregular street frontages and buildings of many dates and styles, must have made quite a contrast to the new

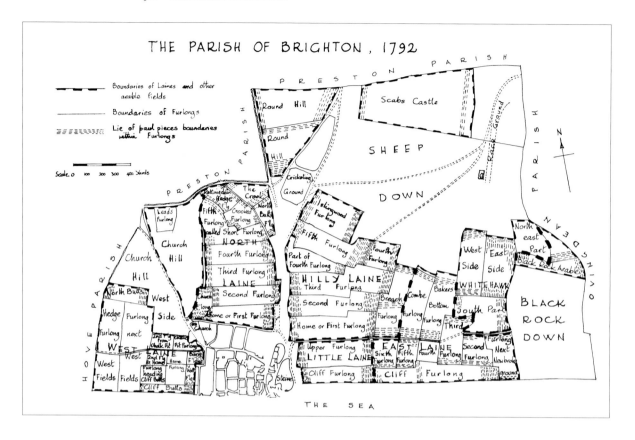

49 Map of the fields in 1792 by Ron Martin.

suburbs that surrounded it in 1800, most of which were built as narrow terraces with a limited range of building materials. A similar contrast between the old core and the new terraces in the later 18th century is still discernible in many seaside resorts, including Scarborough, Hastings, Weymouth, and at Bath, our largest Georgian spa resort.[3]

Brighton's growth is of particular interest because of the way in which the demand for resort housing beside the sea or near the facilities on the Steine influenced the growth of the new suburbs. Arable land with the advantages of proximity to both attractions on the eastern side of the town was built on first and attracted the more expensive housing. The land to the north of the town and away from the sea became a service area intermingled with market gardens and paddocks for the many working horses that were essential for road transport. In 1800 Weller auctioned 84 lots of land, which included walled gardens for fruit, a stable and other urban fringe developments on fields close to the town.[4]

The growth of the new suburbs shared problems with the town centre and other towns, such as terraced houses toppling over during the course of construction. A house being built in the old town fell down in 1771, but far more fell down in the suburbs while awaiting support from the construction of the property next door. Along the eastern cliff tops high winds were the greatest cause of losses. The loss of ten houses in a storm in 1806 was sufficiently unusual to warrant a report in the *Gentleman's Magazine*.[5]

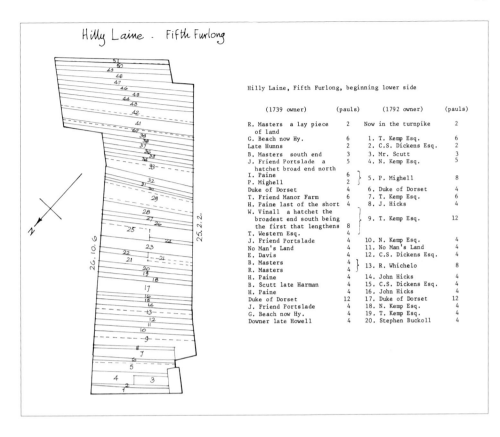

Hilly Laine . Fifth Furlong

Hilly Laine, Fifth Furlong, beginning lower side

(1739 owner)	(pauls)	(1792 owner)	(pauls)
R. Masters a lay piece of land	2	Now in the turnpike	2
G. Beach now Hy.	6	1. T. Kemp Esq.	6
Late Hunns	2	2. C.S. Dickens Esq.	2
B. Masters south end	3	3. Mr. Scutt	3
J. Friend Portslade a hatchet broad end north	5	4. N. Kemp Esq.	5
I. Paine	6	} 5. P. Mighell	8
P. Mighell	2		
Duke of Dorset	4	6. Duke of Dorset	4
T. Friend Manor Farm	6	7. T. Kemp Esq.	6
H. Paine last of the short	4	8. J. Hicks	4
W. Vinall a hatchet the broadest end south being the first that lengthens	8	} 9. T. Kemp Esq.	12
T. Western Esq.	4		
J. Friend Portslade	4	10. N. Kemp Esq.	4
No Man's Land	4	11. No Man's Land	4
E. Davis	4	12. C.S. Dickens Esq.	4
B. Masters	4	} 13. R. Whichelo	8
R. Masters	4		
H. Paine	4	14. John Hicks	4
B. Scutt late Harman	4	15. C.S. Dickens Esq.	4
H. Paine	4	16. John Hicks	4
Duke of Dorset	12	17. Duke of Dorset	12
J. Friend Portslade	4	18. N. Kemp Esq.	4
G. Beach now Hy.	4	19. T. Kemp Esq.	4
Downer late Howell	4	20. Stephen Buckoll	4

50 Hilly Laine Fifth Furlong, owners in 1738 and 1792. This extract shows how the terrier could be used in 1792 to look up the landowners and match the information with 1738. The 1798 terrier was produced as books with pages laid out so the map of the Furlong was on the left side and the key on the facing page. The first paul piece is in the valley and the highest number is on the ridge.

The Developers

There were two main types of developer in and around Georgian towns. The most usual in Brighton was the builder who acted as a developer. He bought the land and employed either his own people or sub-contractors to start the development of the site and rarely built more than a couple of houses before he tried to sell off the rest of land. The second type of developer (which included both men and women) was not involved in the building trade but in another occupation. The majority within this group purchased land from a builder and then employed the vendor or another builder to construct one or two houses on it. Thomas Howell was one of the builders who successfully invested in development. He owned not only houses but also brickfields. J.B.Otto, said to be a plantation owner in the West Indies, was the only developer who would supervise his own project until all the houses were built: Royal Crescent was started in 1799 and took about two years to complete. It still stands, resplendent in black mathematical tiles, but most of the bow windows have been replaced by bays.

Builders played the major role in the risky job of raising the capital to buy and to set out land for development in Brighton. The risks they undertook were considerable because of the scale of the projects they were trying to manage. In addition, their contacts could be unreliable and fail to provide the promised funds or to buy the property. In addition, building was subject to cycles of progress and of decline.

Builders often diversified to try to protect themselves against the vagaries of their business but many were bankrupted at least once. Notices of bankruptcy appeared regularly in the local press and in the *London Gazette*. Richard Harman owned a large lodging house with a frontage of 41 feet in the old town when he was declared bankrupt in 1779. When John Philcox was declared bankrupt he owned a lot of property and land in East Laine, two shops in St James's Street, three cottages, two stables and a lime kiln, as well as other land awaiting development. The bankruptcy of Benjamin Bennett was possibly caused by his failing to manage his debts, for he owed 39 people more than £4,500. His assets were valued at £1,000 and included the unsold carcase of a house on London Road, two cottages in Middle Street and a lime kiln and land in Ditchling.[6]

Thomas Budgen was a builder in Brighton who also supplied goods to others. He borrowed £530 from a relative, a brick maker in Ramsgate, to set up business in Brighton probably some time after 1800. Declared bankrupt in 1811 with liabilities of £2,500, but still trading in 1814 while the bankruptcy petition wound its way through the courts, he is the epitome of both the Georgian builder and the small businessman of the period.[7] He was heavily dependent on credit and on extending credit to others. Budgen rented a brickyard from Mr Attree at Wick in Hove where most of the bricks for Brighton were made. In December 1811 he owed £100 in rent and Attree inventoried and sold his assets at the yard for £117. The stock included 70,000 bricks and tiles, two sand sheds, ashes, manure, straw, a pug mill, 50 tile boards and 90 brick boards. Budgen also occupied the *White Swan* in High Street and the landlord sold the contents for £140 to pay the due rent and taxes. Budgen claimed that the true value of the contents was £350.

The title of Budgen's freehold plot for a house in Devonshire Place was sold in 1812 and his creditors gained £250. His 36 share of the Brighton Union Building Club was valued as a cash asset worth £45 15s. 4d. and that was sold too, along with the assets of his carting business. Budgen was also owed money by debtors such as people for whom he carted goods but his creditors were only partially successful in realising the debts and Budgen's assets were valued as £500. He thought that £750 was more realistic, but his creditors did not agree.

Budgen's brick accounts for 1808-11 survive but are fragmentary. He paid his bricklayers 10 to 18 shillings a day between 1808 and 1809 for a six-day week. His workforce varied in number from five to 17 and he made clamp and kiln bricks and tiles. He used his own carts to collect mould (waste) from the town, sand and chalk from unspecified locations, harbour clay from Shoreham, ashes from the town and the barracks, and straw from a local merchant. For fuel, he bought faggots from a supplier in Falmer and coal from local merchants.[8]

Budgen's other carrying activities reveal the sources of other building materials. He carried deals, clapboard, oak plank, lead, slate and building stone from Shoreham. Clinker, from the town scavengers, was also supplied by Budgen to a builder and to brick makers for adding to brick clay to make bricks. He hauled oak from Ditchling, Buxted and Washington, elm from Washington and ash from Munton. He also pulled coal brigs on to the beach at Brighton, but his records do not tell us about the costs of operating the carting side of the business.

Others did well out of the building business. When John Howell died in 1804, he was described as a prosperous builder and lodging house owner.[9]

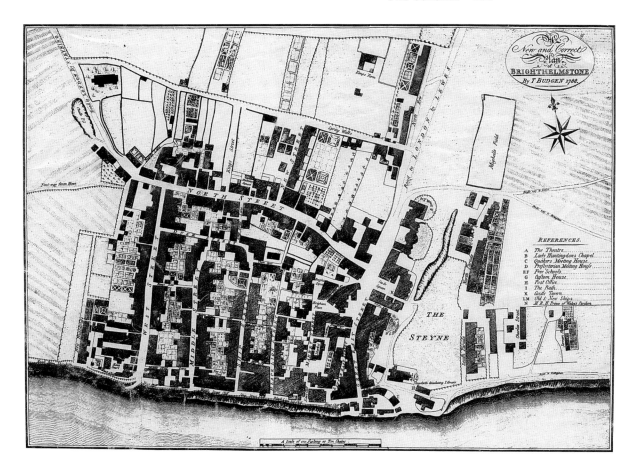

Building Cycles

Builders and developers had to cope with the impact of national influences. Building cycles were linked to the performance of the economy and resorts were always very susceptible to slumps which reduced the numbers of visitors. Brighton prospered between 1765-71, during a national building boom, and again between 1788 and 1793. The second half of the 1790s was a short period of recession when development faltered, as can be seen in the case study of Little Laine in Chapter 10. Some phases of the Napoleonic Wars made house building expensive because the costs of materials and labour rose because of the construction of barracks and the expansion of the naval base at Portsmouth. Materials from any demolished buildings were recycled; the former dog kennels, belonging to the Prince of Wales, just north of Brighton, were auctioned in 1807.

Building Materials

The builders of Brighton's Georgian houses used a mixture of imported wood and slates and local materials. If they needed help they could turn to other builders or refer to one of the many reference books such as *The Practical Builder* by William Pain (1774).

51 Budgen's Map of Brighton in 1788 showing the eastwards expansion.

The houses in the suburbs had timber frames which supported the stair ways and floors and, in some instances, much of the weight of the roof and the walls. Most of the early terraces had party walls made of lathe and plaster rather than the thin rough walls of broken brick and other materials covered with plaster that were used from the late 1700s. Such walls around chimneys posed a major fire risk, so, with very limited water supplies, most urban authorities tried to prevent this practice. Brighton acquired legal authority to supervise party walls in 1808.

Most of the timber used in Brighton was imported from the Baltic and generically called deals. The timber was sawn locally as required. At first most seaborne wood was either off-loaded from boats on the beach or carted from Shoreham; from about 1800 most came via Shoreham. Timber was also carted from inland. Slates were imported by sea from Wales through other ports.

Many houses had brick facings to their front walls and their return (end) walls, if they were visible from the front. The back walls were normally a rough mixture of old broken brick, flint (silica lumps) from the fields and cement. Bricks were made in Hove by the 1720s when many were carted to Stanmer for the rebuilding of the main part of the house.[10] In the mid-1770s Thomas Scutt and Richard Kent were in partnership at Wick and supplying the town with bricks.[11] By August 1790 Scutt and Kent had ceased to work together but both still produced bricks. Other builders and brick makers such as Thomas Budgen (described above) also had kilns in this area. The honey-coloured bricks still visible in parts of Brighton came from kilns such as these. Amongst the best examples are the houses in Regency Square of around 1818. The quality of the bricks varied. Most were made from clay mixed with ash from the town's many coal burning chimneys that was collected by scavengers and sold to the brick makers. The scavengers would bid to the Commissioners for the contracts to collect the ash.

Mathematical or 'rustic' tiles were also common in Brighton, many of the houses around the Steine having them. Little is known about their production but

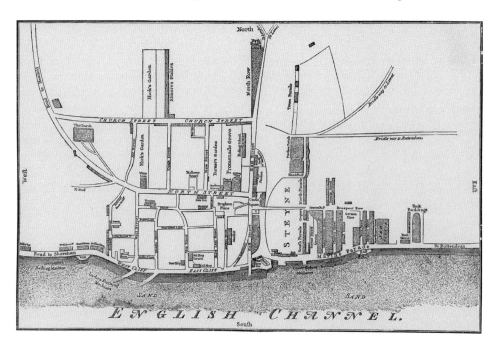

52 Cobby's Map of Brighton, 1800.

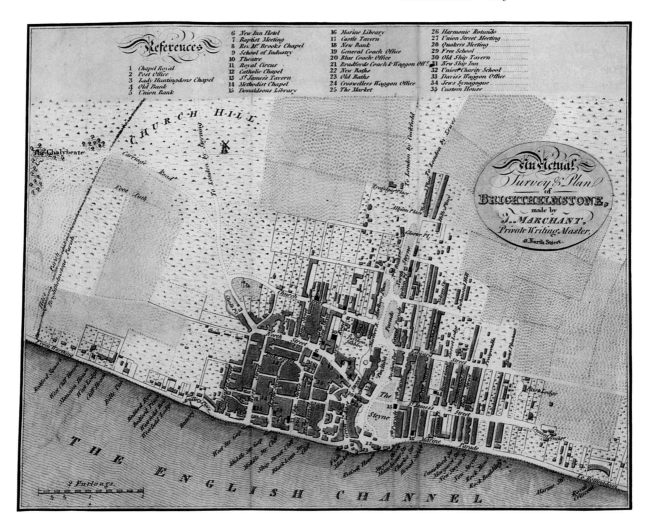

References

1 Chapel Royal
2 Post Office
3 Lady Huntingdons Chapel
4 Old Bank
5 Union Bank
6 New Inn Hotel
7 Baptist Meeting
8 Rev. Mr Brooks Chapel
9 School of Industry
10 Theatre
11 Royal Circus
12 Catholic Chapel
13 St James's Tavern
14 Methodist Chapel
15 Donaldsons Library
16 Marine Library
17 Castle Tavern
18 New Bank
19 General Coach Office
20 Blue Coach Office
21 Bradfords Coach & Waggon Off.
22 New Baths
23 Old Baths
24 Croswellers Waggon Office
25 The Market
26 Harmonic Rotunda
27 Union Street Meeting
28 Quakers Meeting
29 Free School
30 Old Ship Tavern
31 New Ship Inn
32 Union Charity School
33 Davis's Waggon Office
34 Jews Synagogue
35 Custom House

An Actual Survey & Plan of BRIGHTHELMSTONE, made by J. MARCHANT, Private Writing Master. 40 North Street.

53 Brighton in 1808. Thomas Marchant.

they were used both for new buildings and for refacing old ones. Holland used unglazed honey-coloured ones for the Royal Pavilion in the 1780s but they were also produced in red and with a shiny black glaze. The tiles were nailed onto lathes (strips) of wood and the spaces between each filled with a little lime cement. One view is that they were cheaper to use than bricks and required less skill.[12]

Doors and window frames were made locally. Most of them were inspired by the classical design copied from builders' books. Only a few had gothic details, the best of these being in Bedford Square.

The majority of houses did not have gardens, which occupied too much space and also required maintenance that short-term lodgers were unlikely to undertake. So yards with wells and in some instances cesspits were provided. Some cesspits were built under the house towards the front so that they could be emptied from the street, rear access not being a common feature of Brighton's suburbs. The majority of gardens were provided as squares, the cost of which freeholders and leaseholders met in return for access for themselves or their tenants. These were fenced off and simply landscaped. Such communal gardens gave the town valuable open spaces and lent privacy to the main rooms at the front of the houses which private gardens to the rear could not have done.[13]

Laines, Furlongs, Paul Pieces and Leak Ways

In 1776 all the land within the parish but outside the resort was farmland. Five large arable fields called Laines surrounded the town on its landward sides, four of which, Little, Hilly, North and West, had boundaries impinging on the Steine or the old town. All of these were subdivided into smaller fields called furlongs. Each furlong was subdivided into long narrow strips of land that ran the entire length of the furlong and were called paul pieces. By 1792 the 7,000 paul pieces were held in 84 yardlands by nine 'yardlanders' who owned either the freehold or leasehold. In the late 1700s a yardland comprised some seven acres held as about 20 specific paul pieces, with a stint for livestock on the pasture. The yardlanders knew precisely which paul pieces belonged to their yard lands and either let them to tenants or (unusually in Brighton) farmed them. Occupiers would secure adjacent paul pieces to make a bigger plot and sometimes hedge them.

During the 1770s the landowners of the majority of the farmland considered enclosure, so ending the management of the arable as paul pieces and the joint operation of the pasture land. They decided not to do so, possibly because none wanted to lose their hugely valuable land alongside the Steine. Consequently land was sold as freehold or let for building on long lease as paul pieces, that were often long but too narrow to build on. For instance, an auction in 1798 included a paul piece in the Upper Furlong of Little Laine which was 25 feet wide and 600 feet long, and another in North Laine, Second Furlong of the same width and 459 feet long. Some paul pieces were only 12½ feet wide and 500 feet long.

In West Laine most of the landowners sold their paul pieces to Thomas Kemp before development began on the Laine. He then sold each furlong rather than sets of strips. His decision to deal in land in this way exerted a fundamental influence on the development of West Laine, enabling more squares to be built than anywhere else.

The system of landholding dictated the layout of the streets. The wide paths called leak ways which separated one furlong from the next usually became important east-west roads such as St James's Street or Western Road, for developers built along the length of the paul pieces from one leak way to the next.

From the mid-1770s developers had to identify likely locations for development and then find out who owned the paul pieces, which they then needed to lease or buy. In 1792 the yardlanders paid Thomas Budgen for a new survey which was produced as a map and in book form. This survey (or terrier) enabled possible buyers to find out more easily who owned which piece of land.[14] The book form was especially useful, for each furlong was drawn on one page with the paul pieces being numbered. On the facing page was the list of freeholders, and copyholders who owned the paul pieces had the same key. Many deeds then referred to this survey as their starting point for the citation of the proof of title to the land.[15]

The survey was a record of rural land ownership and did not refer to most of the land sold for building or that was being been built on. It gives the impression that in 1792 little land had been sold off. The surviving deeds and records of transactions in the manor court books show that it had been.

Owners of Yardlands 1780 and 1792

Name of owner	1780 Yard lands	1792 Yard lands	Freehold or Copyhold	Manor from which they were held
Kemp, T. (L)	18.00	Unchanged	F	Brighton-Lewes
	10.25	Unchanged	F	Erlyes
	00.25	Unchanged	C	Brighton-Atlingworth
	1.00	Mitchell, J.C.	F	Portslade
Western, T.	8.25	Kemp, T.	F	Brighton Lewes
Scrase, C. (L)	4.25	Scrase-Dickens, C.	F	Brighton-Lewes
	1.00	As above	C	As above
	1.5	As above	F	Not stated
	1.00	As above	C	Rusper
	1.00	As above	C	Brighton-Atlingworth
Kemp, N.	1.5	Unchanged	C	Brighton-Lewes
	4.00	Unchanged	F	Harcourts
Tree, I.	1.00	Askerson, J.	C	Brighton-Atlingworth
Mighell, P.	2.00	Unchanged	C	Brighton-Lewes
Duke of Dorset (L)	8.00	Unchanged	F	Brighton-Michelham
Tidy, R.	6.25	Scutt, B. and Whichelo, J.L.		
	1.00	As above	F	Rusper
	6.5	As above	C	Brighton-Atlingworth
	2.00	As above	F	Not stated
Hicks, J.	4/5.00	Wall, J	C	Brighton-Lewes
Howell, J.	0.5	Wall, J.	F	Not stated
10 Owners	**84 yard lands**	**9 Owners**		**7 manors**
		6 sets of yard lands changed hands		

The yardlanders supervised their land closely. In 1785 a group of five warned farmers that they would be prosecuted if they ploughed up pasture land on the Round Hill without the consent of the freeholders and leaseholders who had the right to use it.[16]

Buying Paul Pieces for Development

When a developer had identified who owned the paul pieces he wanted to buy, he had then to negotiate with the owners. The freehold paul pieces were bought outright for a fixed sum. Each side normally paid their own costs if a solicitor was involved. Copyholders had their ownership registered in the court book of the manor from which they held the land. For the costs of recording his admission as the new leaseholder, a developer had to pay in addition to paying the outgoing leaseholder a purchase price which was normally recorded in the book. To enfranchise the land (buy the freehold), the developer had then to pay the lord of the manor a fee which was normally a multiplier of the rental value of the land.

A standard printed record of the sale of copyhold land was developed during the 18th century which the vendor filled in. That information was then entered in the manor court book, which acted as an effective register of land transactions for copyhold (leasehold) land. The buyer and seller had to pay the costs of the registration of the transactions and again a standardised form was developed. The land agent who ran the system for the landowner was entitled to a fee and so was the owner of the land (the lord or lady of the manor).

Manor of Brighton

I Henry Kelsey do declare that the surrender which I propose this day to make in the court of the Manor of Brighton to the use of James Dent Ruddock of Brighthelmstone stationer is upon a sale, and that the purchase money or consideration agreed upon for the Copyhold Hereditaments and Premises to be surrendered is the Sum of four hundred and sixty pounds.

Witnesse my hand the twenty second day of April 1824 Henry Kelsey.

Source: ESRO SAS BRI 85

Having bought the paul pieces the developer then had to decide whether, after laying it out as building plots, to sell it as freehold or as leasehold. Obtaining freehold or enfranchisement was quite expensive but builders and developers preferred freehold for it was easier to sell on. If the developer was unable to ensure that the land on which building was to take place was commutable from a network of different landownership into a single freehold, then he or she would sell the paul pieces across which the property stood as separate leaseholds, the buyer having a deed for each piece or a deed that listed each piece. Dorset Place was sold like this:

The Process and Cost of Registering Copyhold (leasehold) Title

Manor Of Brighthelmstone 4th December 1781	Cost		
Action by the solicitor who acted as the steward of the manor.	£	s.	d.
Special Court [charge for the steward to enter the transaction]	1	1	0
Surrender Mr Mackreth to Mr Bateson 2 tenements	0	8	0
Imolling [recording the transaction, similar to Land Registry]	0	8	0
Copy [of transaction for each copyholder involved]	0	13	4
Stamps and parchment	0	5	0
Proclamatn [announcement of transaction to ensure that no other claimants existed]	0	2	0
By attorney [one person not present and appointed someone to act for him or her]	0	13	4
Imolling Letter of attorney	0	4	0
Heriots [charge for selling land]	0	1	0
Admission Mr Bateson	0	8	0
Imolling [entering in the manor court book, similar to Land Registry]	0	8	0
Copy [Copy for the purchaser]	0	13	4
Stamps and parchment	0	5	0
Fealty respited [record of allegiance to the lord of the manor]	0	2	0
Fine [charge for buying land]	0	1	0
Surrender to will [to protect inheritance]	0	8	0
Imolling	0	8	0
Copy	0	13	4
Stamps	0	5	0
Total	7	13	4
Paid postage of letters of Attorney from Mr Shergold twice	0	1	0
Total	7	8	4

NOTE: At the bottom there is an endorsement that Brighthelmstone Manor received £4 13s. Endorsed (signed) by Charles Gilbert (the steward or agent of the owner of the manor).

Source: ESRO SAS BRI 85

Compared with the small-scale developments in the old town, building on the fields demanded more resources and organisation. Having assembled enough land for building and ensured adequate access to all of it, the developer prepared to start the

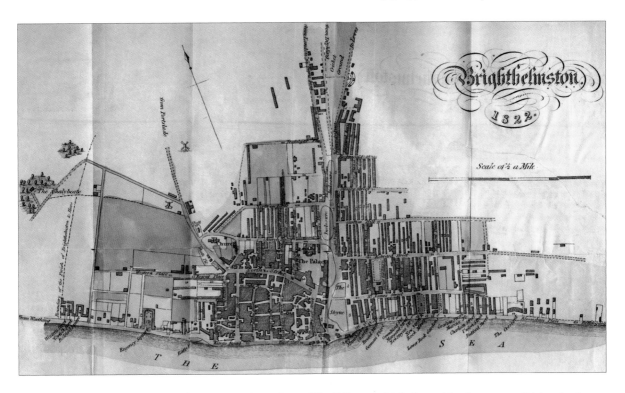

54 *Brighton in 1822.* Published in Baxter's *Stranger in Town and Brighthelmstone Directory,* 1824.

project. His decisions about the type and quality of buildings which he wished to build or wished others to build were influenced by how much money he had spent on purchasing the land, its location, the level of demand, how quickly he wished to dispose of it, and whether he was intending to build and sell property or to sell off building plots on which others would build.

A successful developer had to assess correctly the potential of the area for the type of development he wished to undertake. In the early stages, when the overall pattern of land use on the fields was not clear, development was particularly speculative because the developers could not use what had already been built as a guideline for the potential of farmland close to it.

Land in favoured locations, such as near the Steine and the sea in Cliff Furlong in Little Laine, was the most expensive to buy. The developers there expected to sell most of their land to people who would build houses to a price and style specified in restrictive covenants contained in the deeds of the leasehold or freehold sale. The price referred only to the cost of building the exterior of the house, not fitting out the interior. Many of the higher value properties had bow windows. They were probably devised to give light to rooms that were narrow and often quite deep. The stairs were built towards the back of the house to give the main rooms, which were at the front, depth to compensate for the narrowness. The inside layout and quality of interior fitments was decided by the person who built the house.

In the locations suitable for more expensive houses developers, such as Stephen Wood in Charles Street, sometimes built a few houses themselves in order to start off the project, but local people, particularly builders, then completed it. In many instances, having tried to raise the value of the land by investing in a few houses

55 Pavilion Parade, elegant lodging houses facing the Royal Pavilion, *c.*1790.

of the quality they had in mind, the developer sold it and failed to enforce the covenants in the deeds of sale, having no further interest in the land. This explains why most of the terraces and houses in valuable locations do not have rows of almost identical houses as in Georgian Bath or in the more expensive parts of Brighton and Hove that were built after 1820, such as Brunswick Town.

Elsewhere developers were less concerned about setting the tone of the project and frequently sold on all the land as building plots without restrictive covenants.

Laying Out Streets – Paul Pieces and Leak Ways
Having bought his long and narrow stretch of land, which normally consisted of between two and five paul pieces, the developer would lay a road straight down its entire length, either down the middle, if there were sufficient land to allow for houses on both sides, or along one side. If the developer were laying out only one

side of a road, the next building project would face the new road and its developer would be expected to widen it by dedicating part of his land.

Roads were normally 15 feet wide and this standard helped to make development more homogeneous. The need to lay roads down the length of the paul pieces in order that land in the middle had access had an important effect on Brighton's street plan. Most of the developers assembled long but rectangular blocks of land that stretched the entire width of a furlong so the streets were laid from one side of the furlong to the other, which ensured that the developer and his purchasers could use the leak ways between furlongs, as rights of way, in order to reach their land and then proceed down the new street to the plot. This avoided disputes over access across other people's land but reinforced the influence of the old field system on the new suburbs, the leak ways becoming the main thoroughfares in the new suburbs.

The Impact of Suburban Development

The list of new streets reveals how much infilling took place in the Old Town whilst the new suburbs were being built.

Street	Old Houses	New Houses	Total Houses
North Street	88	62	150
Bond Street	0	32	32
Church Street	0	34	34
King Street	0	51	51
Air Street	6	11	17
East St including Castle Square	90	27	117
Poole and Stein	12	68	80
Stein Street	0	15	15
Manchester Street	0	6	6
Charles Street	0	19	19
Broad Street	0	22	22
York Street	0	20	20
Margaret Street	0	12	12+
Mount Street	0	9	9
New Steine	0	17	17
Rock Buildings	0	5	5
East Cliff and Lane	58	19	77
Bartholomews	6	4	10
Knap	44	12	56
Black Lion Street	62	15	77
Ship Street	70	4	74
Middle Street	67	13	80
West Street	95	51	146
Russell Street	0	78	78
Battery Place	0	17	17
Jew Street	0	12	12
TOTAL	598	635	1233

[Dunvan, P.], *Ancient and Modern History of Lewes and Brighthelmstone* (Lewes, 1795), 553. He notes on the same page as this table that, 'On a late survey it has appeared that in the above 1233 houses there are 11,786 windows'.

The streets in *italic* were first laid out after 1776. The *King and Queen* and the lodging houses just north of Church Street were probably included in East Street, which ran northwards past the Royal Pavilion until the road was closed in 1803.

56 A mathematical tile, showing the glazed front, the profile and the pin for the nail. The tiles were nailed onto wooden lathes (strips of wood) and lime cement was used between each one.

By 1800 at least one-third of Brighton's houses stood in the suburbs and about two-thirds of these were either let as lodging houses or used as lodgings. The majority of the town's 7,339 inhabitants still lived within the old town. Between 1801 and 1811 the number of houses in the parish of Brighton rose from 1,420 to 2,380, or by 61 per cent, and as 80 houses were also being built in 1811 the rate of building was about commensurate with the increase in population. By 1811 the suburbs contained over half the town's housing and a large proportion of the fast-growing population. Between 1811 and 1821 the rate of building dramatically accelerated and many streets which had been started before 1800 were completed.

In 1814 a valuer listed 3,070 buildings as eligible to pay rates, of which 39 per cent were small and worth less than £20 per annum. The top 33 per cent were rated as worth between £41 and £150 per annum and these were the houses on which the income for the town depended. If they were unoccupied and not paying rates then the town's ability to cope with vital urban functions such as street cleaning and basic care for the unfit poor was handicapped.[17] By 1821 the suburbs probably housed two-thirds of the town's population, a remarkable shift in the balance between the old and new areas. The demand for housing also resulted in the development of villas around the spa at Wick.

The growth of the suburbs altered the shape of the town. For centuries Brighton was more or less square. By 1808 the town was roughly triangular in outline with its base along the coast and its apex at North Steine, and by 1820 building on West Laine had accentuated that shape. In 1820 most of Brighton's buildings were under 30 years old.

East Street and the south-western side of the Old Steine began to lose their importance in the early 1820s when resort facilities such as baths and libraries were built in the suburbs; these were preceded by the arrival of clusters of basic services in St James's Street and Western Road which are shown in the valuation of 1814. From about 1820 the development of estates of villas and large terraced houses, such as Kemp Town to the east of Brighton, Brunswick Town (Hove), and the Montpellier area of Brighton, which were intended to provide space for entertaining in the home, signalled the changed attitude of the wealthy towards seaside resorts and a new stage of Brighton's development, with far larger houses.

The developers who built on the fields of Brighton between 1776 and 1820 produced a medley of projects, many of which have survived. They did remarkably well, given the complex system of land ownership and the short seasons within which rented accommodation had to make money. After 1820 land in large blocks became available and the way in which visitors used resorts altered considerably. Access to a central location, where almost all the activities for visitors were run, was no longer a major priority and views of the sea became far more important. The town also built the much needed link road along the front, which enabled more development on the land west of Brighton to take place.[18]

10

The Terraces and Villas
of Eastern Brighton

By the early 1780s Brighton was short of houses to let to visitors and of accommodation for the many people and services that were needed to make a Georgian town work. The lack of a seafront promenade and a road to connect the farmland west of the town with the fashionable Steine helped to determine that the eastern side of Brighton would become the centre for lodging houses. Staying on the eastern side of the town was convenient for people who wanted easy access to the main resort facilities dotted around the edge of the Steine.

The demand for houses pushed development along the fringe of Little Laine facing the old town. This had just started when the Prince of Wales decided to develop the Royal Pavilion and the attraction of views of the Pavilion further stimulated demand for houses along the edge of the farmland. Developers recognised the attraction to the socially ambitious and by 1814 the rentals of terraced houses here were some of the highest in Brighton. Sea views combined with close proximity to the Steine were almost as popular.[1]

This new suburban development altered the image and relative location of the Steine, which became a more central and enclosed area, and by 1790 promenaders could only see the sea from its southern end, looking out towards where Brighton Pier is now.

Little Laine – a Traditional Arable Field

The terraces and villas of eastern Brighton were built mainly over a large area of arable land called Little Laine. The Laine's western boundary overlooked the southern end of the Steine and its southern one ran eastwards along the cliff top track towards Rottingdean. Little Laine was divided into two furlongs (large fields), Cliff and Upper Furlong, and stretched eastwards to where Bedford Street is now. The Laine's topography helped to give the developments on it some variety. The land rises gently both eastwards towards Bedford Street but also northwards, so the streets all rise gently from their seaward ends.

The Houses along the Edge of the Steine

When the Prince of Wales made his first visit to Brighton in 1783 terraces of houses were already being built on the western fringes of both Cliff and Upper Furlongs overlooking the Steine. They were called the North (or Blue and Buffs due to their colour) and the South Parade. In 1789 a piece of freehold land divided into 14 lots opposite the Pavilion was advertised as suitable for middle-sized houses.

As a compliment to an uncle of the Prince of Wales, the land was to be divided by a street through its centre called York Street. This would give access to the mews and other developments to the rear of the two small terraces. The owner followed the normal system for selling such land by accepting half the price in cash and the rest as a mortgage, to enable purchasers to raise more easily the cash needed to build on the land they were buying. A plan of the site and designs for the fronts of the houses were available at the office of Mr Stiles the auctioneer or at Mr Dulot's library.

In 1790 a new freehold lodging house at the upper end of Prince's Street was explicitly advertised as facing 'HRH's Pavilion'. Built by Stephen Gourd, a local man, its layout was typical of the time. On the ground floor the two parlours were located at the front of the house with the servants' hall and kitchen behind them. The first floor contained three bedrooms, a dressing room and closets; the attic floor had three servants' bedrooms. To the rear, attached and detached offices such as a privy were constructed. On the adjacent lot, which may have been behind the house, stood a stable with two stalls for horses and a coach house with three servants' bedrooms in it. Numbers 1 and 2 Pavilion Row were advertised as 'opposite the Pavilion' and as substantially built with elegant bow windows, to be used separately or as one mansion. Mrs Best the owner was prepared to accept a mortgage for a quarter of the cost of the houses but expected the rest in cash. In 1794 some more houses were described as 'fronting the residence of the Prince of Wales'. Houses further south along the Steine were said to have a view of the Pavilion and of the sea.

Building the Early Suburban Streets – Steine Street to Rock Gardens

Cliff Furlong, the farmland along the cliff top, attracted developers who aspired to build lodging houses. From the mid-1780s Steine, Charles and Broad Streets and Jermyn (German) House and Place (now Madeira Place) were being built along

57 Piggott's map of Brighton in 1826 showing the development on the east side of Brighton by then.

the cliff top between the Old Steine and what became Rock Gardens (named after some rocks that were visible at high tide just below the cliff).[2] All of the streets were built at right angles to the cliff top, following the orientation of the paul pieces and extending the full width of the furlong. The interest of fashionable visitors in the social activities in the Steine areas was reflected in the value of property, that farther out being cheaper to rent.[3]

The most expensive properties to buy or to rent were in Marine Parade, along the cliff top (in spite of the fear of cliff falls), and along the eastern side of the Old Steine.[4] The second most expensive lodging houses were in the most spacious streets in Cliff Furlong, New Steine, German Place and Broad Street. So important was a location by the sea or by the Steine that most of the streets in Upper Furlong that lacked these advantages failed as resort development.

58 *A view of Brighthelmstone*. F. Jukes aquatint etched by S. Watts, 1785. This shows the eastern side of Brighton just as the town is about to expand.

The development of Cliff Furlong in Little Laine illustrates both how many Brighton people became involved in the building process and the speed with which paul pieces could be prepared for building on. Of the 11 yardlanders who held land in Little Laine in 1780 only one, John Hicks (of the old *Ship Inn*), attempted to be a developer. The rest either sold their paul pieces or granted building leases, which were normally of 99 years' duration. Developers were so interested in land in this furlong that by 1792 at least 70 per cent was laid out ready for building. A terrier of the open fields made in 1792 notes that only South Parade and the Royal Mews were built and lists the rest as though it were still farmland. By then, though, several streets had been started and at least 17 people were involved as developers, of whom 12 were gentlemen, professionals or shopkeepers and five were builders.[5] Twelve lived in Brighton and five were described as Londoners, but one or two of these were probably resident in Brighton. Though some of them borrowed money in order to buy land, all the Brighton residents were amongst the town's most prosperous citizens.

The developers who were not builders, such as John Hall, a local doctor, normally ordered only one or two houses to be built for themselves by builders to set the tone of their project and sold the rest of the plots. The developers who were also builders, such as Stephen Wood and Thomas Howell, built more houses on their own land to sell or rent and sometimes built houses for clients who had already bought plots from them.

The development of Charles Street began in 1785. Built across four paul pieces by Stephen Wood (a builder), this plot of land measured about 108 feet wide from east to west and 200 feet in length from the cliff top leak way, that became St James's Street, to the furlong's northern boundary. Wood purchased the freehold of two paul pieces. He leased the rest until after he had started to develop the street in the mid-1780s and could afford to buy the freeholds.[6]

The people who purchased houses or plots on which to build houses in Charles and Broad Streets were mostly local shopkeepers and craftsmen. Purchasers normally paid cash, or part cash and part mortgage, and then some raised a mortgage on the value of the land in order to build a house, while others waited until they had sufficient capital themselves. This practice meant that streets were unfinished for long periods and even by 1792, when both Charles and Broad Streets had been under development for nearly ten years and Wood and Howell respectively had sold most of the land, only about six houses stood in each. In 1800 Charles Street had 13 and was almost complete. Broad Street consisted of 15 houses down one side and 32 in 1814 when the other side was completed.

German (Jermyn) Place

Only two villas in large gardens were built on the eastern side of Brighton, German Place House and East Lodge, also known as Egremont House or Place. Both faced the sea. German Place stood on Little Laine Cliff Furlong and Egremont Place stood in East Laine. Both developers successfully combined several paul pieces. German Place House was the earlier of the two villas and probably the first seaside villa that faced the sea in the town, as the first Marlborough House and the Royal Pavilion both faced the Steine.

John Daniel Richards built Jermyn Place in about 1781-2. A substantial detached villa, it faced the sea and was surrounded by its own grounds. The local newspaper was among many local sources that spelt the name of the villa as German Place. Richards, the owner, bought or leased 16 paul pieces before rapid suburban development had started and the land was probably cheaper. He held the land with different types of tenure and had to negotiate with eight owners. The frontage of the four-acre plot ran for just over 200 feet along the north side of the road to Rottingdean, now Marine Parade. Richards leased four paul pieces to the west of the house and built his house across the 50 feet which spanned the next four, of which he purchased the freehold, acquiring the seven remaining pieces to the east as leaseholds.[7]

The plot for German Place was very deep, running the full depth of Cliff Furlong to the leak way on the north side which became St James's Street. In the late 1780s Richards began a terrace of lodging houses near his own residence but following the typical north-south street pattern of streets in Cliff Furlong.[8] On Richards' death in 1791 his wife advertised the estate as a block of land suitable for house building. By then streets running north-south were being built on both its western and eastern sides. No one was willing to purchase this prime site as a single block of land, as it was too large for the typical Brighton developer who rarely speculated in anything more than one side of a street at a time.

From the early 1790s Richards and then his widow decided to sell land for houses, and Mrs Richards continued to do so after she had remarried and became Mrs Pullen. A plan shows the paul pieces across which the development was built.[9] In 1793 Mrs Richards divided the land into small lots based on the original paul

Little Laine, Cliff Furlong from farmland to streets

Number on terrier 1792 numbers	Developer	Street	Earliest Date	Number	Street of Pauls 1800	Street numbers 1814	Street numbers 1822
A		South Parade	1786 (LT)	16	16	16	19
B		Royal Mews		8	11	9	
		Steine St	1785 MCB				
1-3 Sold by John Hicks	Stephen Wood 1785 leasesMCB	Manchester St. Steine Lane in 1785	1792	12	3	20	20
5-7 All Brighton Lewes (S)	Stephen Wood	Royal Mews	1788 map	14			
8-11 8-9 is west	Thomas Howell	Charles	1788 map	15	14	14	17
12-24	J. D. Richards	Broad	1792 MCB	50	15	32	32
		Jermyn (German) now Madeira Place	Jermyn St 1788 map				
25-27	Thomas Howell	Camelford St. by 1798	York St. 1780s MCB	14	7	24	24
28-30		Margaret St.	1792 LT	20	37	37	38
30	Edward Thunder	New Steyne St.(Wentworth)	1798 LT	10	12	27	27
32-35		New Steyne	1797 SWA	32	16	12	12
36-38		Rock Mews	Rock Pla 1808 map	16		31	31
39		Rock Buildings		8			
40-43		Rock Gardens		12			
51-52		Adingworth St.		12		12	27
53-56		Grafton St.		10			13

Abbreviations
LT Land Tax
MCB Manor Court Book
Maps Budgen, Cobby, Marchant (see illustrations 51, 52 and 53)

pieces and buyers were soon found. Thomas Howell was able to buy a strip of land on which to build the east side of Broad Street. German Place (now Madeira Place) and the east side of Camelford Street (first called York Street) were built on the rest of the land.[10] By 1798 the rears of the houses in Camelford Street were being altered. Frances Coombes agreed to build a wall 12 feet high and to pitch the yard, and to lease the property and the walled yard to John Walder. He was to insert a door or gates at the end of the yard and pay a rent of eight guineas for eight or 14 years.[11]

The land was too valuable to survive as the garden for a villa. A few more attempts were made to build detached villas elsewhere on the fields of Egremont Place in East Laine and along the cliff top in West Laine.[12] Most of them survived for only a few years before being demolished or submerged in a tide of high-density terraced housing.

New Steine

The cost of buying land along Cliff Furlong meant that developers did not want to sacrifice the space to communal garden squares. The only development that was built incorporating a square in the design was New Steine, where houses with 'black rustic tiles' (mathematical tiles) and white quoins were standing by 1790.[13] By 1795 the New Steine had rails around it.

60 *Camelford Street (originally York Street).* Camelford was a title of the Pitt family. Being built before 1800.

Edward Thunder acquired the paul pieces and laid out the square, roads and building plots but Philcox, a local builder, was also involved and his name is on the surviving sketch plan from the early 1790s. It shows 15 numbered plots on the west side and 14 on the east, but more land without plot numbers and names, and the garden square marked out in the centre of the scheme. The frontages of the house plots were 20 and 22 feet wide. Local people such as Mary Crawford, Elizabeth Downs, Edward Thunder, George Woods, Matthew Walker, and Thomas Vine are named as the purchasers of plots. The northern part of the communal garden is marked on the plan as a former chalk pit and that may explain why the decision to lay out a square was taken, an infilled chalk pit being too risky for house building,[14] although clay pits from brickfields west of the old town and chalk pits dotted about on the farmland were built over elsewhere in Brighton and Hove.

Marine Parade, Cliff Furlong

At the end of most terraces on Cliff Furlong a house or two was built facing the sea to take advantage of the high value of properties with sea views. These became known as Marine Parade. Pictures show the front as consisting largely of bow-fronted and bow-windowed houses with balconies.[15]

During the 1790s land at the western end of Cliff Furlong in East Laine (adjacent to Cliff Furlong in Little Laine) was bought by developers, but most of it was not built on until the following decade.[16] In 1799 a block of land from Rock Gardens in Little Laine as far east as Royal Crescent in East Laine awaited houses, but the momentum of eastwards development slowed down during the late 1790s as the

61 *Marine Parade from the east in c.1827.* C.& R. Sickelmore Aquatint. The buildings on the right along Marine Parade were built before 1820. The *Albion Hotel* (site of Russell House) and the Chain Pier are after 1820.

developers left their land on the town's eastern fringes dormant and concentrated upon existing building projects.[17]

Upper Furlong, Little Laine: the First Suburban Service Area

Upper Furlong in Little Laine is now the land between St James's Street and Edward Street. This area developed more slowly than the Cliff Furlong described above.[18] The development of St James's Street from about 1804 as the shopping centre for the fashionable houses on Cliff Furlong (on its southern side) stimulated building on Upper Furlong, where many craftsmen and retailers had their workshops and warehouses.[19] Most of the streets were being developed as artisan housing and workshops by 1800, the only successful upper-class housing on Upper Furlong, North and South Parades, being built in the early 1780s along its short western fringe facing the Steine.

Developers showed little interest in the rest of Upper Furlong until after 1792 because projects on Cliff Furlong were still being laid out. By 1792 land in Upper Furlong was being laid out as upper-class streets in imitation of Cliff Furlong, but only Craven Buildings, Prospect Row and part of Dorset Gardens were built as the lodging houses that the developers originally intended.[20]

Dorset Gardens

The ground plan for what was No. 13 Dorset Gardens survives. It reveals the complicated arrangements that faced developers and buyers on the unenclosed areas of arable farmland. The original plan was for two terraces, both facing the garden square. A considerable number of the houses on the east side of the gardens, looking then towards the Royal Pavilion and the Steine, were built and still stand. These were tall narrow houses typical of the town in this period. No. 13 was characteristic, the plot for the terraced house being 19 feet wide but 74 feet deep. It ran across three paul pieces leased by the developer: the first was 37 feet wide and leasehold for 98 years, the next was 12 feet and leasehold for 17 years, and the final paul piece was 25 feet wide and leasehold for 98 years.[21] The developer sold the plots leasehold with a clause granting the owner use of the communal garden provided he or she paid a levy equal to that paid by other occupiers of houses towards the upkeep of the gardens. This clause was common to the leases or sales of all houses that faced communal squares in Brighton (and elsewhere). Dorset Gardens was still being completed in 1807 when Benjamin Hunt, one of the builders, was made bankrupt.[22]

62 Door, North Parade. This house, though refaced, is visible in Lay just north of the library. The door is typical of the late 18th-century and early 19th-century town house.

By 1798 the Upper Furlong was being used to meet the rapidly growing demand for housing and workplaces for shopkeepers, craftsmen and their employees serving the new developments along the seafront and the Steine. St James's Row, hidden behind South Parade, was an excellent example of the higher density development typical of the Upper Furlong. In 1807 the Row was advertised as nine new houses with the privilege of the use of a portion of St James's Garden, a detached garden on the other side of a path that serves as the entrance to these houses, but at a charge of £14 a year. All the houses in the Row stood on leasehold land and the ground rent charge for the 98 years remaining was 1s. 6d. for all except the southernmost (nearest to St James's Street) for which it was two shillings.[23]

George Street, Cumberland and High Streets were all begun before 1800 by developers who had originally intended to build more superior projects.[24] Smaller houses and workshops were soon successful and George Street, for example, was built in seven years, faster than many upper-class streets. There was very little building control exerted over any of these streets and consequently land use was very mixed; the 1814 rate book lists in George Street a mews, a pub with its own brewhouse and workshop, and housing that had a greater range of valuations than was normal in streets on the seafront. Infilling behind the street fronts was common on Upper Furlong because it made low quality buildings profitable, and by 1807 the land to the west of George Street was occupied not by gardens but by St James's Court and Row, Little George Street and Howell's almshouse. High Street also became a development of small-scale houses, shops and pubs, one of which was called the *Susan* in 1810.[25]

63 George Street, west side. Development began in the late 1700s.

As early as 1822 some streets on Upper Furlong were becoming notorious for prostitutes and disturbances were frequently reported by the night watch. Development on Hilly Laine to the north and on East Laine to the east had hemmed in the Upper Furlong and this contributed towards the deterioration of most of the property upon it. From 1840 most of the streets were identified in reports as being serious threats to public health.[26] The initial role of the area as a 'service' zone, combined with the low quality of the development, contributed to its environmental decline.

In Georgian towns high density working areas and slums were often hidden behind prestigious streets. The leak way between Cliff and Upper Furlongs became St James's Street, an important shopping centre and a respectable boundary of high quality shops. The western end was graced with grand shops with apartments above and behind for the owner or tenant. 29 St James's Street was built in 1817 for a wine merchant, with costly marble chimneypieces and seven bedrooms, a piped water supply and water closets.[27]

East Laine

East Laine lacked access to the Steine but had some land beside the sea, and the upper areas had superb sea views. Some very distinctive developments appeared on East Laine from the very late 1790s which were owned or occupied by people who could afford to keep carriages and horses to get into Brighton.

The cessation in new projects along the cliff top in Little Laine in the late 1790s is the reason why Royal Crescent, the first project built in East Laine, appears so isolated on Cobby's map of the town in 1800. Royal Crescent was built on East Laine's Cliff Furlong, where the paul pieces were orientated north to south. The Crescent is uncharacteristic of the eastern suburbs because it is built across the paul pieces in order to face the sea and the same developer built every house.

The Crescent's generous layout can be partly explained by an accident of landownership. Unusually, the freehold of most of the land was owned by one person, only one small but central paul piece having to be purchased from another owner. Two other factors are also important. The project was started at a time when the town had temporarily reached its eastwards limits and land prices in this area may well have fallen. Thus a crescent facing the sea was built in order to attract a clientèle to this peripheral location. In addition, the developer, J.B. Otto, a West Indian plantation owner, did not have most of his money tied up in the Crescent and so could afford to take time developing it. Although the project was under way in 1799 and is depicted on Cobby's map in 1800, none of the houses is listed in the *Directory* of 1800 and the first was probably completed around 1800 to 1801. All of them were standing in 1809 when they were described as elegant but marred by their bow windows and the resulting loss of privacy. The space between Rock Gardens and Royal Crescent was not filled until 1814 and even as late as 1820 the Crescent marked the eastwards extent of continuous building along the East Cliff.

Royal Crescent was one of the largest projects to be built on the fields before 1820 and the only one that was entirely financed by one person. It is notable for the similarity of the houses, all of which have fronts made of mathematical tiles, and for having its own mews at the rear. The whole project shows what was possible when the same person supervised a development until it was completed. The land to the rear of the Crescent was only suitable for building services or low value housing because the sea view and air were blocked off. Tenements were built there by 1821, so reflecting the loss of value.[28]

The Crescent successfully attracted wealthy residents such as the Rice family, whose wealth came from distilling in London. The Reverend J.M. Rice married Elizabeth Holmes of Westcombe Park in Greenwich and they became the first of the family to live at No. 6 Royal Crescent. [29]

Competition from development in Brighton's other suburbs affected both the speed and the quality of the building between Rock Gardens and Royal Crescent. Although the development of the streets which infilled this area began between 1800 and 1809, the low valuations of many properties in 1814 suggest that the developers relaxed their control on the land in order to dispose of the plots. This resulted in a very uneven pattern of development.

In 1814 Grafton Street had not been named, but building work had started before 1816 when houses were being sold.[30] In 1820 No.1 Grafton Street had only recently been built. The house faced east and stood either at the top or the bottom end of Grafton Street with a view of the Downs. The dining room measured 26 feet by 17 feet, quite sizeable for a house in this street, and in the drawing room marble chimneypieces had been installed. The house had eight bedrooms with ten beds in them, a servants' hall (or room) and piped water and water closets, but land nearby was still for sale in 1820.[31] Atlingworth Street was developed at about the same time.[32] Houses and land in Charlotte Street were advertised for sale in 1820.[33] In 1821 land just east of the Crescent was advertised for sale, the plot having been cultivated as a garden and having a farmyard; the plot now offered an ideal site for a house.[34]

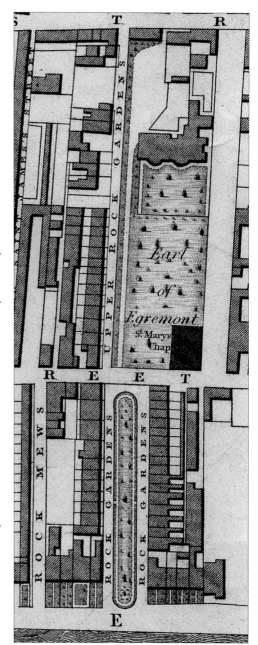

64 Site of Egremont Place, on East Laine. When built before 1800 by a Mr Neville, this was a villa in the fields, but by 1826 it was surrounded by development. Section of map from Piggott, 1826.

East Lodge, the Earl of Egremont's Brighton Home

Other than along the front by the Royal Crescent, building on East Laine tended to be small scale. Development was sporadic because of the area's relative isolation from the main part of the town. The low cost of land may explain the development of East Lodge, which was also called Egremont House or Place. This was the only villa built on the east side of town that survived as such until after 1820.[35]

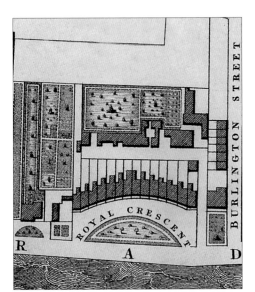

The two-acre plot, spread over about eight paul pieces, was largely purchased by Mr Neville, an Oxfordshire gentleman, before 1800 and he or his family sold the Lodge in 1807 to Lord Egremont of Petworth House in West Sussex.[36] Lord Egremont extended the house on its eastern side and added more stables and outbuildings to the north. By 1830 (and so possibly sooner) he had let the land to the south of the house to a grazier and in about 1808 he gave a plot in the south-west corner for the founding of a chapel.[37] Lord Egremont entertained lavishly and the local tradesmen benefited from his business. Some of the bills for 1811 and 1814 survive and they reveal the running costs for a large house that was only occupied for a few weeks a year. The fixed annual costs included taxes and a housekeeper, garden work and leasehold ground rent. Lord Egremont did not keep his horses on site, but with a liveryman nearby who charged £100 4s. for their keep during the time that the house was used. Heating the house for the season with coal cost £43 13s. The food bill was about £270 due to entertaining, a significant sum for a house that was only little used and for which some of the supplies may have been delivered from the estate at Petworth.[38]

65 Plan of the site of Royal Crescent in 1826 showing the gardens nearby and development eastwards. From Piggott.

By 1820 Lord Egremont's name was honoured in a local street, Egremont Place, which offered terraced houses with bow windows, and views of the sea and the Downs.[39]

Many of the small scale and varied houses that a myriad of small builders and developers took the risk of creating for visitors have survived, although the workshops and smallest houses have now been lost. The high density of the development helps to explain why, when larger houses were built farther out to the east and west of Brighton, visitors who could afford them moved away. The area still retains much of its Georgian heritage and it is at its best between the coast and the south side of Eastern Road.

11

The Squares and Villas
of West Laine

The Furlongs of West Laine

West Laine lay to the south and the north of the modern Western Road, which was named after one of the landowners, Thomas Western (who owned Preston Manor). The smallest of the laines, it contained only nine furlongs by 1780. Although just three people owned all the land in the Laine, the three furlongs closest to Brighton were still divided into paul pieces when building began. The remaining six furlongs were sold as enclosed freehold land by Thomas Kemp after he had bought and exchanged land with the other two owners, the Western family and the Duke of Dorset.[1] Kemp then leased and sold blocks of land and this enabled more squares to be built than was practical along Little Laine, where all the land was sold as paul pieces.[2]

The Development of Tenements

The first buildings on West Laine were erected to meet the needs of workers in the town. Thomas Kent's development of Kent Square to the rear of the houses on the west side of West Street began in the 1770s. By 1787 this tightly packed infill behind the *George Inn* (then on the west side of West Street) had become known as Kent's Court. It included seven copyhold cottages on the site of a former coal yard, a stable for eight horses and a herring house. Some of the same tenants were still there in 1805 when it was sold again.[3] Mr Hilton, a baker, also infilled his large garden on the west side of West Street some time before 1800, when he paid more land tax. In 1805 he advertised his freehold lodging house with five bedrooms that earned £60 a year from summer lettings, his baker's shop with a house and a bake house behind it, and six newly erected tenements with six rooms in each (which became in time Hilton's Court). The court was accessed through a 'tunnel', a passageway which passed along the south side of the ground floor of his house, below the upper floors.[4]

The development of West Laine began on three furlongs closest to the town during the late 1770s or early 1780s. Great Russell and Russell Street, which ran north to south behind West Street following the direction of the furlong, was rapidly occupied by people employed in the town.[5] Farmyard, the top end of Russell Street and the very top west side of West Street, where Wisden's smithy stood for many years, became a tightly packed area of workshops and housing. By the 1840s much of it was densely packed and polluted by cesspits that were overflowing. Two doctors who specialised in public health thought it posed a threat to the rest of the town.

Housing for people who earnt little and spaces for services such as coal yards were essential and this area provided vital trades and labour for the fashionable houses that soon began to cut off Russell Street from the countryside.

Lodging Houses for Visitors

The first terraced lodging houses and villas intended for visitors were built along the cliff top on Cliff Butts in the 1790s. A long unenclosed narrow furlong, Cliff Butts, was used for short terraces such as Artillery Place (1793) and detached villas facing the sea (Belle View, 1794).[6] The development of Cannon Place by the West Cliff Battery highlights the complication of trying to build on the small area of unenclosed land in West Laine. Cannon Place was built in both Cliff Butts and in Home Furlong in West Laine. Charles Elliott, the developer, had to buy a paul piece from the Duke of Dorset and two from Thomas Kemp to build it. An undated plan of the site of about 1800 shows that the first houses were built facing the sea and along the east side of the street where it turned inland. John Myrtle owned the land at the north end of the planned street in Home Furlong and Elliott's grand plan depended on Myrtle's co-operation, which Elliott secured.[7]

66 Map of the West Laine, and the old town in 1826 by Piggott.

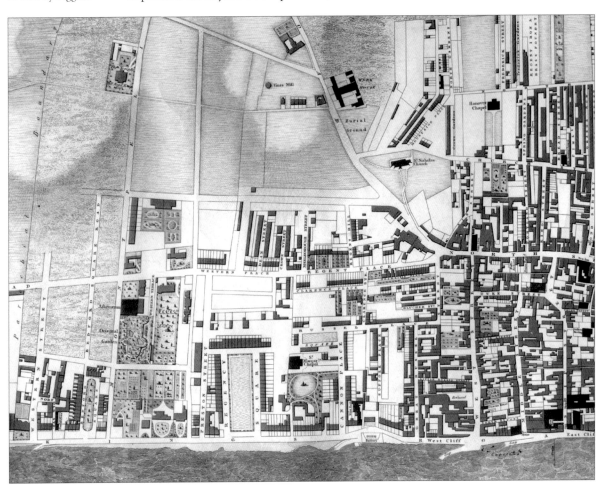

The Villas of West Brighton

Some villas were built along the cliff top and inland before 1800. Belle Vue was standing by 1799 and so was West Cliff Lodge, described in 1802 sale particulars as built of brick and stone with wings, with stained glass in its gothic and sash windows and an elliptical entrance hall with a marble floor. In 1796 one unidentified villa with 17 bedrooms and its own stables stood in eight acres of land.

In 1814 these villas were some of the most valuable residential sites in Brighton. All of them had their own coach houses and stables and so may have occupied large sites. West Cliff House was valued at £180, Mrs Byam's at £200, West Cliff Lodge at £140 and Mrs Norton's house at £150. Belle Vue was £110 and Mrs Brown's house £180. Just over the parish boundary, at Wick in Hove, Scutt, the owner of Wick spa, built himself a house with a sea view. It became the centrepiece for the plan of Brunswick Town in the early 1820s. Inland, Thomas Kemp built his villa with sea views over agricultural land to a design by Amon Wilds and called it the Temple. One visitor remarked that it was a square building with a dome which did not look very comfortable.[8]

As land values rose, so most of these villas were either subsumed into terraces before 1820 or demolished and their sites redeveloped. The Temple was the only villa to survive as a detached building.

67 *The Temple Grammar School Brighton.* Drawn by G. Earpe. Steel engr. by H.A. Hogg, 1835. Designed possibly by Wilds and built in 1818, and still looking in 1835 as it was when built. In spite of the development of Brunswick Town, in 1835, The Temple still looks isolated. It was let for use as a private school.

68   *Brighton a bird's eye view from Preston Road.* Drawn by R. Cordwell. Engr. by D. Havel. London and Brighton 1819. This shows the use of North Laine as market gardens, and the steepness of Hilly Laine to the left of the picture.

The Squares of West Laine

Almost at the western end of the parish, past the string of villas, Bedford Square was started in around 1801 in an enclosed field.[9] This was Brighton's second Georgian square, New Steine (to the east of the old town) being slightly earlier. Bedford Square was the first major project in the suburbs that did not involve purchasing land from more than one owner. Its peripheral location may explain why only 12 of the 36 houses planned had been built by 1814 before a surge in building development on West Laine resulted in its completion by 1818.

Bedford Square had several competitors which were slightly closer to Brighton but without the sea views. Blucher Place (1806), Grenville Place (1805), Clarence Square (1807) and Russell Square (1809) were all built for less affluent visitors and

prosperous local tradesmen on a smaller scale than Bedford Square.[10] Mont Pellier Terrace, first mentioned in 1809, may also have fallen into this category.[11]

When the whole of Brighton was revalued for rates in 1814, the properties along the cliff top of West Laine were assessed as amongst the most valuable in the town, in spite of poor access to the Steine. Thomas Pocock acted as the rating valuer working from the west end of Brighton. He investigated every nook and cranny and recorded his findings in great detail. He valued the six houses called The Paragon at £60 and £70 and Johnson's Library, beside them, at £100.

In 1814 only part of Bedford Square was standing, numbers 1-7 at one end and 21, 22, 34, 36 and 38 at the other. As Pocock began on the west side of Brighton it seems reasonable to assume that No.1 Bedford Square stood at the south-west corner. The houses were either 20 feet or 18 feet wide and all were 32 feet deep. Pocock valued them at either £80 or £90 and so amongst the most valuable terraced houses in Brighton. Sensibly, the development had coachhouses and mews for horses and these were tucked behind No.36.[12] The 18 smaller houses in Bedford Row were either 14 or 18 feet wide and 28 feet deep and typically valued at £45.

The development of Regency Square from 1817 was both a response to the completion of Bedford Square just to the west and a sign that the road was going to be built. Little is known about this elegant and unusually coherent design. It is one of the few in the town built before 1820 that gives any indication that the freeholder

69 Cottages built in the late 1790s on the south side of Church Street (then called Spring Gardens) and the corner of King Street.

70 *Bird's eye view of Brighton from the new church, at the entrance of the town*. Drawn and engr. by Ino Bruce, Brighton, November 1839. Aquatint. This shows the northward march of Brighton over Hilly and North Laines.

may have enforced the building covenants over a substantial number of the houses before selling on the rest. Joshua Fletcher Hanson laid the square in 1816 or early in 1817 filling the whole of Belle Vue Field with the handsome scheme. The houses are bigger than any others built before 1820 and they met the need for houses in which people could entertain. [13] They may well have sparked off the idea of building Brunswick and Kemp Towns, both of which were first conceived around 1820. The demand for larger houses with sea views also resulted in the development of villas around the spa at Wick to the north-west of Bedford Square and in the parish of Hove, but these were built after 1820.

12

Hilly and North Laines

illy and North Laines had much in common. Both rise quite steeply from the south and from the Steine, besides which lay the flattest and most sheltered land belonging to them. Although building on North Laine began in the early 1770s, little then happened, most of the developers finding that the land on these laines took a long time to sell, sometimes several years, and being anxious to let it meanwhile. Although local farmers were uninterested in renting small areas that were intermixed with housing, the plots were suitable for other land uses always found on the fringes of Georgian towns and already existing on both Hilly and North Laines, such as limekilns, stables and paddocks, cow houses, fruit growing and market gardening. Some of the latter used greenhouses to ensure they could provide a wide range of produce all year round. Well into the 1820s the combination of 'town fringe' land uses and partly finished streets was characteristic of the outer parts of these laines and some of that activity is shown in the picture of Brighton from the north by Havell.

The laines' topography and location explain the triangular pattern of urban development on both, which is discernible on the maps of the town during this period. In both laines the paul pieces were orientated north–south and building houses which faced the sea was difficult because of the cost of buying enough land, so the laines had narrow and often quite long streets that run from south to north, many of which have been lost to large-scale developments since 1945.[1] The difficulty of achieving a sea view helps to explain why these laines were developed as small houses and courts and light industry. Without accommodation for workers and workspace the town could not have functioned, many goods being produced locally in Georgian towns.

North Laine

The pattern and sequence of development on North Laine was also influenced by its proximity to the old town and, particularly, to North Street and Castle Square, which was a busy and prosperous shopping centre and thoroughfare from the 1780s.[2] From the 1770s the crofts between North and Church Streets were developed to provide workshops and cheaper housing for the businesses in North Street. By 1780 access to North Laine from the Old Town had been improved by the development of roads through the crofts such as Bond and King Street.[3] Land uses that had formerly occupied the land between North Road and Church Street, such as stabling, paddocks and large gardens, were displaced northwards onto the first furlong of North Laine.

71   North and Hilly Laines in 1826, section from Map of Brighton by Piggott.

The earliest building development on North Laine was North Row (called Marlborough Place by 1814) which was started in 1771 on the laine's south-eastern corner, facing the Steine, and is shown on the Yeakell and Gardner map.[4] John Paine sold some of the land to a bricklayer called Samuel Paine and then sold some of it to John May, a boat builder. May then bought adjacent land from Richard Tidy. By 1773 houses were being sold and mortgaged by May. North Row consisted of a mixture of houses and stabling such as the *King and Queen* inn. In the late 1790s, when the crofts behind North Street were built over, urban development really started on North Laine. By then the North Steine on the eastern fringe of the laine was becoming an attractive site for lodging houses.

In 1779 John Hicks, owner of the *Old Ship Inn* and partner in a stage-coach service, recognised that the chance to sell land in the fields for development might have arrived. He advertised 10 yardlands and a barn and croft just north of North Street, pointing out that several pieces of his land were convenient for the building of houses. Some of it was copyhold and the remainder was freehold. He paid a shilling in rent for the croft and a rent of £2 10s. for the farmland that was also copyhold. He expected to pay a fine (a levy) on the croft and also the farmland to the lord of the manor when he sold it, and the purchaser would also be fined. The levy was 'a heriot in kind', such as the best cow or a horse, but by the 18th century this had become a cash payment. Hicks managed to sell some of the land but only that fringing the Steine was developed.

In 1800 lodging houses extended as far north along the Steine's eastern fringe as Gloucester Place. On the main part of the Steine only a few buildings stood on the First Furlong, and they consisted of some small rows of cottages along Church Street, Wigneys Stables, and market and pleasure gardens such as Hicks' Gardens (later Spring Gardens) and Prospect Place.[5] There was a racing stables somewhere along Church Street.[6] On the First and Second Furlongs, which were closest to the town, market gardens gave North Laine some of the street names familiar today, such as Kensington Gardens.[7] In 1805 a row of buildings stood along what eventually became the east side of Tichbourne Street. Gardener or Gardner Street was under way before 1806 on land which had been bought by Thomas Furner, a gardener.[8]

By 1808 a street pattern had emerged on the First Furlong between the two leakways on its southern and northern boundaries which became Church Street and North Road. Building had also begun on the eastern end of Second Furlong where St George's Place, Cheltenham Place and Kensington Gardens were in progress. Jubilee Street was emerging and had a candle factory operating by 1809.[9]

72 Bedford Square. Development began before 1800.

Bread Street had also been started.[10] Building along the Steine fringe was progressing northwards faster than development on the Laine as whole, for Gloucester Place and Trafalgar Place were already under way by 1808 and building had also started on North Butts on the eastern side of London Road, where houses in Oxford Place were for sale.[11] Between 1808 and 1820 ribbon development continued up the London Road while earlier developments were infilled. In 1808 William Weymark or Wymark, a bricklayer, was building numbers 2-5 at the south end of York Place, and immediately behind these houses small cottages and a yard were built.[12] The close proximity of different land uses was typical of Georgian urban development.

By 1818 stabling for houses in the town, cowhouses and market gardens were disappearing and being replaced by small processing businesses.[13] The clustering of workshops on North Laine which had developed by 1822 was characteristic of early 19th-century towns, and was convenient for the different stages of manufacture common in, for example, furniture making or coach building.[14] Brighton's largest manufacturing concern, the Regent Foundry, was also developed on North Laine because of cheap land and access to shops and other services in North Street.

Purchasers of land for development in North Laine were often over-optimistic. By 1814 land near the parish boundary at the north end of North Laine and so too far away from the town centre for workshops was used for market gardening, keeping horses and fattening livestock, which suggests that it was awaiting buyers for building. But there was a long delay before buyers were found and in 1822 much of it was still in the same use. The ranks of small houses and workshops that have become a well-known feature of North Laine were mainly built between 1820 and 1845.

Hilly Laine

Hilly Laine lay north of Little Laine, the leakway or path between the two laines becoming Edward Street. Hilly Laine's western boundary ran northwards from Edward Street to overlook what is now called The Level. Before Hilly Laine succumbed to streets of houses and workshops there were already suburban activities. In 1801

Humphrey Paine sold eight pauls to John Hicks and his associates, together with the chalk pit, limekiln and granary that stood on them. The land was developed as Lime Kiln Row and Darby Place, and in 1814 William Mott, a builder, was still operating the limekiln.[15]

The development of the fringe of Hilly Laine for lodging houses had started before 1789, for then Town Parade (or Pavilion Parade) stood on the south-western corner of Hilly Laine, looking across the Steine towards the Pavilion. Numbers 1 and 2 Pavilion Parade were already erected and were advertised as freehold houses of four storeys including the basements. Each had a complete kitchen in its basement and a housekeeper's room, servants' hall, pantry, wine cellar and yard.

73 Russell Square.

The first (ground) floor contained a 'handsome hall', an elegant drawing room and a dining parlour. Both had four bedrooms on what was described as the second floor, and servants' rooms in the attic storey. By 1800 a meadow enclosed with a rail fence was for sale at the northern end of Hilly Laine, but development took more than a decade to reach that point.

Town Parade was still incomplete in 1806 when the first houses in Carlton Place to the north (which was started in 1806) were ready to sell.[16] Both terraces were almost complete when Richmond Terrace, Richmond Villa and Albion Place were started further north. Some development there is indicated on Marchant's map of the town in 1808. The Wilds (Amon and Amon Henry) were associated with Richmond Terrace and so probably with the villa, too.[17] In 1819 Waterloo Place was built on a piece of land called the Gold Butts which belonged to the Fourth Furlong in Hilly Laine. This copyhold land passed from the Masters family to Richard Lemon Whichelo who sold it to Thomas Attree. Attree paid for the land to be made freehold and laid out Waterloo Place and the two streets behind. By 1820 houses were standing in Waterloo Place. The architect of some of them is said to be Amon Wilds.[18] North of Waterloo Place, Hanover Terrace on Islingwood Furlong was the brainchild of Henry Brooker, who employed Amon Henry Wilds to design a crescent of connected Palladian villas which was probably started right at the end of the 1810s and certainly completed after 1820.[19] Most of these places can be seen on the view from the north of 1819 by Havel which includes Richmond Villa and Terrace. Hanover Terrace is just too far north to be included in this view.

Carlton Place – Grand Parade

By 1811 all the houses along the front of Hilly Laine as far north as Carlton Place were known as Grand Parade.[20] The development of Carlton Place between 1806 and 1808 shows how the lodging houses along this stretch of the Steine were developed and the way in which developers with large plots of land laid out the

less accessible land behind the more prestigious houses with a network of smaller streets. Remarkably, the rough sketch plan by the developer for this whole project has survived, which shows how the streets were drawn over a copy of the survey of the laines by Budgen in 1792.[21] Many of the street names and some of the buildings have also survived and so the area can still be traced in the modern landscape.

The owner of the land around Carlton Hill was Dr Benjamin Scutt. He inherited yardlands in the fields surrounding Brighton and also houses within the old town. Scutt also owned the land on which the Wick Spa stood in Hove and sold the land which became the Brunswick Estate in Hove in the 1820s. He acted as the developer of the land on which Carlton Place was built and of the land to its rear. When he decided to sell plots for building houses, his land formed the western edge of the second furlong in Hilly Laine and its boundary lay along the North Steine. The development of the plot fitted into the expansion of the town in 1806, by which time the perimeter of the common fields overlooking the Steine to the south and the Royal Pavilion had been built up.

Scutt was only interested in Carlton Place, the most prestigious part of his project, and named after the Prince's house in London. In 1806 he marked up plots for 20 terraced houses, each house and yard having a frontage measuring 17 feet and a depth of 60 feet. In the centre of the Place he allowed the development of a riding school called the Royal Circus. The houses backed onto Circus Street, a 25-foot

74 Carlton Terrace, on the fringe of Hilly Laine.

wide road named after the riding school.[22] Scutt must have sold the land for Royal Circus to someone else for he did not raise the money to build it.

To fund the construction of the houses he raised mortgages, the average sum being £410. The 12 southern houses were standing by the end of 1805 and in 1806 some were sold to their occupiers. In 1814 the new rating of the town assessed them as worth £55 and £60, which was in the top quarter of valuations for the town but lower than those along the southern part of the Steine. Numbers 1 and 2 Carlton Place were sold for £700 in 1806 to the Reverend Frederick Hamilton. The sale enabled Scutt to pay off the mortgage to Robert Nott from whom he also borrowed the money to build No.4. Hamilton also bought Nos.11 and 12 and then let them. Three ladies, Letitia, Sarah and Charlotte Digence, bought No.6 and paid £350, raising some of the money by borrowing, but this was not unusual. By the end of 1808 Scutt had sold all of the houses.

He sold the land to the rear of Carlton Place in parcels, and it developed more slowly than the frontage. Scutt did not seek to control what happened there by using covenants or by charging large sums of money for the land. He named some of the streets but left the rest for the developers to decide. Circus Street, Carlton Mews, Carlton Row and Wooburn or Woburn Place were named by him. The sketch plan of his projects shows not only the layout of the paul pieces over which the developments are taking place but also the varied land uses.

Numbers 1-16 Carlton Place and the Royal Circus were built on a paul piece that was 'late Kemps', Circus Street to the rear stood on 'late Mighells' (paul piece 71) and the yards, lime yard, tenements, warehouse, granary and stable beside it on paul piece 70 (late Western's and late Kemps). Carlton Mews and a garden and a coal yard were developed on eight pauls (late Friends and Kemps), Carlton Row straddled paul pieces 62 and 63 (late Kemps). Woburn, or Wooburn as spelt on his plan, straddled paul pieces 60 and 61 and an unnamed road to the north was laid along paul piece 59. A sketch map of about 1815 shows the rapid development of the crowded courts on the north side of Woburn Place.[23]

The Development of Small Terraces and Workshops

Scutt timed his sales of land well for between 1804 and 1808 there was a minor building boom on Hilly Laine, during which Edward Street emerged along the leak way. By 1804 Edward Street had several stables and workshops and at least one kiln for the making of clay pipes along its length. By 1804 the *Thurlow Arms* stood on the edge of Upper Furlong Little Laine, facing Hilly Laine across Edward Street. The inn was used as a base for auctions of local houses and land, especially on Hilly Laine.[24] From 1808 building on Hilly Laine continued more sedately and few new streets were started. In 1814 half-finished streets of artisan housing and workshops were scattered all along the lower slopes of the laine behind the upper-class terraces, including Carlton Street and Row, John, Nelson, Thomas and Chesterfield Streets (the latter long demolished, near Thomas Street).[25]

A few examples illustrate the process of development of the Laine. It involved large numbers of small speculative builders and developers and some land changed hands several times before building began. John Street (also called St John Street in the 1810s) stands on the First Furlong of Hilly Laine. The developer was John Hall and two of his purchasers were also called John, and Hall probably named the street for that was the common practice. The east side of the street stands on land that once belonged to the manor of Brighton Atlingworth. In 1805 Hall laid out the house plots, each 11 feet wide and either 14 or 15 feet deep depending on their location, before he sold some of the land for building to John Mantle, a gardener, and to John Baker, a victualler. Building began almost as soon as Hall sold the land for in 1805 two of the tiny houses were sold.[26] The rate book for 1814 suggests that John Street was almost completed.

Cornelius Paine began developing Carlton Street after 1800 and in 1807 was the owner of the entire street, having had a licence to use the land since 1793. He bought the freehold in 1821 and then sold the properties, copyhold title not being popular with house purchasers.[27]

Second Furlong, Hilly Laine

Carlton Hill was being built on four pauls in the Second Furlong of Hilly Laine by 1819 but developed very slowly. Christian Kramer, master of the Prince's private band, was amongst the speculative developers involved.[28]

Third Furlong, Hilly Laine

On the third Furlong in Hilly Laine, Benjamin Scutt sold his plot of eight pauls which he held as the copyholder from the manor of Brighton Atlingworth for development from 1809. Sussex Street was laid out by the end of 1809 and Claremont Row (also called St Stephen's Row) was also under way. William Boxall was one of the builders involved in this development and he funded the building work by mortgaging land to John Martin, a linen draper, and by selling land. The typical plots were 45 or 50 feet by 50 but by 1816 some had been divided to 25 feet frontages because Boxall needed the capital. [29]

Chesterfield Street was laid out as small houses, the plots being sold with 12 or 24 feet frontages. They were built on '4 pauls or half a customary acre' belonging to the Manor of Brighton Atlingworth, which passed from Sarah Boyce to Thomas Kemp and then in 1807 to J.S. Smith gent who paid a herriot (transaction fee) of 5½ shillings (in lieu of a horse), and on four pauls which had been owned by Benjamin Masters.[30] Smith immediately sold some of the copyhold land to William Philips, a builder who then sold most of it to the Reverend Jeremiah Smith of Peasmarsh and to Thomas Evans, a shopkeeper.[31] All of the land was being developed by 1816 when Mott was selling his lime works nearby for building.[32]

Behind the elegant façades along the North Steine and the Lewes and London Roads, Hilly and North Laines provided space for essential housing and services. The long narrow streets imposed by the paul pieces were economical for the small-scale houses which could be fitted in quite neatly. On North Laine the leakways such as Trafalgar Street and Gloucester Road are with us still and so are many of the streets laid out between them, even though most of the housing has either been rebuilt or lost to later development such as large Victorian warehouses. On Hilly Laine many of the small Georgian houses and workshops survived until the 20th century when big local improvement projects such as the Fruit and Vegetable Market and the Law Courts claimed them. But Carlton Hill, Sussex Street and Richmond Street are still there, developed along the old leak ways between the furlongs, and so the fields beneath are still detectable in the landscape.

13

Population and Employment

Between 1750 and 1821 Brighton's population increased from about 2,000 to just over 24,400. Of the resorts, only Bath's population grew faster. Brighton's population increased faster than those of industrial northern towns such as Blackburn, Bolton and Oldham whose populations were twice as large in 1750. Many county towns with populations two or three times as large as Brighton in 1750, such as Canterbury, Salisbury, Warwick and Worcester, were considerably smaller than Brighton in 1821. Lewes and Chichester, the county towns of East and West Sussex, were larger than Brighton in 1750 but in 1821 each town had only about 7,000 inhabitants. By 1793 Brighton advertised a wider range of services advertised in the *Universal Directory* of that year than Lewes and the county town's role as the developer of trades and services in Brighton had been supplanted by London.[1]

The cause of the rapid increase in Brighton's population was the high level of expenditure by visitors. Although the resort facilities and activities described in Chapter 3 did not employ many people, and by themselves would not have resulted in population increase, they played a major role in attracting visitors. Encouraged to stay in the town by leisure amenities, visitors spent on other things such as food, accommodation, clothes, luxury goods and services (such as artists) and travel in the area, all of which generated employment. The direct beneficiaries in the town spent some of their profits locally, so adding to the economic value of the visitors' expenditure. As the number of visitors rose, the average length of stay increased and the season extended, so the element of the population which could depend upon the visitors for its livelihood increased.

Even by 1821 the increased volume and range of mass-produced consumer goods made available by industrialisation had done little to reduce the importance of local production of many goods in most towns. Thus, visitors provided employment for dressmakers, shoemakers, milliners, jewellers, artists and other providers of fashionable services. Their liking for the town provided employment in the building and furniture trades. Catering for visitors provided work for butchers, bakers and confectioners, as well as for wholesalers who supplied livestock, flour and other foodstuffs and for 'eating houses' (restaurants).[2] Domestic servants were employed not only by the visitors but also by those townsfolk who prospered.

The Development of the Town's Economy; the Influence of the Region and of London
From 1750 the number of occupations in Brighton increased, reflecting the rise in demand for trades and services which the change of function from fading maritime town to

Brighton's Population and Employment by Occupational Sectors 1783-1824

Sector	Year and Percentage Employed in Each Sector			
	1784	1793	1800	1824
	%	%	%	%
Professions	29	16	14	12
Services excluding Accommodation:				
Distributive and personal	29	24	31	35
Transport	2	8	3	3
Inns	8	10	10	4
All services (excluding accommodation)	39	42	44	42
Manufacturing				
Food	10	5	6	5
Clothing	2	13	12	15
Other	14	10	14	13
All Manufacturing	26	28	32	33
Building	6	13	8	11
Agriculture		1	2	2
TOTAL (100%)	51	340	474	2090
Total above as % of all entries in directory	100	84	61	81
Accommodation as % of all entries		3	37	2
Commercial as % of all entries			1	1
Private income as % of all entries		13	1	16
All entries (100%)	51	407	774	2560
Number of families	690 (est)	1230 (est)	1390 (1801)	5580 (est)
Population (year)	3620			
(1784)	5669			
(1794)	7339			
(1801)	29300 (est)			
Possible number of families represented		33%	50%	40%

fashionable watering place brought. It is possible to detect two stages in the development of employment that match those described in Chapter 3 for the development of resort facilities, the first from 1750 to 1780 and the second from about 1781. The increase in employment and the growth of population in each phase were closely linked.

Whilst the region played a major role in the development of services for visitors between 1750 and 1780, London became more important later as the services required became more sophisticated and fashion-conscious. Sussex continued to play a major role in the supply of basic goods, food stuffs and labour. As other resorts developed they began to compete for the same resources. Semi- and unskilled labour continued to be drawn from the region but other resorts such as Worthing and Hastings began to absorb it as well.

1750-1780: Regional Support and the Development of Services

In 1750 there was a limited range of occupations because of the town's poverty and the lack of a regional clientèle because of the nearness of Lewes, the county town.[3] The crafts represented in Brighton included ropemakers and shipwrights, who supplied the town's maritime needs, and blacksmiths, cordwainers, joiners and tailors for domestic requirements. The limited number of retailers reflected the low level of expenditure within the town, which provided only basic necessities: brewer, baker, innkeeper, haberdasher. The teacher represented the professions.

Between 1750 and 1780 a wider range of the trades and services common in most busy small towns of the time was attracted to Brighton. Amongst the new arrivals were linen drapers, tanners, tallow chandlers, plumbers, cabinetmakers and grocers. There was also a rapid increase in the number of people who offered the basic services and trades that the resort already had, such as innkeepers, malsters, bakers, carpenters and grocers. Before 1750 Brighton was so poor that the town lacked the more specialist employments, such as peruke makers, a hatter and a milliner, but after 1750 these soon arrived, and so did professions such as doctor surgeons. By 1780 the resort supported a wider range of luxury trades and services and professions than would normally be expected in a town of this size, including boarding schools, cutlers, doctors, drapers, a gold and silver smith, hatter, jeweller, librarians, portrait painters, surgeons and apothecaries.[4] By 1819 some local businessmen such as 'Mr Izard of Brighton' were so well established that their deaths were recorded in *The Times*.[5]

Most of Brighton's inhabitants in the 1750s and 1760s lacked the expertise and the money to start new businesses. People who came from the surrounding region, most especially from Lewes, established many of the new occupations that Brighton had by 1780. Semi-skilled or unskilled work, or tasks which required little training, included working in an inn or being a general domestic servant, so the numbers of inhabitants who found new jobs, initially even as apprentices, were probably quite small.[6] The large numbers of people who received aid from the Overseers of the Poor until the late 1760s suggests that opportunities for semi- and unskilled employment did not keep pace with population growth. By 1780 Brighton's continued success resulted in plenty of suitable jobs for the townsfolk and for immigrants from the region.

1780-1820: London's Dominance

From about 1780 a considerable number of London tradesmen were attracted to the town, some opening branch shops for the season, others moving their entire businesses. Before then the London trades had been few and tended to stay for only a few weeks during the peak of the season. Amongst the names that now appear in the town is that of Hannington, who in 1780 auctioned the stock in trade of a linen draper and hosier at the *Three Tuns* on East Cliffe. By 1800 the Hannington family were on their way to becoming wealthy tradesmen by developing the shop that became a well-known department store in North Street.[7]

Brighton Population and Occupations from the census 1801-1821

Decade	Total Pop'n	Male	Female	Agri	Occupations Manuf	Others	Family All Occupations	Av Family Size
1801	7339	3274	4065	94	3050	4195		
1811	12012	5069	6943	61	1301	1054	2416	6
1821	24429	11019	13410	92	3834	792	4718	5

Population and employment 1811 and 1822

	1811	1821
Inhabited Houses	2077	3947
Houses now building	80	360
Houses now empty	301	352
Number of families	2416	4718
Number employed in agriculture	61	92
Numbers employed in trade	1301	3834
Families neither	1054	792
Average Household size (Baxter)		6.20

From: *The Stranger in Brighton and Baxter's Brighthelmstone Directory* 1822, p.xiv, 29 May 1821.

Cobby's *Directory* of 1800 and the extensive lists of members of the local freemasons' lodges with a wide range of occupations reflect a sophisticated urban economy which continued to develop into the 1820s. Then, the next street directory provides an opportunity to see what has developed and where.[8]

Seasonal Accommodation as a Source of Employment and Income

For any study of Brighton, a town within which many people made a living from seasonal lettings, the exclusion of accommodation from most of the directories is a major limitation.[9] *Cobby's Directory* of 1800 is the only one of the period to include accommodation and it shows the major role played by lettings in the town's economy by that date. Nearly two-fifths of the people listed in entries are there solely because they owned lodgings or lodging houses to let. In addition a significant group owned accommodation but also had other occupations. In 1800 about a fifth of the people with a business in North Street also had lodgings to let.[10] The accommodation sector must have been a major source of employment for servants. It was also very important to the building trades for, like all expanding towns in this period, Brighton employed a large number of people in the supply of building materials and in the actual building industry, such as bricklayers, plumbers and glaziers.

Age structure of the population of Brighton in 1821

Age Structure	Males	Females
-5	1849	1789
5-10	1492	1491
10-20	1189	1416
20-30	1024	2849
30-40	1902	1862
40-50	1517	1132
50-60	1025	641
60-70	593	364
70-80	304	133
80-90	96	41
90-100	-	2
105		Phoebe Hessel
Excess of females		2391
Total	11019	13410
All	24429	

The Stranger in Brighton and Baxter's Brighthelmstone Directory 1822, p.xiv 29 May 1821

75 *Fishermen with a breeze going to sea.* Engraving by Rouse, *c.*1810.

Retailing – Castle Square and North Street

It is clear from newspaper advertisements and from addresses in directories that by 1780 services were starting to cluster. Specialists such as booksellers and stationers were close to the Steine and it was through them that most of the male and female artists, teachers of fencing and others of this type normally advertised. Mr Jukes sold his engravings through Paines, the stationers at the bottom of North Street who also produced an *Almanack* for Sussex. Libraries competed against each other and the stationers for business, catalogues being amongst the marketing tools used to show who had the best choice of books. Librarians also sold paper, pencils, books, maps and presents such as Tunbridge Ware. Before 1780 some also sold pills, such as Dr James' Pills at four shillings a box and a family medicine for most diseases including 'over drinking'.

In the 1780s and 1790s Castle Square and the eastern end of North Street became the town's fashionable shopping centre and East Street specialised increasingly in high quality food shops and drapers at the Castle Square end. By the mid-1790s people who described themselves as high-class drapers, such as George Elmore, were coming from London to establish businesses and settling in North Street and Castle Square. Some, such as William Lloyd, built their own houses and shops and advertised their goods in the local paper. Some shops were on the ground floors of houses, others were detached. The displays in the windows along the main streets had to be quite sophisticated for, by the 1750s,

London, Bath and the wealthier provincial towns had created a clientèle who expected as much.[11]

The affairs of drapers who became bankrupt give an insight into how retailers acquired goods and credit. In 1818 G. and T. Curme, Drapers were declared bankrupt. They had moved to Brighton in 1817 and may have been drapers in Dorchester or Gosport because they owed money to suppliers in both places, one of the creditors being T. Curme of Dorchester, presumably a relative.[12] The pair owed Benjamin Gott of Leeds, the textile manufacturer, just over £23, T. Curme of Dorchester, a cabinet maker and upholsterer, almost £109, and a host of suppliers in London between £10 and £12 apiece. The total debt amounted to £7874 3s. 6d. and the pair had assets worth £578 2s. 10d. Peter Powell of North Street, silk merchant and linen draper, was declared bankrupt in 1823. He probably arrived in Brighton in about 1818, to judge from the length of the lease of his premises. Powell not only owed a lot of money but also had issued a considerable number of unpaid bills. His suppliers were mainly in London and in the West Midlands, pins, for example, coming from Redditch in north Worcestershire. He owed £5,884 but had some £1,169 of 'good debts' owed to him that the creditors thought could be made to pay and other assets worth £4,049. Most of his debtors were women who lived to the east of the Steine, but others had also been allowed to run up large bills. Madame de Cotee in New Road owed him nearly £21 and Miss Evans in Boyces Street nearly £16. Some of his assets were sold off and the many ladies who had yet to pay were pursued.[13]

Jewellers and watch and clockmakers also gathered in the vicinity of Castle Square where, at No.2, S. Pearce was located. Dressmakers and other fashion traders came to Brighton for the season from prestigious London shopping streets, such as Bond Street, but also sought shops near Castle Square and the south end of North Street. Hairdressers, who advertised quite often for skilled staff and offered apprenticeships, liked to be near the dressmakers.

Cobby's Directory confirms how important North Street and Castle Square had become by 1800, especially near the Steine, where the roads were filled by coaches going to the inns and passengers waiting at the coach offices, and the town's banks, fire insurance offices, larger shops and town houses were intermixed.

Food Supplies – Market Street and Brighton Place
Market Street and Brighton Place were the main locations for food shops, particularly porkmen, poulterers, cowmen and butchers, because of their proximity to the market where meats and dairy products were also sold. The market was established in Market Street in the 1740s to replace the previous one lost to erosion. In 1773 it came under the control of the Commissioners who were established in that year. They rebuilt and laid out the market and set the tolls for those who wished to have stalls there. The tolls were a valuable source of income and the Commissioners borrowed money secured against them.

Retailing in the Suburbs
There were few services or trades in the suburbs in the 1790s although housing was being built quite quickly along the East Cliff. Two of the earliest shops to open outside the old town sold luxuries: in 1794 a millinery and haberdashery shop opened at the 'Sign of the Grand Sultan', South Parade and Jones's Music Warehouse opened at 13 South Parade. They faced the Steine but were on its eastern side. In the early 1800s employment in services and trades became more dispersed although

the professions continued to remain clustered in the 'old town'. By 1810 St James's Street was the shopping centre for the new suburbs on the eastern side of the Steine and by 1822 the ranges of shops at the western end of the street near the Steine were similar in status to those in North Street, although fewer in number.[14]

Little shops opened in the streets to the north of North Street and St James's Street. In Bond Street, King Street and the streets that emerged north of Church Street, networks of workshops developed which supplied retailers on the main shopping thoroughfares. By 1820 the high rents on main-street frontages meant that the relationship between retailers and workshops was changing as the retailers ceased to maintain their own workshops and sent their business to craftsmen who supplied more than one retailer.[15]

Legal and Financial Services

Financial and other services were necessary and insurance agents, solicitors and other ancillary services advertised, but with a few exceptions little information about them has survived. The insurance agents normally represented firms based in London. Thus, in 1784, Edward Cobby represented the Royal Exchange Assurance and Mr Earle the New Fire Office of Lombard Street. In 1793 William Pollard advertised the London Assurance Co. By 1775 the Royal Exchange Insurance Company and the Sun Fire Office insured a considerable number of places in the town.[16]

Brighton also needed a bank to help with the flow of cash between businesses and to provide a facility for visitors but the first one did not last for long. Founded by Thomas Harben, Samuel Shergold, Thomas Scutt, Stephan and John Rice in 1787, it was joined by John Lanham of Horsham who had already agreed in 1791 to manage a bank at Horsham for 21 years which was run as a separate venture.[17] Both the Brighthelmstone and the Horsham Banks failed in 1793 but there was enough to pay all the debts and to leave a surplus. An agreement was set up to repay creditors as much as possible, any money left being returned to the bankers. Shergold, Scutt and the Rices delivered a schedule of their private assets vaued at £67,000. George Courthope of Whiligh and Nathaniel Kemp of Preston agreed to act as trustees, Courthope for the obligations of the Horsham Bank and Kemp for Brighton. The Horsham Bank owed the Lewes Bank money and so the impact of its failure was quite widespread, Thomas Harben of the Lewes Bank being very concerned about liquidity.[18]

The Brighthelmstone Bank was replaced by the Brighton and Horsham Bank in 1794.[19] Rickman and Wigney were partners in this bank, both having run a bank in Lewes. Rickman died in 1801 and his son continued the business with Wigney, whose family remained involved with the bank until 1842.[20]

The Brighton Union Bank opened its doors in North Street in 1805. The partners came from the Brighton area and from London. William Golding, James Browne, Nathaniel Hall, Richard Lashmar and Thomas West invested £2,000 and invited subscriptions of £200, offering five per cent on each share before the profits were divided. By December 1805 there were 70 accounts held at the bank and by 1820 the number had increased to 350 accounts.[21]

Solicitors dealt with business matters such as buying property, formalising partnerships, making wills and handling the litigation that sometimes resulted from business affairs. By the 1770s they were settling in Brighton so local people no longer needed to go to Lewes. William Attree from Ditchling set up his practice before 1775, when he bought the land for both 8 and 9 Ship Street and probably rebuilt them, the latter becoming his house and office. Attree became an influential man; from the 1780s not only was he Clerk to the Vestry but also the local agent for land purchases for the Prince of Wales. When he died in 1810 aged 61 he was a wealthy man. His assets included the *Old Ship*, which he purchased in 1802 and where he installed a tenant as manager.[22] Henry Brooker (1758-1848) also flourished, having set up his practice in 1782.[23]

Auctioneers

Auctioneers played an important role in town life. They usually rented space in the inns for their sales, auctions being the main way of disposing of houses, horses and any other expensive items. Henry Stiles was both an auctioneer and an innkeeper. Verrall and Co. specialised in auctioneering but would sell anything that required their services. Sometimes auctioneers sold the contents of houses in situ. The firm of Attree and Kent, now in Church Street, Brighton, began as Attree and Co, auctioneers and valuers and then became undertakers.[24] The company's first premises were in Ship Street.

Staple Trades – Coal

By 1780 coal was a major import. Brighton had been importing coal since at least the early 1600s but the volume increased after the town became far wealthier and needed a considerable amount of fuel for the bakers and other traders and to warm homes. The town was dependent on coal and imported it by sea. Views of Brighton show coal boats unloading on the beach already occupied by bathers and fishermen. Concern about the dust and noise from carting helped to push the coal trade into Shoreham, as did taxation of the loads by the Commissioners looking for income towards the cost of the town's street cleaning, lighting and other services.[25]

Coalyards, brewing and transportation were often linked. Several owners of coalyards owned vessels based either in Shoreham or at Brighton, where most of the coalyards were close to the seafront to reduce the cost of moving this weighty commodity overland.

Robert Davis became a very prosperous coal merchant and when he died left Mary, his wife, a post chaise that was being built and two carriage horses called Tommy and Billy. She was given £1,000, Robert's clothes and the contents of their house, plus a house in Middle Street and another in Duke Street for life, after which the property went to John Davis, Robert's nephew. Mary was also given £100 that was secured on the town rates as a loan to the town in her name. Robert's brother-in-law Thomas Scutt inherited a coalyard and house 'late Measors', and John was to have the use of the warehouse and two great stables in return for a rent of £125 during Mary's lifetime. He also received the coalyard in Middle Street, shares in Tubb and Davis (the coach business) and the carrier wagons for the London carrier business. John had to pay legacies to his sisters and to four old servants.[26]

In 1796-7 John Davis sold or let the coalyard at the bottom of Middle Street to James Gregory, who advertised that the Newcastle Coal Company was the supplier, specifically stating that the coal came from Bykers Street, Anthons and Heaton Main and was all 38 shillings a chauldron. Gregory had been a partner in the Brighthelmston Coal Company of Ship Street which in 1796 announced that it had purchased two

boats to overcome the shortage of coal in the town and was dissolved in 1797. Matthew Whichelo and Thomas Mitten owned a coal company in Ship Street.

In 1804 the Constable and Headboroughs investigated a charge that Izard had been selling coal short weight and said the claim was unfounded. Merchants were also the victims of crime such as the theft of coal by their own employees. In 1799 James Gregory proved in court that four of his coal porters were stealing one of every nine sacks they were entrusted to deliver. Two of the quartet went to prison and two fled. The counting house of Grover, Killick and Buckoll, coal merchants and

76 *The Fish Market on the Beach.* Drawn and engraved by R. Havell, 1824. This shows the Chain Pier in the background which was not constructed until 1822-3.

brewers, was broken into. Some advertisements suggest that the financial situation of these partnerships was unstable. In 1804 the Brighton Union Coal Company ceased to trade and asked for all bills to be settled, the four partners apparently in debt to Mr Levy who decided that he wanted payment.

Staple Trades – Brewing
Most of the inns did their own brewing, and commercial maltings and brewhouses do not appear in Brighton until the later 1700s. Brewing was a dangerous job,

77 *Pavilion, Statue of the King etc.* Aquatint by G. Atwick. Pub C.&R. Sicklemore *c.*1830. These were built on the site of the *Castle Inn* in the later 1820s.

accidents being reported in the paper of which the worst was the death of John Nevill, who fell into a vat of boiling wort and struggled out only to die the next day. Maltings and breweries were especially prone to burning down. In 1799 the prompt action of soldiers who used the fire engine to quell a fire at the *Black Lion* inn and brewery saved the brewhouse and the malthouse, although the stables were lost. The age of the buildings made them especially vulnerable and the commentator thought that, had the fire been at night, the whole place would have been lost.

One of the largest breweries was owned by Isaac Grover and located in West Street. By 1780 it was large enough to be amongst the higher valued sites in the town, at £15 15s., and paid rates of £1 3s. 10d. Brewers used coal and so often sold it, too, Grover owning two coalyards in West Street.[27] At some point in the 1790s Russell Street Brewery was established, but was renamed West Street Brewery from about 1809.[28]

Staple Trades – Fishing
It is easy to imagine from the picturesque images of the seafront that this industry was an important employer, but that was not the case. Although there were still drying houses run by fishermen, most of the fish was sold fresh. The period when Brighton's economy was dependent on fishing was over before 1680,[29] although the inshore fishing of the period did provide a major part of the town's diet and fish was sent inland to Lewes and other communities including London. In 1788 there were about 100 boats, each of which was operated by three people. Some fishermen went to the Medway and to the Thames in the spring for oysters for the London market. Locally, mackerel were caught between May and July, red mullet in May, and lobsters and prawns in August along with flat fish. In September and October whiting were plentiful and herring were caught in November.[30]

Good catches of fish and periods when the price was high were sometimes mentioned in the local newspaper. In 1788 a fisherman called Bishop, who was thought to be at least 70 years old, caught 1,800 herrings in a day and another boat landed 80,000 herrings worth £80. In 1787 some of the fishing boats made about £200 each from sales of mackerel because supplies were short and demand from London high. The local charge for a mackerel was '3d. and a groat', which was thought to be very expensive. In 1789 it was thought that 900 mackerel were caught by one fishing boat and sold on the beach for three guineas per hundred. In October 1791 one herring catch earned the fishermen between seven and ten shillings for 100 herrings. They were sold in London the next day for two guineas per 100. The next morning the catch was good and the price fell to six shillings.

The London market was a major influence on prices in Brighton throughout the 1790s, partly because some of the fish was sold directly to dealers who sent it there. Drivers sometimes sold fish off carts before they reached London, and the impact on the profits of the owners was such that in the 1790s advertisements asking for information about this practice offered five guineas' reward. The wide fluctuations in price continued to be a problem for the fishermen, in June 1800 the cheapness of mackerel making them more attractive to purchasers than butcher's meat. This was good news for the consumers but not for the fishermen who faced the same problem almost exactly a year later. Sometimes good catches of john dory, turbot or sole were advertised.

Imported fish was available in the town but it was salted or dried. Mighell and others sold large and small barrels of cod from Newfoundland and New Iceland

and salted Newfoundland salmon, dried and pickled herrings. Some fishmongers sold eggs.

The fishing families were not numerous by the 1770s when they first appear in references in the local paper. The majority of the notices are about accidents, a reminder of how dangerous fishing was. Mockford was drowned in 1771, leaving a widow and a large family, when a strong wind overturned a fishing boat on its way into Shoreham harbour. In the same year two more men were drowned off Hastings when their boat overturned. The remainder of the references to fishermen mainly concern bad accidents and drownings either just off Brighton or Shoreham or towards Hastings.

Press gangs were repudiated whenever possible, the wives and daughters of fishermen once chasing a recruiting officer out of the town. Their concerns were real because nine fishermen were impressed in 1800 on their way back from a fishing trip. That they were all part of the Sea Fencibles under Captain Sprowle was thought to have helped speed their release.[31] Fishermen had a hard life and if the sea or the Navy did not claim them then there was always the possibility of being captured by a French privateer and forced to crew the ship or be imprisoned in France. In 1800 Mrs Shrivell was in the fortunate position of knowing what had happened to her husband, one of 12 fishermen captured by a privateer. He was among the three men sent to the prison at Valenciennes, the fate of the remainder being unknown.

The only insight into fishing methods is from a description of a trip in 1791 when 11 fishermen, fishing with hooks as the French did, found this was more successful than using trawls.

The market for boats and nets at Brighton may have shrunk because of the development of Shoreham. Nets are advertised for sale in 1787 and 1790 which is unusual: 52 large herring nets suitable for the Hastings fishery and 90 mackerel nets were auctioned on the Steine in 1787; 60 mackerel nets were auctioned in the West Field in 1790. From 1786 sales of boats are referred to in the local paper, which suggests a high turnover of boat owners who were either investors or owner-fishermen. Dean May, a boat builder, may not have been paid for the two hog (fishing) boats that he sought to sell by private contract in 1786. Both were ready to sail and complete with nets. The biggest was called *The Young Cockatrice* and was 28 feet long; the other was 22 feet.

When Thomas Piper died in 1786, no one in the family seems to have wanted his three-year-old boat and it was advertised with its nets. Dean May advertised another hog boat in 1787 that was fitted out and about 18 months old at his base, the Sign of the Royal Oak, in Brighton. William Piper tried to sell his eight-month-old hog boat called *Neptune*, which was 25 feet long, in 1789. May and Pocock employed Harry Stiles, a local auctioneer, to sell two hog boats in their yard at the Steine in 1789. From that point on most were sold at auction. Boat building continued into the early 19th century but more and more boats were built in and operated from Shoreham.

In 1813 a scheme was drawn up for a fishing community in Hove. The promoters sought to raise £25,000 in £50 shares. The intention was to erect deezes for the nets and curing houses for the fish on the shingle and about sixty houses for the fishermen and curers. The three-sided plan was almost a square which faced the sea and had a fire beacon as its centre. The scheme failed in 1815.

78 Refacing the old town, early 19th-century Ship Street.

Staple Trades – Agriculture

Agriculture shares with fishing a capacity to appeal to the romantically inclined. Piles of rotting manure and town waste, or the smell from the piggeries, dairies and chicken coops in the town in the later Georgian period are conveniently ignored.

Brighton had a market place in Market Street, right in the town centre, but by the 1770s the area was becoming too congested for weighty loads or large herds of animals. The *King and Queen* in North Row, just north of the Royal Pavilion, became the focus for much of the dealing in agricultural produce. The Hay Weight was set up outside the inn before 1792. Anything could be weighed and the toll was 20p a ton excluding the weight of the wagon; the buyer and the purchaser were each to pay half of the toll up to two tons. Above that weight the seller was charged an extra 5p for every excess hundredweight.

A lot of produce came from the land surrounding Brighton which was quite intensively farmed, the owners carefully supervising their tenants' activities. In 1789 tenants were told that if they ploughed up any part of Round Hill or the land on the east or south of Whitehawk, or anywhere else that was sheep down or common pasture belonging to the manor of Brighton, they would be prosecuted.[32] Pasture was valuable and let with the associated arable land.

The arable farmland around Brighton produced wheat and rye for bread, oats for the many horses that were so vital to transportation, and barley for brewing. Flour was normally ground close to the market because grain was easier to transport. As Brighton expanded so the number of mills providing flour from both local and imported grain increased, but not all of them stood within the parish of Brighton.

79 Shop fronts in Little East Street.

Grain was moved to Brighton along the coast and either landed (presumably in sacks) from beached boats or unloaded at Shoreham.

The capacity of mills varied considerably. In 1815 a fantail mill which stood to the north-west of the town was advertised for sale. Built on a brick base and standing within an acre of land, it was capable of grinding 15-18 cartloads of grain a week. The vendor hoped to obtain £40 p.a. for the remaining 90 years of a 99-year lease.

Not all of them were flour mills; one that stood to the west side of West Street in the 1760s was a wood mill for trimming and cutting timber. They were moved when necessary. In 1801 only two mills were listed in the parish: Thomas Beard's smock mill lacked cloth for the sails but Thomas Botting's post mill was operating. Both stood on Beacon Hill. [33] The rest had been relocated to Hove or to Preston parishes, the smaller post mills being moved by dozens of oxen arranged in teams.[34] Smock mills were built of brick, to the first floor, which part was demolished, but all the timber parts such as the sails were reused.

Staple Trades – Market Gardens

The growth of the town resulted in the development of market gardens producing fruit and vegetables, but references to the gardeners rarely appear. Most of them lived on the outskirts of the town, in North Street up until the 1790s and then, as the suburbs spread onto the fields, they moved to the terraces of cottages developed away from the more expensive parts of Brighton.

Large market gardens were advertised in the newspaper for sale or to let. In 1800 Mr Hicks was advertising to let gardens between North and Church Street, one of about two acres and the others having greenhouses and fruit houses. This garden also had a dairy with a hayloft. The combination of dairying and market gardening on the edge of towns was not unusual. Farther to the east, on Tenantry Down, some 40 acres were advertised for building, and within the site several gardens were enclosed by lofty walls, which shielded the contents from thieves and from the south-westerly winds.

The *Gardeners' Arms* was close to market gardens when it opened and held competitions for growers. In 1800 the cup for first prize at the melon show was worth four guineas. By 1814, when a new rate book was compiled, the market gardens were extensive. To the west of the town, in West Laine, some were an acre in extent. Around Church Street to the north the typical size was between a quarter and half an acre and some of them included greenhouses. On Hilly Laine to the north-east were plots up to an acre. One was called Lavender Garden.[35]

The Profits of Businesses in Brighton

Most of the material about Brighton businesses is too emphemeral for balanced judgements to be made about profitability. Mrs Dring may have been one of the wealthiest residents in 1780 but the valuations that suggest this also show that her wealth was in goods and property that depended heavily on good seasons, coming partly from the grocery business she ran with her husband, who died early in 1780. On 15 February 1780 Henry Stiles, an experienced valuer, completed an inventory of the fittings within the empty shop and valued it at £53 17s. He listed shelves made of deal, a counter of deal, deal steps, a mahogany desk, three irons to hang scales on, and other essential items.[36]

The Drings followed the usual practice of living in an apartment above and behind their shop, the contents of which were valued at £88 9s. The comfortably furnished rooms were probably typical of the period. In the dining room were five walnut chairs and two mahogany elbow chairs, a mahogany dining table, china tea pot and other items of best china. The middle bedroom was furnished with a four-poster bed bedecked with a crimson check fabric. Placed around the bed were three beech chairs, a night stool and a mahogany chest of drawers. Their bedroom behind the shop had blue-checked cloth on the four-poster bed and a matching festoon window curtain. The other furniture included a double chest of oak drawers. In the maid's bedroom the stump bedstead had half-tester cotton bed fittings. She had a chest, a table and a looking glass. The kitchen range was fully equipped with the panoply of implements then expected, such as bellows, a jack pulley and lead weights, and was furnished with a large square deal dining table and six ash chairs. Here the everyday earthenware and the brewhouse equipment was kept. In the cellar and in the yard stood ten large and small casks and four gross of bottles.[37] The Drings owned a lodging house which they let furnished.[38] Stiles valued the contents of the shop and the lodging house and the debts owed to Mr Dring from traders at a little under £2,000. Mrs Dring inherited the two houses and so became a very wealthy widow who continued to run the businesses.

Thanks to expenditure by wealthy visitors, Brighton had a very wide range of services, the success of tourism ensuring that the basic trades, essential to town life, were also present.

14

Local Government

By 1770 a well-run small Georgian town had street cleaners and a basic drainage system, gas lighting, a rudimentary system of law and order, a gaol, a poorhouse and a market place or market house. During the first twenty years of the town's development as a resort no one in Brighton was responsible for the regulation of most of these. In 1740 it had a poorhouse with a gaol and a market place and little else by way of local government. This remained the case until the early 1770s. The wealthier residents would have been well aware of the need to keep up with the progress made elsewhere in civic improvements but Brighton's short season probably contributed to the reluctance to commit to the extra capital and operational costs that improvements required, with the inevitable consequence of higher rates.[1]

The Brighton Parish Vestry – the First Town Administration

Until 1773 the Parish Vestry, a body consisting of the head of each household paying parish rates, was responsible for the conduct of most parish affairs. Its tasks included the annual appointment from amongst themselves of the churchwardens, the overseers of the poor and the surveyor of highways, levying parish rates, and the supervision of the accounts of all parish officers. These volunteers ran almost all local government. The only employee was the master or mistress of the workhouse. In 1740 the business of the Brighton Vestry was the same as that in any rural parish, principally the care of the poor, some maintenance of highways and keeping the parish church in repair. The collection of church and poor rates enabled the Vestry to undertake these tasks.

Between 1744 and 1761, 12 men were required annually to fulfil all the parochial offices and two more to act as the King's tax collectors, and they were chosen, by open election if needed, from the taxpayers at an annual meeting of the Vestry. Although the population was about 2,000 in the 1740s and increased thereafter, between 1744 and 1761 there were still only about 100 ratepayers.[2] Women, minors, old men and absentee ratepayers could not hold the unpopular, unpaid parish offices, which could take up a lot of time and bring the post holder into conflict with neighbours over the collection of rates and taxes and distribution of the poor rate. Inevitably, a small group of men, who were literate and numerate and who, as taxpayers, had a keen interest in the cost of running the parish, ended up serving regularly.[3]

In the late 1700s the Vestry's influence in the town declined following the setting up of the Commissioners. In a town with so many nonconformist churches and chapels of ease, a substantial number of residents did not see why they should pay Church Rate to support the parish church (St Nicolas) when they did not attend the services there, and the Vestry had great difficulty collecting the rate.

The parish Constable, who was also called the High Constable in this period, acted not only as the head of the small voluntary 'police force' called headboroughs but also as the mouthpiece of the Vestry and the head of formal events such as processions. In 1796 John Baulcomb, the Constable, announced that the Vestry had agreed to try to reduce the consumption of wheat by reducing the amount put in bread. How this was to happen was not made clear. He also summoned people to public occasions such as a procession to the *Castle* to show loyalty to the King in 1792, when a meeting was chaired by a member of the local gentry, Sir John Bridger. On 15 October 1798 Stephen Gourd was the High Constable who signed a notice that the Vestry members agreed at the Town Hall that a fund to assist the widows, and men injured after the Battle of the Nile should be raised by voluntary contributions to accounts held at the town banks.[4] After the Commissioners were established the Vestry used public meetings as a way of expressing views, one such voting against a jetty in front of the town in 1807.

The Town Commissioners 1773-1820

The lack until 1773 of an administrative body responsible for the care and regulation of Brighton had probably aggravated one of the major local problems, erosion. No one was responsible for the maintenance of the groynes, which had been built in 1723-24, and by the late 1740s they were badly decayed. Nothing was done until 1757 when letters patent were issued permitting the collection of house-to-house donations towards the cost of new groynes, estimated at £2,250, but there is no evidence that any money was collected. The need for street cleaning and lighting and a proper market house must also have been recognised. By the 1760s many English towns established Commissioners by private Acts of Parliament who were responsible for the streets and markets and by the early 1770s Brighton's townsfolk must have raised the money to pay for their Act of Parliament, which was passed in 1773.[5] The 64 residents named in the petition for the Act became the unpaid Commissioners. They chose themselves rather than election by local ratepayers.

The 1773 Act's preamble is a succinct summary of the Commissioners' responsibilities:

> An Act for paving, lighting, and cleansing the Streets, Lanes and Places within the town of Brighthelmstone, in the county of Sussex; for removing Nuisances and Annoyances, and preventing the like for the future; for holding and regulating a Market within the said Town; for building and repairing Groynes, in order to render the Coast safe and commodious for Ships and Inhabitants of the said Town; and for laying a Duty thereon, and for other purposes.

The Commissioners' powers to improve were confined to the town's area and not the whole parish and the need to deal with nuisances outside that boundary became an issue. The next Act extended their powers to the parish as a whole.

The Act empowered the Commissioners to remove nuisances and annoyances, which included stopping butchers preparing meat in the street and coach companies from cleaning their coaches there. They could also remove obstructions and occasionally did so, including the hog sties and stables on Bartholomews. It was customary in this period to keep pigs, horses and dairy cattle within towns, and such blitzes became necessary to remove the resulting odours. The Commissioners were also enabled to collect a rate on the town to pay for administration, to fine or prosecute people who ignored their regulations, to levy a rate on coal brought into the parish, and to borrow money.

Most of the original Commissioners were important people in the town. Shergold and Hicks were leading innkeepers, Tidy owned property and Kent was a builder, and all had experience of running businesses and so of the cost of getting things done. Only a small group were active and they supervised the employees, which included a clerk who kept records of meetings and followed up decisions. Most of their responsibilities were put out to contract, including scavenging (street cleaning), lighting the streets, collecting the tolls at the market, repairing and building groynes, and collecting the Coal Tax. The collection of dung was seen as a valuable office. Occasionally, the Commissioners had to issue an advertisement telling the town that only those contracted to move the dung could do so because of the potential loss of income. Dung was spread on the surrounding market gardens and fields.

The Commissioners enlarged the market and ran it by leasing the tolls to an operator. They also determined the standard corn measure by holding an open meeting with local farmers and corn dealers, choosing the Winchester Nine Gallon Bushel. A pound for stray stock was set up. Within the town their activities were less successful, partly because of the limited scope of the Act, which did not include building regulations that might insist on uncluttered street frontages free from excessively protuberant buildings or windows to help street cleaning. They acquired that authority in 1810.

The efficiency of the rubbish collection did not impress visitors; one visitor observed that they had the powers to sort it out but the cliff area smelt.[6] Residents felt that cesspits should be cleaned more frequently than the number of scavengers made possible.[7] The town's system of street cleaning was similar to, and probably no worse than, other places but may have been unable to cope with the rapid growth in population during the season. There is no evidence that contractors were expected to provide more resources during the busy season.

The Commissioners installed Brighton's street sewers, which ran under the main roads and were devised to drain rainfall and effluent from animals off the streets. Because of the cost, the Commissioners installed them only when they were felt to be necessary, and local people were encouraged to pay for their own. Houses were supposed to include cesspits below or to the rear that scavengers could empty but some were illegally attached to the town sewers. Householders could be fined and forced to detach their houses from the town sewers, but first they had to be caught.

Lighting the streets must have been a vital necessity, not least because of the risk of falling down the many holes left by Brighton's busy builders. By the early 1790s there were 150 lights on main streets, which the Commissioners wanted lit for 120 nights. Outside the peak resort season, residents used their own lamps.

The control of erosion by building and maintaining groynes was improved with revenue from the Coal Tax, but the Commissioners found this an endless task.

House owners and developers along the coast agitated for the construction of more groynes and even offered to pay towards the initial cost, provided the Commissioners maintained them. By 1791 groynes between East and West Streets were considered to be effective, but residents of the new houses on the cliffs to the east of the Steine were expecting groynes to be built to protect them. Work began in 1792 but a large fragment of the East Cliff fell just as masons were going to work on the wall, 1,000 [cart] loads falling right where they were going to work. The Commissioners paid in two stages, half at the start and half on completion.

Relations between the Commissioners and the ratepayers between 1773 and 1810 were not always amicable, partly because the former did not have to subject their accounts to scrutiny by the latter, and some ratepayers thought the rapidly increasing income which the Commissioners gained as the town expanded was not being well spent. By 1799 some townsfolk thought the Act needed amending. In the early 1800s there was pressure to have a police force and the town applied to Parliament to establish one.[8] The town lacked a fire engine and its residents had sufficient faith in the Commissioners to support them in their successful efforts to raise the funds for one, its care to be paid for from the rates.

In 1810 a new Act of Parliament replaced that of 1773. Although one hundred Commissioners were listed in it, new post holders were to be chosen by election from the town's ratepayers. To qualify as a Commissioner the applicant had to pay at least £50 in rent or occupy a house rated at £50. Alternatively, he had to receive at least £50 in rent from property in the parish. The Act provided that ratepayers were given access to the annual accounts.

The Commissioners' powers were increased and they were permitted to appoint more paid employees, including watchmen and coal meters (Coal Tax collectors). They raised the duty on coal to three shillings and became the licensing authority for hackney carriages, bathing machines and other vehicles that plied for hire which provided another source of income. Some control over the quality of building was given in 1810. The new regulations included provision that party walls should be nine inches thick and that buildings obstructing the street by being built over the building line were to be rebuilt and correctly aligned. Care of the poor was transferred from the Vestry to the Directors and Guardians of the Poor, who were nominated by the Commissioners from amongst their number. The Act enabled the Commissioners to enlarge the workhouse or to build either a new one or an infirmary.

The Commissioners also included in the Act a list of properties they wished to purchase in order to widen roads. In so doing they began to change the appearance of the town's main thoroughfares by cutting back the frontages of properties. Middle Street, St James Street and Ship Street Lane were amongst the streets listed and the back of the Act contains a detailed schedule of planned purchases which shows how significant their impact would be.[9] The Act also banned bow fronts, all buildings except shops having to be flat-fronted, and the Commissioners had the power to order the demolition of non-compliant buildings. Bow windows were acceptable provided they did not encroach over the owner's building line and the same applied to the bowed fronts built within the boundaries of the owner's land which did not protrude over the 'area' or basement into the road.

The Commissioners sought to develop street gas lighting rather than provide it privately but did not consider piped water supplies.[10] They also worked on the plans

eans of a road along the seafront. In

w road, from Middle Street to
bmitted to the Commissioners.
pon 12 arches along the beach.
oo. The present thoroughfare
recated, as the communication
so much intersected.

ew developments were not paying
ematically valued in 1814 to find
ssessment survives and shows that
hen on the collection of rates was
some of which survive) were laid
be easily monitored.[12] By the later
ned printed demands and receipts.
urch Tax to which he added the
and the sum due, and his address

authority after the Act of 1810
residents and visitors considered

uardians of the Poor took over,
care of the town's poor and the
of the Poor were members of
collecting and distributing the
he taxpayers at an annual public
and Guardians of the Poor were
6th century and was codified in
in the 17th and 18th centuries
olunteers.[14]

from the poor rate (levied on
year. Even though more than
only 115 paid, the rest being
arge number of unrated town
e of land in the town before

for the care of the poor. On
their care and the arrears of
lings, half a year's rent, from a
om land in Rottingdean now
of 40 shillings was owed from
1732 George Beach left the
minister to preach a sermon
d housekeepers who did not

Poor Rate Assessments for the Town in 1744

Street	Total	*Number of Houses* Rate due from		Total rate collected (£)
East Street	58	17	(29%)	19 4s.
East Cliff & Little East Street	41	4	(10%)	5 8s.
Knabb	38	5	(13%)	5 8s.
Steine	12	3	(25%)	8 8s.
North Street*	84	20	(24%)	26 8s.
West Street	75	23	(31%)	36 8s.
Middle Street	60	13	(22%)	22 16s.
Ship Street	39	26	(87%)	49 16s.
Black Lion Street	47	6	(13%)	8 4s.
	454	117	(26%)	182 4s.

* There were probably more houses than the rate book suggests as some were subsumed under the section headed 'lands' in the rate book. Most of the properties listed as houses stood on North Street's south side.

receive alms from the parish, and the last two–fifths to the Treasurer of the charity school. The practice of public meetings to examine the expenditure continued.[16]

Although the sums of money collected rose as the town grew in size and prosperity, the number of poor also continued to increase.[17] In 1791 the Vestry met to consider a request from landowners who wanted their taxes reduced to reflect the sale or letting of farmland to others.[18] In 1798 Thomas Pelham of Stanmer advertised a meeting to explain his plan to employ the poor of Brighton and help them to maintain themselves. He stated that the expenditure on the poor exceeded £3,000 a year.[19] The town's problem was the seasonality of tourism, which meant that there were long periods with little work,[20] but many industries in England were seasonal and in this respect Brighton's problems were not unique. One of the concerns of Georgian towns was food riots. Brighton had one in 1757, and poor relief was seen as a means of reducing or preventing such disorder.[21]

The surviving evidence suggests that before 1820 a lot of effort was made to deal with the needy as economically as possible but with some degree of compassion, both by the Overseers and, after 1810, by the Directors and Guardians.[22] The Overseers (and their successors) provided help in several ways. Weekly allowances were paid to applicants who remained in their own homes; Mrs Simpson, who lived in Elishor's Hole on Bartholomews, was allowed to stay there as long as the parish chose. When George Best, a shepherd, committed suicide by jumping into a well, his wife and children were cared for in the same way, by keeping the family together in their house. Similarly, James Crossweller received five shillings a week and Mary Godman was allowed two shillings a week to stay in her home but Mary Priest, a widow, was struck off the poor book. Such a step normally indicated that the person had found another way of supporting herself and not that she had fallen out of favour, as is sometimes believed.[23] A considerable amount of aid was given in the form of clothing and at a meeting in February 1797 clothes for the children of Widow Hills, John Gillam, Emma Pocock, Thomas Pellings' two sons and Susanna Hobbs were allowed.[24]

These practices were only intended to relieve short periods of seasonal unemployment, but in Brighton payments were made for longer periods until the resort season lengthened from its initial four months and began to provide more long-term employment. Help in kind was given to families and to individuals who did not qualify for regular payments but who needed periodic assistance with clothing, coal, food or medical care or a contribution, for example, towards the cost of burying a relative. The poor rate book in the 1740s and 1750s contains occasional lists of the people entitled to poor relief because Brighton was their place of residence.[25]

The overseers distributed subsidised food during periods when the grain prices were high. The money was raised by public subscription advertised in the paper and the wealthiest visitors and townsfolk were expected to contribute. The Prince of Wales filled the role of philanthropist, which the town would have expected of any wealthy regular visitor, and gave an annual bounty, although it was only £50. The number of people regarded as in need of help from this sum in 1791 was thought to be 540 families because the weather was so bad that fishermen could not work. Donations to supplement the Prince's gift were sought. Thomas Kemp, Geoffrey Webster and Charles Scrase Dickens were amongst the subscribers who in 1799 helped to buy food and coal.

Vagrancy and Desertion of the Family

Vagrancy and desertion of the family were both treated as crimes because they were thought deliberately to foist costs onto the local community. Fit people who did not work were regarded with suspicion, too, not least because they were regarded as most likely to steal. The normal punishment for vagrancy was to be sent to a house of correction. The threat of imprisonment was also used to persuade people to move on.

People with disabilities or regarded as too old to work were accepted as the responsibility of the parish within which they had lived longest, an approach to the care of the poor that was established by the Act of Settlement in 1601. Disputes about the place of settlement of those in need of help could end up at the Quarter Sessions, and the Order Books which list the decisions made at the Sessions show how people were moved about the country as the small proportion of society that paid taxes sought to keep the demands of the needy under control. Between 1740 and 1770 eight applications resulted in people from Brighton being sent elsewhere and ten people from other parishes sent people to Brighton. The cost of obtaining such orders tended to keep the number of applications down, for the Overseer had to transport himself and the people involved to courts held well outside Brighton, and temporary support could be cheaper. The majority of the removal orders were to parishes within twenty miles of Brighton. The removals in November 1740 of Elizabeth Massey 'rogue and vagabond' to Broughton and of Daniel and Susanna Maslin to Heddington in Wiltshire in 1761 were exceptional.[26]

Rewards were offered for the detection of men and women who left their families chargeable to the parish. Carpenter, cordwainer and labourer were amongst the occupations of the men who disappeared. Most of them were in their twenties. Alleged fathers of bastards were also sought in order to reduce the parish's liability, but the bill for support of the poor rose in this period. Children, especially orphans, were placed as apprentices but some absconded and the parish sought them, the tax payers having paid the costs of the apprenticeship.

80 *Phoebe Hessell.* Lithograph published *c.*1830. She was one of the Brighton residents who periodically received help from the Overseers of the Poor.

The Workhouse

The workhouse and town hall on Bartholomews took the sick, aged and young. In 1745 it consisted of a kitchen, a workroom with ten spinning wheels in it, a pantry, a brew-house, two cellars and, on the upper floor, chambers with 'eighteen fether bedds with their Appurtenances as they stand'.[27] The number of inmates probably fluctuated depending on the time of year and the amount of employment, but in 1761 there were about 35 people. Even when the workhouse was enlarged in 1800 it could only accommodate 150, which suggests that more families could afford to care for their needy without recourse to the parish. Inmates were expected to work if they were fit enough, make their own clothes and prepare the food. In the 1740s the workhouse inmates picked oakum and in the 1780s they made mackerel nets for sale.

The Overseers appointed a workhouse master or mistress and put out to contract the supply of food and medical care; these were advertised in the local paper, with a date for the opening of the letters for tender. In the 1770s the advertisements for the workhouse master required a male, but later the Directors and Guardians of the Poor advertised for a man or woman. Shoes, meat, butter cheese, candles, coal, Waterford butter and oatmeal were amongst the items supplied, the contractors all apparently being local people because their names appear in other documents and advertisements.

Changes to the workhouse were also undertaken by contractors using notes of public tender and the decision to build a new 'necessary house' was advertised in 1791. An additional workroom was added to the workhouse yard in 1794.[28] There was a plan in 1791 for a workhouse to replace the one in Black Lion Street, and requests for estimates for a new one were advertised in 1810 after the sale of some property left to the town to assist the poor. Eventually, between 1818 and 1822, a new one was built just north of St Nicholas Church.

From the late 18th century a small block of almshouses took a few of the poor. The Percy and Wagner Almshouses still stand at the bottom of Elm Grove, once well north of the town centre, a small terrace with a Gothick façade which is a little known feature of the town.[29]

The Poor and Disease

Georgian England had to contend with many unpleasant contagious diseases, such as measles and chickenpox. Smallpox was regarded as especially dangerous and, if a resort was known to be suffering from it, then visitors were unlikely to appear. In 1761 Charles Herser (Heasor) of Shoreham wrote to Mr Paine of Brighton and informed him that he would only meet him outside the town due to an outbreak of smallpox.[30]

From a population of about 3,600 around 1,800 were inoculated. The Vestry organised a head count to establish how many people needed to be paid for by the parish; the churchwardens, the Overseers and 12 residents undertook the survey. They reported on 26 January that the population numbered 3,260 (allowing an extra 30 for those who might have arrived since the count) of whom 1,887 needed to be inoculated. In a few days all had been done, the parish paying £68 2s. 6d. for 545 poor people aged from one day to 80 years old to be so treated by Messrs Lowdell, Gilbert, Pankhurst and Tilson at the rate of 2s. 6d. a person. All others had to pay their own costs and were charged 3s. 6d. each. According to one source 34 people in Brighton died from their inoculation and seven of the disease. The minutes of the Vestry recorded that ten people paid for by them had died and so the Vestry paid for their burials. Those affected by their inoculation at the expense of the parish were attended by Dr Sanders at the taxpayers' expense and anyone who was too ill to work received extra food and coals. The total cost of the inoculation and the care of those who needed it amounted to £150.[31]

In January 1794 there was a meeting about a general inoculation at which it was said that around 2,500 people had been successfully inoculated in nearby Lewes. Smallpox was still an endemic disease but this outbreak was more serious than most. There had been a panic and three surgeons and apothecaries published an affidavit claiming they had not brought smallpox to the town, and Mr Cocks, who was also a surgeon, offered to suppress his affidavit claiming otherwise 'for the sake of preserving peace'. In February 1794, 2,000 people were inoculated and the cost was charged to the poor rate, albeit with some opposition. Most of the 25 who died were children. In April 1794 Dr Henderson was presented with a silver cup for his work with the poor during 'an epidemic of smallpox' earlier in that year.

The issue of public health care continued to be periodically controversial, especially attempts to eradicate the scourge of smallpox. The Overseers of the Poor were not the only people trying to eliminate it and in 1803 and 1804 the Brighton Royal Jennerian Institute for the Extermination of Smallpox offered to inoculate the poor free of charge. In 1804 no one took up the offer.

Medical care for those in the poor house was usually contracted to a doctor. Claims were made that the treatment was inferior but doctors who did not win the contracts may have made these assertions. In 1797, for example, Dr Scutt alleged in the *Sussex Weekly Advertiser* that 'farming' the poor to medical men was inhumane; his allegation was built around the death of a person in the care of the Overseers and attended by Dr Watson. Watson and Newton held the contract for the poor and were paid £35 a year. The same paper then carried a series of letters and advertisements which alleged that Scutt had neglected his patients when he had care of the poor.

When applicants for help were interviewed the Overseers would establish whether they were residents of Brighton or if they were still chargeable to another parish. If another parish were liable then the Overseer would either send the applicants back to the parish of residence or let them remain in Brighton if their own parish agreed to pay their allowances. Disputes over who should incur the cost of poor relief were resolved by the local justices, who interviewed applicants to establish their place of settlement and then made an order that committed a parish to payment. Fathers who deserted families were sought and mothers of illegitimate children were asked for the names of the fathers so that the latter should bear the cost of maintenance. In 1794 the Vestry ordered that John Patteson paid Mr Vallance £3 4s. for attending the lying in of Elizabeth Coppard and then four shillings a week to the parish for so long as the child remained chargeable to it.[32] Children apprenticed by the parish normally went to masters in the town or in the region. In 1805 some were sent to a factory in Lancashire but this was uncommon.

Overall, the town had to cope with a system of care for the poor that was still managed by volunteers trying to keep intact their public reputations while doing a job they may have found difficult and distasteful. As Brighton became more prosperous so more of the work was taken on by employees. The volunteers became supervisors, having to judge whether the task was being done reasonably well by the people they employed but still faced with concerns about accountability to taxpayers anxious to distinguish between the needy and the undeserving poor.

The Dispensary and Hospital

By 1800 the need for a reliable place to treat poor people who became sick was recognised but nothing happened. Compared with Margate and Bath, residents and visitors alike realised only slowly that helping people before they became a charge on the poor rate was cost effective.

The Middle Street Dispensary for the poor was opened in 1809 and run as a charity in three rooms over a warehouse in Nile Street. In 1811 it moved to North Street. The Earl of Chichester was the patron by 1812 and at a public meeting gained support for widening its role. In November 1812 it was renamed the Sussex General Infirmary. The Earls of Chichester and Egremont then tried in 1812 to raise money to open a hospital but failed to obtain sufficient funding from other people. In 1813 the Earl of Egremont agreed to put money towards a separate building that would hold 60 patients but again the project lacked support.[33] The Infirmary moved to Duke Street and then in 1819 to Middle Street.[34]

It was still open in 1822, when wealthy visitors and residents were being asked to continue their support for it. Donors of either five guineas as a single gift or of one guinea a year had the right to recommend people to it and only those in possession of a letter or a form which had been provided by the Dispensary for a supporter to sign had the right to help. Vaccinations against smallpox were offered. [35]

State Taxation and Services

Brighton residents paid land and window taxes to the government as well as local rates. Local people were normally appointed as tax assessors and collectors but they were neither responsible to nor controlled by the parish, from the 1750s their appointments by government being announced in the local paper. During the 1780 and 1790s taxes on wagons and carts, horses, hats, hair powder, licences to sell medicine, stamp duty and personal legacies all had local collectors.

An excise officer and riding officers were appointed by the Board of Customs and so were employees of the government. When Chevalier Maupeau committed suicide in 1789 and left valuable goods at the *New Ship Inn*, Mr Simon, the principal officer of the Customs at Brighton, claimed them. The Chevalier had attempted the previous day to jump off the packet on its way to Brighton and his goods appear to have been regarded as imported. Government also controlled the contracts for the delivery of the post between towns, although local people bid for and managed the service. Excise men also stopped travellers no matter how wealthy if there was a report of smuggled goods and, if the owner was not responsible, they could be fined. [36]

National and Regional Politics

The number of residents able to vote for Members of Parliament rose considerably from the 1750s as the rateable value of the town increased. By the early 1800s the resort's residents were a major influence on the choice of regional and national representatives. Brighton also had residents who were sufficiently wealthy and influential to act as Sheriffs for the county of Sussex and in 1790 Thomas Scutt became one.

Many English towns were struggling with the development of a cost-effective system of local government during the mid- to late Georgian period and in this respect Brighton is not unusual. We cannot tell whether the town was more or less effective then but the fact that the strengthening of the Commissioners' powers was not opposed in Parliament suggests that the process was regarded as typical and also inevitable.

15

Keeping the Peace

By 1770 Brighton's population was swelled not only by wealthy visitors but also by itinerant people in search of work or easy pickings from local people and tourists. Crime was reported in the local newspaper more graphically and frequently than good news and the reports are a rich source of information.[1] Although local people committed most of the crimes and were the most common victims, strangers were often blamed. The majority of the crimes reported in the newspaper and elsewhere fell into six categories: absconding, assault, deceit, murder, theft (and robbery) and smuggling. The main offences involving visitors were assault, deceit, prostitution and theft (of possessions and money). Most of these were committed by local people, including migrants to Brighton who were attracted by the prospects. A few were committed by visitors. The range of crimes was similar to those encountered in other towns of Georgian England.

Peace and security in Brighton depended heavily upon public acceptance of the authority of the volunteers who took responsibility for dealing with law and order, and victims' preparedness to prosecute or seek reparation. The town rate covered the costs of infrastructure such as the town hall and its cells which were known as the 'Black Hole'.

The Constable and the Headboroughs – the Volunteer 'Police Force'

Georgian towns were noisy, lively and often quite rough places. One of the most difficult voluntary posts was that of Constable (or Head Constable) of the Parish, a post that survived for the whole of the period. The Constable, and his voluntary assistants called Headboroughs, had to try to ensure that the town was a safe and orderly place. In a small town crowded at times with many strangers this task must have required considerable diplomacy.

The Constable was an important member of the Vestry, whose officials were supposed to be appointed annually by a Court Leet. This was a meeting of local people (mainly local farmers) from the three parishes of Brighton, Patcham and East Blatchington which collectively comprised the Hundred of Whalesbone, an ancient but no longer effective administrative area.[2] The Court Leet had once dealt with petty offences but by 1750 it was convened so infrequently that in some years the Constables and Headboroughs were formally appointed by the local Justices of the Peace, to whom they were accountable.[3]

The Constable's expenses were met by the parish and negotiated by the Vestry. In 1754, at the request of the Constable, the payment was revised from £1 10s. a year plus the right to graze a horse and 20 sheep to £1 10s. and the right to graze 30 sheep (but no horse).[4] The farmers had to agree to the reduction of their own rights to allow the Constable his.

A volunteer night watch was organised in 1812 and the Commissioners paid night-watchmen from 1815. A record of their night reports from 1821-3 survives which suggests that their presence acted as a reassurance and as a deterrent. At the end of most nights nothing was reported. Occasionally there were disturbances which the watchmen sorted out and then noted, as on 4 May 1822: 'There has been a great many drunken men about the streets but nothing worth reporting happened during the night.'

By 1822 the town had eight watch areas each of which had a watch box within it. The watch box at Camelford Street served the whole of the east side of the Steine and all the streets to the east which were to the south of St James's Street. The watch box at Cavendish Street covered the area north of St James's Street and the south side of Edward Street including Princes Street and Pavilion Parade. The watch box at the *Richmond Arms* took care of Gloucester Place and the streets to the north and all the streets north of Sussex Street.

Justices of the Peace and Local Courts

Until the late 1700s, unless one of the visitors to Brighton were a Justice of the Peace from Sussex and prepared to help, the Constable had to take any suspect that he wanted to charge to a Justice of the Peace resident in one of the local villages, at Patcham Place or Stanmer House. Justices who belonged to other county Commissions could not assist in Brighton.

Having been charged, defendants before 1812 were taken to the Petty Sessions or the Quarter Sessions at Lewes or Horsham for their hearing. In 1812 Petty Sessions were established in the town to deal with minor transgressions such as drunken behaviour and other actions which did not result in major injury or loss.[5] Licensing of theatres, diverting of roads and other activities that required the approval of Justices were always referred to the Quarter Sessions and so remained outside local jurisdiction until after 1820.[6]

Juries

By 1819 people who could serve on juries at trials when a defendant pleaded not guilty were being listed by the High Constable and published. An annotated copy of a list for Brighton which was produced in 1819 survives.[7] The occupations of those eligible for jury service included brick makers, carpenters, gardeners, hairdressers and milkmen as well as many gentlemen.

Prosecuting Societies

As the town grew the voluntary system became stretched and townsfolk sought more protection. *The Society for the Prosecution of Felons and Thieves* was founded in 1783 and supported by lawyers, shopkeepers, lodging-house keepers and other town worthies. In 1792 the threat of invasion and unrest may have precipitated the foundation of another local body, *The Society for the Protection of Liberty and Property against Republicans and Levellers*, whose membership was countywide.

Punishment – the Public Apology

The parish Constable and his Headboroughs did their best to keep the resort peaceful by persuasion and the same approach was used by the night watch after it was established. Punishment was by public embarrassment. Advertisements were published in the local newspaper by people who apologising publicly for their offensive behaviour towards officials or others. This was probably an effective means of dealing with those who could afford it for no one appears to have had to apologise twice or been arrested and charged for a second offence. Even taking part in what were described in the local paper as 'small riots' outside some houses illuminated for the birthday of the Prince of Wales in 1784 was punished in this way. Prosecutions resulted from the most serious assaults but when William Gorringe, a shoemaker, was threatened with legal action for attempting to rescue Richard Humphrey, who had been arrested by John Dean, a Headborough, Gorringe apologised in a notice inserted in the newspaper.

The Role of Drink

Many of the disturbances in Brighton were fuelled by drink, as in other Georgian towns, and most of the arrests made at night were of drunken people, of whom most were men though drunken women were not uncommon. Drunken behaviour also involved people of all backgrounds. There were cases of drunken aggression towards the nightwatchmen intervening in assaults or noisy behaviour. The punishment depended on the response of the drunkards to intervention. Both the Constable and the night watch were prepared to press charges when they thought it was necessary and neither tolerated assaults on themselves.

Drunkenness also contributed to the end of more than one marriage:

> On the night of 6 May 1822 between 12 (midnight) and 1 o'clock Gunn [nightwatchman] found a woman in Russell Street destitute of a home and brought her to the [town] hall. She says her name is Knobes and that she parted with her husband yesterday. She was very much intoxicated. I sent her to the Black Hole [cell] for the night. This morning Tree the watchman [at the John Street watch box] informs me that she is in the continual habit of getting drunk so much that her husband cannot live with her.

Theft and Burglary

Theft was considered a very serious crime in a society where most wealth was not in pensions or savings but in goods. The majority of the population did not own their own homes and few had secure places for possessions for which they had worked hard but could not afford to insure. The very low incomes and irregular employment of even the hardest working of people made the loss of the most basic possessions a tragedy. Theft from a house when occupants were attacked was treated most seriously, and the number of occasions on which the defendant was known to have stolen goods and their value was also taken into account. Theft from shopkeepers was the most commonly reported offence, particularly of clothes, money, cloth, food and plate.

The following are broadly representative of the punishments for theft. Eleanor Davies was branded and imprisoned for 12 months for stealing 30 guineas from

Robert Travers, and James Gibbon was whipped and discharged having been tried for stealing a coachman's coat. James Murrell, John Lilliott and William Cousins each paid a fine of five shillings and were sentenced at Lewes to hard labour, James for a year and the others for two.[8] William Stevens was transported for seven years for stealing from a house in Kent and also from the house of Henry Wilbur in Brighton. The same sentence was passed on Luke Newman, who broke into Sarah May's house and stole clothing, a mahogany tea chest, a spy glass and other goods, and also on William Kinshott, who stole a considerable amount of cereal from Roger Welsford.[9] Amongst the articles stolen by John Gardiner of Preston from Beach Roberts were books; his sentence of hanging was commuted to transportation for life.[10] Thieves known to the Bow Street Runners were apprehended in Uckfield, having been caught stealing in Brighton, and received the death sentence. The press coverage suggests that Mr Kipping, a surgeon who lived in Brighton, was assaulted during the theft and this would have decided the fate of the thieves.

A significant number of defendants was acquitted or discharged at Quarter Sessions when the judge was not satisfied that the evidence was good enough. William Martin was acquitted when charged with stealing a part-finished felt hat from William Miller, and Thomas Wimble was acquitted for the theft of a looking glass from Ann Skinner.[11] Sometimes the outcomes of illegal entries into properties are not reported, and so we may never find out what happened to the man that Widow Mercer found under her bed.

Some shopkeepers also cheated, for example, by selling goods at short weight. When such an accusation was proved the rest of the produce was given away, so the shopkeeper lost his profits. The Constable normally took charge of the public dispersal of such goods. Fraud was also heavily punished, James Brown Dignan being sentenced to five years' hard labour on the River Thames.

There were a few instances of highway robberies of local people either carrying cash to London to restock their shops for the next season or bringing back the goods. One robber, described as a highwayman, relieved a visitor of nine guineas somewhere near Stanmer.

Murder

A few murders were reported and in the cases where the murderer was identified both parties were normally local people. The earliest recorded case is the committal of 'May' for trial for the murder of 'Howell' in 1759. Lord Barrymore, who visited Brighton quite regularly, was sent for trial at the Quarter Sessions and found guilty of intending to kill Mr Simpson, a local linen draper, who intervened to help Mr Donadieu when Barrymore attacked him. Anne Boon threw her dead child into a pigsty behind the market place, presumably in the hope that it would be eaten, and was found guilty of murder. The penalty for murder for either sex was hanging.

There were also unsolved deaths. A dead baby in a box was ploughed up in a local field but the mother was never found nor prosecuted for killing it. Men cleaning a well found the body of a murdered prostitute. Suicides were normally reported, too, and explanations sought: Mary Upchurch was thought to have hung herself because her lover had left her.

Smuggling – the High Profile Crime

The crime with the highest profile was smuggling. Historians sometimes depict this as a romantic crime, in spite of the brutality of many of the people involved and the adverse impact it had on the national economy. Brighton's wealthy visitors must have made it an attractive prospect for smugglers in spite of the risk from the French during periods of war. It resulted in huge losses of income for the government. Keenly aware of the unrest that the levying of additional taxes to make up the deficit could create in all classes, the state tried to stem the smuggling, and Excise (Revenue) Officers were based at Brighton because of the great deal of shipping activity.

The resort had a cross-Channel service to Dieppe from 1761 and a very large beach trade. Dragoons, who usually came from the cavalry barracks at Preston, assisted the Excise Officers in some forays against the smugglers. Sometimes the smugglers got away with their hauls and it was not unusual for both revenue men and their horses to be injured. The blockhouses on the cliff contained cannon that could be turned against the smugglers' cutters, and frigates of war patrolled the vulnerable stretch of coastline to intercept them. No doubt the visitors turned out to watch from Brighton's cliff tops.

Some smugglers landed their goods only to have the contraband conficated. A large haul of spirits was found hidden in the dovecote at Preston. Thomas Dennet tried to protest his innocence by publishing a complaint against the Excise Officers for entering the dovecote without his permission. Another group got as far as Lewes before the Excise Officers, with the assistance of a party of Dragoons, arrested them. Smugglers also arranged false trails, a cutter running onto a sheltered beach just east of Brighton and 200 horses collecting the goods after the Revenue Officer had been diverted to the west. But in 1777 two Excise Officers and four Dragoons seized nine hundredweight of tea and ten casks of brandy and Geneva (gin) and arrested the smugglers.

The brick kilns to the west of Brighton appear to have been quite a popular spot for smugglers. In 1786 they lost contraband there to a group of Excise Officers and Dragoons. In 1789, 1,680lbs. of tobacco and 39 casks of Geneva were seized on the beach and another haul was captured near the brick kilns after a skirmish with the smugglers. In another incident two smugglers attempting to evade capture made for Roedean to the east of Brighton and rode over the cliff. Only one survived to be arrested. Even the Customs House in Brighton was a target for thieves, a few French Crowns and Half Crowns being stolen on one occasion.

Excise Officers sometimes got into trouble if they used what was thought to be unreasonable force against someone. Thomas Walters was fined £10 for a violent assault on Mrs Phillips, and Mr Barnfather was fined the same for a similar offence against an unnamed widow. A fine of £10 was a very considerable sum then, especially for these people, and prompt payment was expected.

British and French travellers on the Brighton to Dieppe ferry were caught smuggling and some of their more creative efforts to conceal goods attracted the attention of *The Times* newspaper. In 1816 a young man was caught trying to smuggle cotton stockings and thread in stone bottles with with false bottoms filled with spirits. He overdid the weight in the bottle and the bottom of one fell out.[12]

Lace was discovered under fruit in chests belonging to a French gentleman when he landed from the ferry at Brighton. Sometimes the Excise men stopped the packet in the English Channel and found contraband when they searched it.

Escaping on the Ferry

Occasionally the town's ferry service was reported as the means of escape by criminals involved in crimes elsewhere. One man was arrested as he attempted to leave the country having gained £700 with a forged set of army commission papers. Another was apprehended whilst he masqueraded as an M.P. A Bow Street Runner and a bank official caught 'one Clutterbuck' as he tried to leave Brighton by the same route with bank drafts amounting to £6,930.

The Development of Public Regulation

People in Brighton recognised that crime deterred visitors, who heard about it from friends or read about it in the local and national papers, and sought to develop proper policing, street lighting and other means of reassuring them that Brighton was a safe place for residents and visitors. The concern for order and a safe, well-lit town resulted in wealthier residents banding together to obtain an Act of Parliament to set up Improvement Commissioners. The Commissioners may not have been perfect but they did begin the hard task of persuading people to pay for town improvements through local taxes, and they ensured that progress was made.

Lord Dudley wrote in 1811 that the town contained between 12,000 and 15,000 people when full but lacked a police force and any sign of local government. Yet he had not heard of any crime. He was rather sanguine about the issue of crime, for the newspapers and other sources show that he was wrong – but his point about the lack of local government was true.[13]

16

Education

By the end of the 18th century basic literacy and numeracy were accepted as essential for almost all forms of employment but another major concern was the reform of manners and morality, for which education was regarded as a vehicle.[1] In Brighton visitors supported both free and subsidised public schools by donations, and the importance of the wider civilising role was emphasised. The small number of townsfolk who could afford it sent their children to private schools, which also hoped to persuade visitors to board their children. Little evidence of that happening exists until the 1820s, which resulted in most private schools failing to survive more than a year or so.

Little is known about their pupils, the few references to them indicating that most of the custom was local. The majority occupied only one house and were therefore very small, comprising typically some 10 to 20 pupils, a master (or mistress) and an assistant. Many claimed to teach a wide range of subjects, especially to the boys, and teachers of music, languages, art and other skills advertised in the local newspaper. Some of the self-employed teachers tried to open schools, a 'sober steady young man' proposing one such in 1771, but there is no evidence that he succeeded. Messrs Poely and Thring tried to set up a school in 1779 but nothing more is heard of them.

Free schools supported by charities were rare and often did not last long. Even the basic costs of running a school, such as paying rent for or buying a room, a teacher, seating, heating, lighting and slates required a large and steady income from endowments or constant fund-raising. The value of the stocks, shares and property that often formed the core of donations fluctuated and this contributed to instability in the provision of free or subsidised education.

The National School for Boys (Springetts' and Grimmett's Charity Schools)

In 1740 a charity school for boys was provided by Anthony and William Springett in a house which they bought for this purpose in Meeting House Lane (facing down Union Street). There the school remained until 1828, the school funded by Grimmett's Charity merging with it. The Springett Charity was endowed with an exchequer annuity that ran until 1806. Both George Beach and Lady Mary, Countess Dowager Gower left bequests.[2] The Anglican school had links with the SPCK from whom, in 1752, 300 books and pamphlets were ordered. Anthony Springett set up a separate school for girls but it shut and was then re-opened in 1726. It may have lasted until 1770 before closing again.[3]

William Grimmett was taught by John Grover at the school funded by the
Springett endowment. He became a wealthy London merchant and when he died in
1749 left a bequest in his will for the establishment of a charity school in Brighton.[4]
Not until 1768 were his affairs sorted out by the Court of Chancery and the school
was set up. This was another school for 20 poor boys aged between eight and 15
who were to be clothed as well as educated and brought up in the principles of the
Protestant religion as agreed with the Church of England. In 1779 the school was
on the south-west side of Craggs Lane (now Duke Street) and it was marked on the
Yeakell and Gardner map of Brighton published during that year. Between 1801 and
1818 Springett's and Grimmett's charities were combined at the Springett School's
site in Meeting House Lane. In 1818 it became the National School for Boys when
140 boys were enrolled, the numbers increasing to 200 in 1821. It was then subsumed
into the Central National Schools which opened in Church Street in 1828.[5]

The Royal Union School (latterly Middle Street School)

In 1805 Edward Goff of 'Scotland Yard, St Martin's in the Fields' gave £400 to
found the Union Charity School (reflecting the fact that the school was run by
a union of Congregational churches). This became the Royal Union School and,
finally, Middle Street School. The trustees included five members of the Countess of
Huntingdon's Congregational Chapel, five independent Congregationalists and five
Baptists. Goff, a coalman who owned houses in Brighton, bought the freehold land
for the school from Hargreaves, who was using the site as a coalyard.[6] The school
opened in 1807 with a capacity of 300 boys and enrolled 140. The trustees decided
to use the Lancaster method of education to teach reading, writing and arithmetic
and that the school would be inter-denominational. They permitted anyone who
subscribed a guinea to present a poor boy to be educated. The master was paid £50
a year to teach and to run the school and boys were allowed three holidays a year,
each of a week, and had to attend one of the Congregational churches or chapels
noted above on Sundays.[7]

The Union Street School for Girls

The Union Street School for Girls was opened in 1808 and in 1813 received a
legacy of £200 from Goff. The schoolmistress was to be paid £40 a year but no
one suitable was found and so the salary was increased to £50. Run by a ladies
committee, which consisted largely of the wives of the trustees of the boys' school,
the girls' school had difficulty raising money and, until 1825, a rapid turnover of
schoolmistresses.[8]

By 1815 the Lancaster teaching method was not in use and the teacher had
resigned. The next permanent teacher arrived in 1817 from Borough Road School
in London and reinstated the Lancaster method. The school roll then numbered 141,
but in 1821 there were 200 pupils and the trustees decided that the school was full.
By then pupils were charged 1d. a week to attend.[9]

Church of England Sunday Schools

Sunday schools were mainly concerned with moral education but reading was also
taught. The first Sunday school supported by the Church of England was opened in

January 1788 using 20 guineas raised to run a school for 200 children. On the first day 54 boys and 74 girls were enrolled. Nathaniel Kemp of Ovingdean Hall, a Town Commissioner, is credited with playing a major role in its foundation.[10] To raise its profile, the Prince of Wales became patron in August 1788. Local and visiting clerics helped the school by donating the collection raised by preaching. High profile preachers included the Reverend George Pelham, a relative of Thomas Pelham of Stanmer Park.

The teaching was largely by women, responding to advertisements for a schoolmistress and for ladies to help with the teaching of reading in the local newspaper. On the first anniversary of the opening of the school a report noted that the fund raising had been so successful that the school children could all have a uniform and that a School of Industry for Girls could be founded. An offshoot of the successful Sunday School, the School of Industry was opened under the patronage of Mrs Kemp (wife of Nathaniel of Preston and Ovingdean). By 1813 it had moved to Church Street and was educating 46 poor girls. In 1818 there were 150 girls and some were clothed by the charity.[11]

Boys Private Schools

From 1757-77 Marchant's School for Boys seems to have lacked competitors. From the late 1770s more private boys schools were opened but the fragmentary evidence suggests that no more than three stayed open at any time for more than a year. The total number of boys in the schools could not have exceeded 100 for they were so small. The first girls' school opened in 1769 and few were opened subsequently. Again, the total being educated in Brighton may not have exceeded one hundred.

The patchy provision of private schools before 1800 is a huge contrast with developments afterwards and it was the expansion of education after 1800, well portrayed in the directories and guidebooks, which ultimately resulted in the opening of Brighton College and St Mary's Hall as well as other long established private schools.

The earliest private school for boys that is advertised was opened in 1757 by Richard Marchant, 'late of Truly in Edburton', the curriculum including typical subjects for the time such as algebra, arithmetic, writing, navigation and trigonometry.

Cornelius Paine's private school for young gentlemen was opened in 1777, the delights of sea bathing 'with proper attendance' being advertised in 1778. The school survived into the early 1800s and is listed in *Button's Directory* in 1805. Paine prospered and in 1800 served as High Constable of Brighton, then regarded as a prestigious post.[12]

A school run by the Reverend Thomas Hudson and Hugh Owen was opened in Middle Street in 1778 but the partnership was dissolved in 1782. In 1787 the Reverend Mr Mossop took over Hudson's school and renamed it the Grammar School, by which time it was in West Street. Grammar schools were regarded as offering a classical education which was the intention here. Successful local tradesmen such as the Tuppens, Lashmars and the Attrees sent their sons.[13] Mossop offered sea bathing as well an education and charged more if the bathers used a bathing machine. Advertisements of the dates when the school opened and closed for holidays were included in the local newspaper as an opportunity to remind people of its presence. Mossop offered Latin, Greek, French, English, writing, arithmetic, geography and different branches of mathematics. When he died in April 1794, aged 38, his assistant Reverend Briggs ran the school until June 1794, when it was taken on by William Brook and relocated.[14]

Buckoll and Son did better than most, their school for young gentlemen opening in West Street in 1791 and still being open in 1796. In 1794 boarders were charged 16 guineas and parlour boarders 20 guineas a year.

Mr Wilbar's Academy opened in Middle Street in 1789 to accommodate twenty to thirty boys but it seems to have closed within months. Measor and Hunter opened their school at 38 Middle Street in 1791 but ceased advertising in 1792. Mr Michell advertised the Steyne House Academy in 1792. Mr Brooks at 31 West Street opened for only a few weeks, from December 1794 to January 1795. Mr Sanders, in spite of the detail offered in his advertisement, also failed to make his school succeed. Located at 44 West Street, the charges for attending were 12 guineas for boys aged 10 or under, 13 guineas for 11-year-olds, 14 guineas for 12-year-olds and 15 guineas for 15-year-olds; sea bathing was free but use of machines cost an extra six pence.

Girls Boarding Schools

In 1753 Grace, wife of William Matthews, surgeon, advertised her new boarding school at Brighton, where,

> young ladies may be instructed in all manner of needlework, in the modern taste; have the opportunity to drink the waters, and bathe in the sea; also to be taught to write, by a person near at hand, and have a dancing master to attend once a week, if required; in a house beautifully situated, with a pleasant garden, and a delightful view of the sea, from east to west.[15]

There is no evidence that the school succeeded and it may have been a little early; the next attempt was more successful. In 1769 Miss Russell and Miss Rickward opened the first school for young ladies that survived. They charged a guinea for admittance to the school and £16 a year for boarding and schooling, with £2 a year extra for French lessons. Then Mary Rickward ran a school for young ladies by herself, in East Street, for a few years, Mrs Beard having purchased the previous school. Miss Rickward seems then to have been joined by Miss Wayte and to have moved in 1788 to 20 West Street where she was when *Cobby's Directory* was published in 1800. Mrs Beard successfully established her school in 1775 and moved it to Seaford in 1794.

Another school for girls was advertised in 1775 when Miss Smith established herself in West Street, but it failed. Miss Pullen and Miss Widget advertised a school in North Row in 1784 without success and Miss Rowe and Miss Watson do not seem to have opened in 1790. A ladies school opened in German Place in 1791 in a large house with space for parlour boarders but no further advertisements for it appear. Mrs Lay's school for young ladies to the age of eight, who would be boarded for 50 guineas a year, also failed to open. Mrs Lay was a local artist who had a print shop on the Steine to which enquirers about the school were to go.

Dancing lessons were offered by private tutors but occasionally someone tried to open an Academy for Dancing. In 1783 Mr Rawlins charged one guinea for two lessons a week for three months at his Academy at 61 East Street. Many offers of

French tuition appeared in the local papers and many of them were anonymous but Mr Baschat was happy to be identified.

Travelling lecturers were popular in this period and a course of lectures was not unusual. The subjects offered in Brighton were typical. In 1761 Mr Silk lectured about philosophy and in 1776 Mr Pitt's subjects were all scientific, including astronomy and electricity.

17

Religious Buildings
and their Congregations

In 1740 Brighton had a diverse range of chapels but only the parish church of St Nicolas belonged to the Church of England. An estimate of the numbers of worshippers in 1740 indicated that there were 500 families living in Brighton of whom 50 were Presbyterians, three were Anabaptists and six were Quakers. No Catholic families were known.[1] The town's nonconformist leanings may have been stronger than the estimate suggests for the Quakers had their own place of worship.

In the 1750s the town attracted nonconformist and itinerant preachers such as Whitfield, who preached twice at Brighton in September 1760. The number and range of religious buildings had increased considerably by 1820. Visitors such as the Countess of Huntingdon and Mrs Fitzherbert supported some of the new establishments directly.

St Nicolas, the Parish Church

The medieval parish church of St Nicolas remained on the edge of the town until development swept past in the 1840s.[2] In 1740 a report to the Bishop of Chichester claimed that the church was in good repair other than the whitewash on the north chancel which Walter Mose, the lay impropriator responsible for the maintenance of that part of the church, had not repainted. However, the vicarage was in such a poor state that it was supported with props.[3]

The vicar was supported by the income from two livings. This began when William Colbran, the vicar of Brighton from 1705-44, also became the rector of West Blatchington in 1712, when Henry Pelham, John Morley Trevor and Peter Courthope presented him to the living of the parish. He held both until he resigned. To enable his successor Henry Mitchell to hold both livings, they were legally combined by a deed of union dated 1 August 1744. The patronage of the united benefice then alternated between the Bishop of Chichester and the Courthope family. On Mitchell's death the Bishop chose Thomas Hudson as his successor in 1789. When Hudson died in 1804 Courthope selected Robert James Carr, who was still there in 1820.[4]

Henry Mitchell's daughter Ann married M.H. Wagner in 1784 and their union launched the Wagner dynasty, which played a major role in the later religious history of the town. The vicarage was in Nile Street where, during the 1780s, Mitchell ran a young gentleman's academy. Arthur Wellesey attended the school from 1784 to 1785 and, as Duke of Wellington, he later became a well-known visitor.[5]

81 *St Nicolas Church, Brighton.* Engraving by R. Havell, 1824. This shows the external stairs to the upper gallery and its windows and the church as visitors to late Georgian Brighton would have known it. The gallery and stairs were removed when the church was renovated in the 1850s.

By 1780 the congregation at St Nicolas had significantly increased from the fifty or so who attended in 1740. The box pews were arranged in the pattern of a cross with the font at their central point and galleries were added which were entered from outside staircases. This still failed to meet the demand even though the Chapel Royal was built in the town as a chapel of ease.[6] St Nicolas also had free pews, none being provided in the Chapel Royal until after 1803. St Nicolas was virtually rebuilt in 1853-4, the outside staircases being removed.

As the town prospered so the church was embellished. In 1777 a new peal of eight bells was cast by Mr Rudhall of Gloucester at a foundry in Bristol.[7] The new bells attracted ringers from the region and the results of bell-ringing competitions were reported in the newspaper. In 1778 four members of the Horsham Society

of Bell Ringers joined forces with four London men to beat the Bolney team who rang 5,680 changes of Bob Major at Bolney at the end of 1776. The eight men wanted to ring 6,160 Bob Majors at St Nicolas but their first attempt was 'obstructed at the door', which suggests that someone complained.[8] They had already rung 5,264 changes but decided to begin again and achieved their goal. In 1779 the Society of Cumberland Youth from London, Middlesex, Surrey and Sussex rang a complete peal of 11,088 Bob Majors at St Nicolas in 1779 which took six hours and fifty minutes and then they had dinner. The Horsham Society were so pleased with the accomplishment that in 1787 they fixed a plaque to the church to record the names of the ringers and then rang a complete peal of grandsire triple.

The burial ground for St Nicolas was enlarged in 1789. Two more bells were added to the peal in 1818 and the additional burial ground purchased that year was consecrated.[9] The graveyard still contains memorials to residents of Brighton who died during the later 1700s and early 1800s, earlier stones having either been lost or neglected so that they cannot now be read. A Coade Ware stone urn commemorates the singer and actress Anna Maria Crouch who was born in Brighton and worked for most of her life in London. Romney and Lawrence painted her.[10] Sake Deen Mohammed, owner of the Shampooing Baths, is buried in the extension ground to the north of the church.

The Church of England's activities attracted little attention in the local press, few events that are noted being likely to excite news readers. The appointment of Henry Mitchell as the domestic chaplain to Elizabeth, Countess of Rothes in 1774 and the unusually large number of baptisms in March 1784, when the Reverends Mitchell and Hudson baptised 43 children, were noted.

The Chapel Royal

The Reverend Hudson was Mitchell's curate before he succeeded Mitchell in 1789. In 1784 Viscount Montague appointed Hudson as his domestic chaplain when

82 *Dr Syntax Preaching.* Drawn and engraved by T. Rowlandson in 1813. A typical Georgian church interior with the emphasis on the pulpit, not the altar.

he was resident in Brighton and helped him to gain further preferment. Hudson then obtained other church posts, which may have helped him in his funding of the Chapel Royal, which he built in 1793 as a 'chapel of ease'. Such chapels were commercial ventures, the income being the rent from the pews. Hudson paid for the construction of the chapel to the design of 'Mr Saunders'. The building was large by the standards of the day, with 1,000 pew spaces. The simple classical building was a preaching chapel with galleries on all four sides, and the focus of the building was the pulpit and not the altar. Hudson's aim was to recoup the costs and then make a

profitable living by letting the pews either for 99 years at 20 guineas each or for one guinea a year for a large pew on the ground floor seating five to six people. Two services were held on Sunday, at 11a.m. and 3p.m.[11]

Hudson opened the Chapel Royal only during the season and the first service was held in 1795 in the presence of the Prince and Princess of Wales. He found the chapel expensive to run and in 1803 sought a private Act of Parliament which would enable it to become a chapel of ease for the parish and the vault below to be let as a wine store.[12] He needed income to offset the 224 free seats which were a condition of becoming a chapel of ease and he sought to charge the cost of a clerk and other overheads against the pew rents from the remaining pews.[13]

St James's Street Chapel

Thomas Kemp erected the brick-built St James's Street Chapel as a free chapel in 1810.[14] It became a chapel of ease in 1817, which enabled it to charge for some of the pews but it appears to have had problems raising income. By 1822 it could seat 800 and held two Sunday services, at 11 a.m. and 6.30 p.m.[15]

In 1813 Nathaniel Kemp of Ovingdean Hall wrote to Thomas Pelham of Stanmer about the 'free chapel of St James' and outlined a suggestion that the education of poor boys to fit them for sea service should be based there in order to use the building more. The Bishop of Chichester accepted the idea and agreed that 'The Naval Institute for the Instruction of the Poor' should be run as a free school. The Bell system of education was to be used and only 'clean and decent youths' allowed to attend. A governor or a subscriber would recommend them. Kemp invited Pelham to the meeting of the governors and enclosed a handbill advertising the meeting to set up the school under the patronage of the Prince Regent, the Duke of Marlborough, Lord Egremont, the Earl of Chichester and the Bishop of Chichester. The meeting was chaired by Nathaniel Kemp and it agreed that there would be 500 boys. Kemp and Sir Thomas Barnard would open the school and advertisements in the local newspaper would attract support and boys. Kemp wrote to Thomas Pelham, that the proofs of the advertisement were awaiting comment, but Pelham responded with a reproof, saying he was surprised to see his name on a paper published to advertise the school when he was not at the meeting. In spite of further correspondence, the school did not open.[16]

St Mary's Chapel

This was opened as a small, classical chapel of ease at about the same time as St James's. The land was given by the Earl of Egremont, whose town house was to the north of the site. The chapel's site is now under St Mary's Church, Rock Gardens.[17]

The Quakers

The earliest nonconformist chapels were the Union Street (or Elim) Chapel in the old town and the Quakers' Chapel. Union Street Chapel existed in the 17th century and continued to have strong local support in the 18th. In 1822 it was described as 'much altered' and capable of accommodating 800 people.[18]

The Quakers were established in Brighton in the later 17th century. In 1700 they leased for 1,000 years at a peppercorn rent part of a croft which is now within the grounds of the Royal Pavilion and partly under New Road. The site of about an acre stretched from North Street to Church Street.[19] The malt house was converted into a meeting house and part of the land became a cemetery; the rest was to be let or sold to earn income to maintain the meeting house and cemetery. The trustees let it to John Furner, a gardener, in the mid-1700s. The meeting house attracted Quakers from outside the town, and in 1749 Sally Shashall from Hurstpierpoint, who had 'a plentiful fortune', married Elijah Warring, a surgeon from Alton in Hampshire here, and after the ceremony they had an 'elegant entertainment' at the *Old Ship*. In 1808 the Quakers moved to Ship Street and their building is now called the Friends' Meeting House.[20]

The Countess of Huntingdon

New nonconformist movements established themselves in Brighton from the 1750s. John Wesley preached at Rottingdean in 1758 and in 1759 Selina, Countess of Huntingdon (1707-91) invited George Whitfield to preach at Brighton.[21] She organised the building of the first chapel in North Street in 1761 and then had it rebuilt in 1774. In 1770, following a dispute with the Church of England, the countess decided that her chapels should become independent of it. Her sect remained popular and the chapel was enlarged in 1810 and

83 The Friends' Meeting House in Ship Street. The Friends moved to this location in 1808 but the building has been altered since.

1822. In 1822, it accommodated 1,000 people and stood behind a row of shops which helped to pay the costs of the ministry, the chapel and the Sunday school. Weekday and Sunday services were held by 1822.[22] The countess took a keen interest in resorts. She had already founded a chapel in Bath and in July 1769 opened one in Tunbridge Wells, an occasion attended by 20 young people from Brighton.

The Wesleyan Movement

In spite of Wesley's presence in the area in the 1750s, the first Methodist group was not established until the early 1800s. The leaders were Edward Beves, a carpenter from Fareham, and William Mitchel, a carpenter from Northampton who worked with Beves and nine members of the North Yorkshire and the South Gloucestershire Militia. In 1804 the group met to worship in a cottage and invited preachers from the Methodist group in Lewes. Then they rented a loft to the rear of a house in Middle Street, and by 1807 there was enough support in the area to found a Methodist circuit.

The Wesleyan Chapel built in Dorset Place in 1808 cost £1,000 of which £460 was raised by a levy on the circuit's members. By 1822 access to it was from St James's Street. From 1808 there was a minister who lived in George Street. A body called 'The Conference' appointed the ministers and no single named person ran the services. The chapel supporters appear to have been mainly local people, some of whom sent their children to the Sunday school which Beves set up and ran in the gallery of the church. Some 500 people could attend the weekday evening and Sunday services.[23]

Smaller nonconformist Protestant congregations

The Providence Chapel in Church Street (1810), The Particular Baptists' Meeting House in Bond Street, the Huntingdonian in Union Street and the Unitarian Chapel in New Road were other nonconformist places of worship. Theophilus Lindsey of Yorkshire, who could not accept the doctrine of the Holy Trinity and withdrew from the Church of England, founded the Unitarian denomination in 1773. The Unitarian Chapel in New Road was designed by Amon Wilds and modelled on the Temple of Theseus in Athens, and the laying of the foundations in 1819 was noted in *The Times*.[24]

Perhaps the most curious foundation was that of Thomas Kemp, who built the Ship Street Chapel in 1817 for a sect for which he was the minister until 1823. Then he returned to the Church of England and rededicated the chapel to the Church.[25]

The Development of a Catholic mission

The Catholic Relief Acts of 1778 and 1791 gave back to Catholics a greater public role, the second allowing them to build churches again provided they did not have a bell or steeple. There is no evidence of any place of worship for Catholics in Georgian Brighton before the Reverend Philip Wyndham, chaplain to successive Dukes of Norfolk, was mainly responsible for the establishment of a Catholic mission in 1798. The first rector was the Reverend William Barnes, who was succeeded in 1804 by the Reverend Joseph Mouchel. The mission was established in a room in Margaret Street until the Reverend Mouchel decided to find somewhere more central. Castle Square, Prospect Row and North Street did not work, and in 1806-7 money was raised to build a church and presbytery on the east side of High Street. The simple church employed the classical design of the period used by most religious groups. In 1811 the new rector was the Reverend Edward Cullin, a friend of Mrs Fitzherbert. He enlarged the church and it remained in use until the present Catholic church was built in 1855-6 at the junction of Upper St James's Street and Upper Bedford Street.[26]

The Jewish Community and Worship

A Jewish community developed from the 1780s. Emanuel Hyam Cohen emigrated from Bavaria and settled in Brighton in 1782. The first synagogue was in use in Jew Street by 1792 and this, like the next one, was probably a room in a family's house. By 1808 the synagogue was on the south-east side of West Street and approached down Poune's Court, one of the alleys in this area. It was still in West Street in 1822 but then moved to the east side of Devonshire Place, where the first purpose-built synagogue was erected, holding fifty people. For the first time there was a ladies gallery.[27] Emanuel Hyam Cohen ran a boys' school in Artillery Place which he had established by 1800. [28]

A Surfeit of Religious Buildings 1800-1820

Between 1800 and 1820 there were few new foundations of any denomination, and yet during this period the population more than doubled. This suggests the town had too many churches and chapels in 1800 and the population had to catch up with the provision, but in 1815 a commentator in *The Gentleman's Magazine* remarked on the insufficiency of churches dedicated to the Church of England in Brighton compared with Lewes and Chichester. He observed that only one was open although 9,000 people lived in the town,[29] and thought that the town could go Methodist due to the lack of provision. By 1820 the Church of England decided to build another church (rather than a chapel of ease) for Brighton. The construction of St Peter's Church to a gothic design by Charles Barry in the early 1820s was the result.

By 1820 Brighton was a thriving resort which attracted visitors from Europe as well as from the British Isles. More prestigious than Bath, and a major influence on the well-being of a tract of inland Sussex, which prospered by providing services to travellers and foodstuffs, the resort needed to change its image. Alert to the influence of London on the expectations of visitors, Brighton had to respond to the challenge of the large planned estate house. New attractions were also needed to keep the town ahead of the competition. As the 1820s dawned, Kemp Town, Brunswick Town and the Chain Pier are the best-known symbols of the changes taking place. But the houses and other buildings refurbished or built between about 1750 and 1820 still played a major role in housing visitors and residents and meeting their needs. Many still play that same important role today.

Notes

Unless stated otherwise the primary source for this book is *The Sussex Weekly Advertiser*, now widely available in Sussex Libraries on microfilm.

1. Brighton: Fishing Town to Declining Town c.1580-1740, pp.1-11

1. Kent Record Office U269/M44/2.
2. For further information see Chapter 9.
3. Brent, C.E., 'Rural population and employment in Sussex between 1550 and 1640', *SAC* 114 (1976), 33-5.
4. *The Book of the Ancient Customs* (1580) published as Webb, C. and Wilson, A.E., *Elizabethan Brighton: The Ancient Customs of Brighthelmstone* (Brighton: John Beal, 1952).
5. PRO SP16/32 f.90; 18/36 f.116; BL Harleian MS 6828 f.223.
6. PRO SP16/32 ff.50, 90; 18/22 22 June 1649; 18/154 f.103; 18/2 f.67; 18/72 f.15; 18/38 f.112; 29/59 ff.16/18; 29/81 13 June 1673.
7. ESRO BRI Goodwyn's Rental; ESRO SAS/BRI Brighton-Lewes Manor Court Books; ESRO W/A 44/116; [Dunvan, P.], *Ancient and modern history of Lewes and Brighthelmstone* (Lewes: W. Lee, 1795) 474, 485.
8. PRO SP 18/38 f.116.
9. PRO SP 12/60 f.73; 16/361 f.47; 18/123 f.110.
10. PRO E190/Port Books.
11. PRO SP29/273 f.45; 29/61 23 April 1672.
12. PRO SP/29/397/2 10 Oct 1677; 29/241 15 July 1672; 29/395 f.60 26 July 1677; 29/228 6 August 1672.
13. PRO SP16/161/17, 141 f.144; 16/171 f.47; 18/35 f.60-64; 18/52 8 November 1652; 18/35 ff.30-2.
14. PRO SP46/116 f.43; 18/204 11 August 1659.
15. PRO SP29/203 f.52 4 June 1667.
16. ESRO HOW/34/16.
17. Bird, R. (ed.), *Journal of Giles Moore* (Sussex Record Society, 1971), 47.
18. See Chapter 9.
19. Farrant, J.H. and S.P., *Aspects of Brighton 1650-1800* (Brighton: University of Sussex, 1978), 44-55.
20. Brighton Area Library Z7443 S9 STA DUB (the original is now in East Sussex Record Office in ACC 6077) and abstracts from Brighton wills ESRO W/A series.
21. Farrant, J.H., 'Brighton Charity School', *SAC* 122 (1984), 139-46.
22. Farrant, S.P. and J.H., 'Brighton, 1580-1820: from Tudor Town to Regency Resort', *Sussex Archaeological Collections*, 118 (1980), 339; ESRO ACC 3597/3 Views of Frankpledge.
23. ESRO HOW/34/16; ESRO QO/EW9, July 1698. ESRO QO/EW12 April 1704-1708; Dunvan, *op.cit.*, 482-3; ESRO DYK 1121; ESRO ACC 3597/1 and 3.

24. ESRO HOW/34/16 unpaginated.
25. ESRO AMS 5889 Poor Rate account 1744-1761.
26. Farrant, J.H. and S.P., *Brighton Before Dr Russell* (Brighton: University of Sussex, 1976), 2-12; Farrant, J.H. and S.P. (1980), 333.
28. Farrant, S.P. and J.H. (1980), 21-4.

2. Why did Seaside Resorts Emerge?, pp.12-18

1. Ellis, J.M., *The Georgian Town* 1680-1840 (Basingstoke: Palgrave, 2001), 7-46.
2. Langton, J., 'Urban Growth and Economic Change from the late seventeenth century to 1841' in Clark, P., *Cambridge Urban History of Britain* (Cambridge: University Press, 2000), 453-90.
3. Ellis, *op. cit.*, 26.
4. Ellis, J., 'Regional and County Centres 1700-1840' in Clark, P. (2000), 673-704; Borsay, P., 'The landed elite and provincial towns in Britain 1660-1800', *The Georgian Group Journal* Vol.13 (2003), 281-94.
5. Hembry, P., *The English Spa* 1550-1815 (London: Athlone, 1990), 66-78.
6. Rosenheim, J.M., *The emergence of a ruling order: English Landed Society* 1650-1750 (Harlow: Longman, 1998), 215-44.
7. Borsay, P., 'Health and Leisure Resorts 1700-1840' in Clark, P. (2000), 775-804.
8. Summerson, J., *Georgian London* (London: Yale, 2003), 10-21, 49-68; Forsyth, M., *Bath* (London: Yale, 2003), 17-25.
9. Hunter, M., 'The first seaside house?', *The Georgian Group Journal*, Vol.8 (1998), 135-42.
10. Lubbock. J., *The tyranny of taste: the politics of architecture and design in Britain* 1550-1960 (London: Yale, 1995) demonstrates the impact of this taste.
11. Ayton, R., *A voyage around the coast of Britain* (1815); Barrett, J., 'Spas and seaside resorts *c.*1660-1780' in Stevenson, J. et al., *The Rise of the New Urban Society,* Open University Course Reader, 1977, 37-70; Brown, B.J.H., *Weston super Mare and the origins of coastal leisure in the Bristol region* (Weston super Mare Conservation and History Group, 1978); McIntyre, S., 'Towns as health and pleasure resorts; Bath, Scarborough and Weymouth 1700-1875', University PhD thesis, Oxford (1973); Smith, W.J., 'Blackpool, a sketch of its growth 1740-1851', *Transactions Lancashire and Cheshire Antiquarian Society* 69 (1959), 98-101.
12. Whyman, J., *The Early Kentish Seaside* (Gloucester: Alan Sutton, 1985) 160-2.

3. Resort Facilities, pp.19-36

1. Decennial Census.
2. ESRO AMS 6279 sketch map drawn in 1773 by William Green shows erosion along the front as he recalls it.
3. Miele, C., '"The first architect in the world" in Brighton: Robert Adam, Marlborough House, and Mrs Fitzherbert', *SAC* 136 (1998), 149-76. The Duke moved to the north of the Pavilion to Grove House and took the name Marlborough House with him. It returned to the original building after this period.
4. ESRO SAS BRI 57 and 58 Manor Court Book, copyhold transactions.
5. Crawford (1788), 19.
6. Farrant, J.H., 'Dr Richard Russell', *Dictionary of National Biography* (2004) is the most recent study of this astute medical man. Some of the profits of his business was used to buy land near Lewes to augment the estate that his wife inherited; details in ESRO/SAS/GAGE.
7. Bucks RO Hartwell Papers D9/10. E. Poole 23 May 1769 to Sir William Lee.
8. ESRO Hook MSS 23/1/13; Vaisey, D., *The diary of Thomas Turner* (Oxford: University Press, 1984), 212.
9. ESRO Hook MSS 23/1/13; ESRO ACC 2409 Hove Deeds/576, 578.

10. Saluka, A., 'Brighton's medical worthies: a miscellany', *Medicine's Geographic Heritage* 6 (1990), 3-13, offprint in Brighton Local Studies Library. ESRO ACC 2409 Hove deeds/575 and 580 conveyances of land in East Street to Dame Denise Hart of the Palace of St James, Westminster 7 July 1768 and 9 January 1769.

11. *An Essay on Seabathing and internal uses of Sea Water* by Dr Kentish, physician of Brighton. Advertised as just published, *SWA* 7 July 1788 price 1s. 6d. Sold by Mr Crawford and Mr Dulot on the Steine.

12. BL Add MS 33658 f27 27 February 1821. *The Public Advertiser* 10 Oct 1769 cited in Bishop, J.G., *Brighton in Olden Times* 2 ed. (Brighton, 1892), 226.

13. WSRO Add MS 30838 15 June 1771.

14. *The Times* 15 October 1812; Mahomed, S.D., *Shampooing; or, benefits resulting from the use of the Indian Medicated Vapour Bath as introduced into this country by S.D.Mahomed* (Brighton: Creasy, 1822); Roles, J., 'Sake Deen Mahomed's Silver Cup', *Royal Pavilion and Museums Review*, 3 (1990), 1-2, Born *c.*1749 and dying in 1851, his visitor books are in Brighton Local Studies Library; a painting of him in 1809 by Thomas M. Baynes is in Brighton Museum and Art Gallery.

15. Roberts, H.D., *Brighton Parish Register* (Brighton: Brighton Corporation, 1932), 198.

16. BL Add MS 33658 diary in 1821.

17. Crawford, M.A., *A description of Brighton and the adjacent country* (Brighton: Crawford, 1794), 16.

18. Chalklin, C., 'Capital expenditure on buildings for cultural purposes in provincial England 1730-1830', *Business History* 22 (1980), 59-60.

19. Sitwell, O. and Barton, M., *Brighton* (London, 1935), 64.

20. Dale, A., *The History and Architecture of Brighton* (Wakefield, 1972, 512) gives Crunden at the *Castle* and Poor (Poore) at the *Old Ship* in 1766 and 1767 respectively. Crawford (1788)16-17 says Golden [Goulden]. Crawford (1788) 17 Awsiters baths.

21. Correspondence between Mr Crunden and Samuel Shergold in Brighton Local Studies Library SB9 CRU 1777-84.

22. Crawford (1788), 12.

23. ESRO HOW 31/1 1825 onwards hotel leases, HOW 44/15 will of Leah Hicks of *Old Ship*, HOW 9/4 *New Inn*.

24. Bishop (1880), 137-9.

25. Bishop, J.G., *Brighton in Olden Time* (2nd edn, Brighton, 1892), 16; *SWA* 18 February, 3 March 1760; Brent, J.A., 'The Pooles of Chailey and Lewes', *SAC* Vol.114 (1976), 75; ESRO Hook 23/1/13 Building account for my house, 1762-1766; ESRO ACC 2049/578 Edward Poole purchase of land south-west of the Stean. Bishop (1982), 113, *SWA* 11 Oct 1762, 6 June 1774, 9 Nov. 1778, 21 Jan 1793. *SWA* 30 Jan 1769 *SWA* 1759 quoted in Bishop (1892), 29. Bath see Pimlott, 21-48. C. Lane Sayer, *Correspondence of Mr John Collier deceased and his family* Vol. 2 (1907), 316, letter 27 July 1762, letter from Mrs Green.

26. Beckwith, F., 'The eighteenth century proprietary library in England', *Journal of Documentation* (1947-8), 81-98.

27. Bishop (1892), 40. Dale (1972) says Whitfield first preached in 1760 in Brighton on a field behind the White Lion at request of Countess of Huntingdon and returned in 1761. By 26 June 1769 company 'flocking to Brighton'.

28. 'Pony Races at the Theatre Royal, Dublin' in Walker's *Hiberian Magazine*, November 1779. Reproduced in Mackintosh, I., *The Georgian Playhouse* (London: Hayward Gallery & Arts Council, 1975), catalogue of an exhibition of the same names, illustration 308.

29. Brighton Library Local Studies Collection S9LEWT34.

30. Middleton, I., 'Cockfighting in York during the early eighteenth century', *Northern History* 40, No.1 (2003), 129-46.

31. Crawford (1788), 20.

32. Bishop (1892), 107
33. Bishop (1892), 123.
34. The detailed history is in Chapter 5.
35. See Chapter 4 for the purchasing process by the Royal Pavilion.
36. ESRO 2409 Hove Deeds /745 15 June 1795, transfer of lease.
37. Brighton Local Studies Library SB792SIC, Sickelmore Play.
38. Costs, Chalkin (1980), 59 and Bishop (1892) based on *SWA*.
39. Dale, *History of the Theatre Royal*, 6.
40. Mackintosh, I., *The Georgian Playhouse* (London: Hayward Gallery & Arts Council, 1975), section XIII (not paginated); Mackintosh, I., *Pit, Boxes and Gallery: The story of the Theatre Royal at Bury St Edmunds* (London: The National Trust, 1979), 9-17.
41. ESRO AMS 5440/147,148.

4. Brighton's Visitors, pp.37-45
1. Berry, S., 'Stanmer and the Pelham family *c*.1714-1820', *SAC* 142 (2004) due 2005.
2. Bishop, J.G., *Brighton in the Olden Time* (2nd edn, Brighton, 1892), 29.
3. Fawcett, T., *Bath Entertain'd* (Bath: Ruton, 1998), 6-10. Sloman, S., *Gainsborough in Bath* (London: Yale, 2002), Fig. 75 Captain William Wade, painted by Gainsborough, was designed to hang in the Octagon Card Room of the Lower Assembly Rooms, Bath, where it is still on display.
4. BL Add Ms 61680 ff.91.
5. *Diary and letters of Madame D'Arblay*, Wednesday 20 November 1782.
6. Her first visit was in 1776, BL Add Ms 331278 f.47.
7. See Chapter 5 for the Grove's history.
8. Chapter 17 contains the details.
9. *The Times*, 30 August 1797, 3.
10. *The Times*, 3 August 1802, 2d, 10 August 1802, 2b.
11. *The Times*, 15 August 1797, 2c, 31 July 1806, 2e, 10 September 1817, 3c, 16 September 1817, 3a.
12. ESRO BAT 4788 8 February 1891.
13. In Brighton Museum's Local Studies collection.
14. *The Times*, 15 September 1794.
15. The best image of the early Pavilion with Marlborough House and Marlborough Row is Jacob Spornberg's 'Old Steine, Brighton from the North, 1796'; it also shows a small army encampment beside Marlborough House and coaches running down East Street behind the Pavilion and Grove House. The original is in Brighton Museum.
16. *SWA* 29 Oct 1792, ESRO H&C 51/2. Brighton Local Studies Library, Negative BAL S2473. Repton, H., *Designs for the Pavilion at Brighton* (1808).
17. Berry, S., 'Myth and reality in the representation of resorts: Brighton and the emergence of the "Prince and fishing village" myth', *SAC* 140 (2002), 97-112.
18. Foreman, A., *Georgiana, Duchess of Devonshire* (London: Harper Collins,1998), 51.
19. Chapman, C. and Dormer, J., *Elizabeth and Georgiana* (London: John Murray, 2002), 193.
20. Hicks, C., *Improper pursuits: the scandalous life of Lady Di Beauclerk* (London: Macmillan, 2001), 245, 247.
21. ESRO SAS BRI Manor of Brighton-Lewes. First reference to Ralph is 20 April 1756; record of death is 6 August 1760 and son Henry admitted. Daughter Cecilia inherits and sells with husband J.M. Mostyn 26 April 1802.
22. The land was purchased by Brighton Council before 1960 and they held the deeds seen by author. Manor of Brighton-Lewes, also ESRO Add Ms 789-792. Shelley sold it on in 1779 to Robert Makreth of Burlington Gardens, London.
23. ESRO ACC 2409 Hove deeds/575 and 580 conveyances of land in East Street to Dame

Denise Hart of the Palace of St James, Westminster 7 July 1768 and 9 January 1769. Sir William, who was described as a goldsmith of Pall Mall, died in 1766 (see Lincolnshire Archives 2 RED 1/8/19).

24. Lane Sayer, C., *The correspondence of Mr John Collier (deceased) and his family* Vol.2 (1907), 27, 316.

25. Letter in *Brighton Herald* 7 July 1884. Churchill was in Brighton on 9 July 1763.

26. Anon, *Gentleman's Magazine* Vol. 36 (1766), 59-60.

27. Vaisy, D., *The Diary of Thomas Turner* (Oxford: University Press, 1983), 43.

28. Jesse, J.H., *George Selwyn and his contemporaries* Vol. 1 (London: 1882), 262-3.

29. Thomas and Ann Pelham of Stanmer were amongst those with very clear ideas as to who was acceptable as 'company' and who was not, the latter including some very wealthy people.

30. Yorke, P.C., *The diary of John Baker, Barrister of the Middle Temple and Solicitor General of the Leeward Islands* (1931), 216-17.

31. Hannah, H.C., *The Sussex Coast* (London: Unwin, 1912), 188.

32. Lloyd, Mary, *Brighton: a poem* (London, 1809), illustrated and with list of subscribers; Anon, *A Summer at Brighton*, 3 vols, 1807; Trelawney, A., *Characters at Brighton*, 4 vols. 1808. Copies of all held by Sussex Archaeological Society, Lewes. Moriarty, H.M., *Brighton in an uproar*, 2 vols (London, 1811); *Journal of a tour from Brighton to Weymouth in 1816* BL Add Ms 331337. Anon, *The observant pedestrian mounted on a donkey tour to Brighton*, 3 vols. (London: Simpkin and Marshall, 1815).

33. The library of the Sussex Archaeological Society, High Street, Lewes has a collection of early music which includes a bound set of later 18th- and early 19th-century dances, several of which are about Brighton.

34. Philips, P., *A Diary kept on an Excursion to Littlehampton near Arundel and Brighthelmstone in Sussex in 1778 and also to the latter place in 1779*, 2 vols (1780), 51.

35. Wilberforce, S. and R., *The Life of William Wilberforce* Vol. 4 (London: John Murray, 1838), 268.

36. Jackson, Lady (ed.), *The Bath Archives: a further selection from the diaries and letters of Sir George Jackson KCH 1809-1816* Vol.1 (London; Richard Bantley, 1873), 322-6.

37. *Gentleman's Magazine*, November 1812, 442-3.

38. BL Add Ms 31337 f.1, Journey from Brighton, 26 August 1816, handwritten with sketch map.

39. *Gentleman's Magazine* Vol. 58 (1788), 455.

5. The Royal Pavilion, pp.46-62

1. This is a revised version of the article which I published in *SAC* 120 (1982), 171-84 entitled 'The physical development of the Royal Pavilion Estate and its influence on Brighton (East Sussex) 1785-1823'. The Royal Archives were used with the permission of Queen Elizabeth II. The origins of the myth of the founding of Brighton as a resort by George is discussed in Berry, S., 'Myth and reality in the representation of resorts. Brighton and the emergernce of the fishing village myth 1770-1824', *SAC* 140 (2002).

2. ESRO Acc 2049/1007 letter of appointment of Edward Scott (1746-1815), miniature painter, to George IV, issued in London.

3. Slater, T.R., 'Landscape Parks and the form of small towns in Great Britain', *Transactions Institute of British Geographers New Series* 2 (1977), 314-31.

4. Brighton Borough Town Hall Deeds 1604/5 now in ESRO; Royal Archives hereafter RA GEO/33507, 33498; ESRO SAS BRI 115; Foreman (1998), 179; Hibbert, C., *George IV* (1972), 59.

5. ESRO ACC 2409/19 lease 60 years 14 July 1790 J. Ackerson to L. Weltje land in John Hicks enclosure.

6. In the north-west segment of land at Preston Circus. The land was sold for development

and the name used to market it.

7. RA GEO/33518.
8. Richardson, *New Vitruvius Britanicus*, has 'weather tiles made in Hampshire, appearance of beautiful bricks, about colour of Bath Stone'. He also notes that work began in March and was finished in July.
9. Holland was working on Althorp Park in Northamptonshire in 1787 when he was working on the Pavilion and used the same coloured tiles there to reface an Elizabethan house, but these may have been made in Essex and sent to Althorp by boat. Hampshire is the more likely source. (Information from Mr Ron Martin.)
10. Stroud, D., *Henry Holland: his life and architecture* (London, 1966), 88.
11. Pasquin, A., *New Brighton Guide* (London, 1796), 16.
12. RA GEO/33518.
13. ESRO SAS BRI 86 and 129, ESRO ACC 2409 Hove 656 (Flint Collection); Bishop, J.G. (1897), 30.
14. Morley, J., *The Making of the Royal Pavilion* (London: Sotheby, 1984).
15. See Longstaff-Gowan, T., *The London Town Garden 1700-1840* (London: Yale, 2001).
16. Stroud (1966), 89; RA 33557; Parry, J.D. (1833), 92. Lapidge had been an assistant to 'Capability' Brown, Holland's father-in-law.
17. ESRO ACC 8642/2/26/5/12 East Street/Royal Pavilion plan. Roberts, H.D. (1939) lists many of the transactions but does not provide sources or relate them to the map which he dates as 1803 but which is enrolled in Quarter Sessions in 1805 as ESRO QR/E 703; see RA GEO/33602, 33563, 33597 and 33602-33620. ESRO ACC 2409 Hove 656, ESRO BRI 129.
18. Farrant, S. (1983), 208-20.
19. Cobby (1800).
20. Cobby (1800).
21. ESRO ACC 8642/2/26/5/12 East Street/Royal Pavilion plan.
22. ESRO QR/E 703, QO/EW 36. Slater, *op.cit.*, 320.
23. Mordaunt Crook, J., *History of the Kings Works* (1973), 124, 678.
24. ESRO BRI 86, 85, 93.
25. ESRO Hove 665, ESRO BRI 127, Brighton Town Hall Deeds Terrier 1604/1, 5, 6. RA 33578.
26. RA GEO/33602-20, 34210, 33671, 33589, 33599, ESRO SAS BRI 130 131.
27. Repton, H., *Designs for the Royal Pavilion at Brighton by H. Repton with the assistance of his sons* (1808).
28. Repton (1808), vi-viii; Davis, T., *John Nash: The Prince Regent's Architect* (1966), 84.
29. RA GEO/33589, 33599.
30. *Gentleman's Magazine* 78 (1808), 126-7.
31. ESRO QR/E 751, QO/EW42. ESRO DB/B/73/73 rough draft of a report on the several appropriations of roads and public lands which have been made from time to time, to the Pavilion grounds at Brighton.
32. BL Add Ms 32686-992, Add Ms 33112 ff.243-52.
33. ESRO Brighton Town Hall Terrier Deeds 1604. RA GEO/33705, 34031, 34035, 34074, 34118, 33658. ESRO SAS BRI 88.
34. Mordaunt Crook, J. and Port, M.H., *The History of the King's Works 1782-1851* (HMSO, 1973), 49.
35. Davis, T. (1966), 83, 84-6.
36. RA GEO/788-33806, Thomas Attree's Account.
37. RA GEO/33686, 33690, 33734, 33827, 33950, 33976, 34021, 34037. ESRO SAS BRI 101, 132, 114, 124, 92, 105.
38. ESRO ACC 8642/2/26/5/13.
39. ESRO SAS BRI 124.

40. Wood, H., 'Number 8 Marlborough Row: A Royal Love Nest Revisited', *The Royal Pavilion, Libraries and Museums Review* July 2000, 7-11.

41. RA GEO/33923, 33810, 33788-806, 33695, 33621, 33582, 34139, 34158, 34160, 33938. ESRO SAS BRI 102, 103, 104, 106, 107-11, 112a, 112b, 124. ESRO BRI Manor of Brighton-Lewes Court Books, ESRO Land Tax 1780-1820. Total purchase price for the houses £19,320. *SWA* 27 November 1820 remarks on the demolition of three houses and the amount of employment generated by work on the Pavilion.

42. ESRO ACC 8642/13. Land was purchased by compulsory order, 1830 Improvement Act.

43. Wood, H., July 2000, 10-11.

44. Wood, H., 11.

45. ESRO BRI 90. RA GEO/33834.

46. British Library Add Ms 33658, Journal of Rev. J. Skinner.

47. Pevsner, N., *The Buildings of England: London* Vol.1 (Harmondsworth: Penguin, 1973), 570.

48. ESRO Brighton Rate Book, 1814.

6. The Influence of European Wars on Brighton, pp.63-72

1. ESRO AMS 2535. *SWA* 3 August 1781.

2. See chapter 8 for details.

3. ESRO AMS 2535 Lord Sheffield to Lt Col Gage 3 August 1781.

4. The alliance was called 'Armed Neutrality' and a key issue was its refusal to let British ships stop and search for goods destined for America.

5. Hudson, A., 'Volunteer soldiers in Sussex during the Revolutionary and Napoleonic Wars 1793-1815', *SAC* (1984), 165-81.

6. ESRO LCG/3/EW1, 2.

7. Grant, R.C., *The Brighton Garrison 1793-1800* (Brighton: Layman's Publication, no date), 21.

8. *BHH*, 27 May 1807.

9. *BHH*, 27 October 1810.

10. *The Times,* 7 July 1796.

11. ESRO Howlett and Clarke 90/2-3.

12. Attree, H., *Topography of Brighton and Picture of the Roads* (Brighton, 1809), 320.

13. Attree, 320.

14. Margary, I.D., 'Militia in Sussex Camps', *SAC* Vol 107.

15. *The Times*, 22 March 1813, 3d.

16. *The Times*, 10 August 1793, p.2.

17. ESRO QUS/1/EW1 Royal Clarence Lodge of Masons.

18. Grant, R.C., *The Brighton Garrison 1793-1900*, 22.

19. Williams, E., 'Trafalgar in Sussex', *Sussex Local Historian* Vol.4 No. 3 (1982), 110-11.

20. *BHH*, 27 May 1807 auction.

7. Transport Networks, pp.73-85

1. Farrant and Farrant (1976) discusses the town's economy before the 1740s.

2. *The Times*, 10 September 1818 2e.

3. *Ogilby's Britannia*; Company of Parish Clerks of London, quoted in Harper, G., *The Brighton Road* (1902 edn.), 8-11; Fuller, G., 'The development of the roads in Surrey and Sussex', *Transactions Institute of British Geographers* (1953), 37-40.

4. Bishop, J.G. (1892), 229.

5. Bishop, J.G. (1892), 238.

6. ESRO, ACC 8642/40. Robins also suggested that the land would suit a new church and a large corn market, both of which he thought the town needed. He was seeking £500 a year for a lease of the site; the current rental of £350 was too low.

7. See chapter 4 for details.

8. *The Times*, 18 August 1802

8. Accommodating the Visitors, pp.86–96

1. ESRO Howlett and Clarke 8/10, ESRO ACC 2499, SAS BRI ESRO 27, ESRO WA59/490 ESRO Howlett and Clarke 8/10, ESRO Acc 2499, ESRO SAS BRI27, ESRO WAS9/490.
2. *BHH*, 24 January 1807, 2 February 1807.
3. See chapter 3 for the history of the site.
4. PRO B1/72 21 March 1780, with Peregrine Phillips, John Isaac.
5. ESRO SAS Bri 27 Brighton-Lewes Manor Court Book, p.234.
6. ESRO/SAT/N682.
7. ESRO W/A66 f.461 20 October 1791 proved 30 October 1792, Will of Susan Lucas.
8. Cruickshank, D. and Burton, N., *Life in the Georgian City* (London: Viking, 1990) gives an overview of urban lifestyles including accommodation.
9. *BG* 7 June 1821, 99 West Cliff, 6 bedrooms, 4–5 months.
10. ESRO HA 310. Lady Pembroke was there in 1762, Lucy Clinton lived at Chailey.
11. ESRO ACC 8642/25/5/6 Plan of No.6 Marine Parade.
12. *BHH*, 6 September 1820 Marine Parade Lodging Houses.
13. Chapter 4.
14. Bishop, J.G. (1880), 151-2 Bishop notes purchase price was £4,000, subject to mortgage to D. Pitcairn not paid off.
15. Bishop, J.G. (1892), 310; ESRO ACC 8642/2/26/5/5.
16. Bishop, J.G. (1892), 310.
17. Philips, P., *Diary* (1780), 83 notes that the house was built in 1779, new and elegant, and that Mr Dring was about to open a glaziers.
18. ESRO ACC 2049/878 Mrs Dring. The accession also includes the inventory of her grocer's shop.
19. Thanks to Jill Seddon and Lou Taylor.
20. ESRO H&C 66/4 leases 1805-60 Pimlico.
21. ESRO AMS 6153/16/1-20 Warden's Buildings.
22. ESRO AMS 6153/7/35-51.
23. ESRO SWA 14 January 1805.

9. Developing the Suburbs, pp.97-110

1. British Library Add Ms 33127 f.49, f.289, staying in Lewes 1776 due to lack of accommodation in Lewes.
2. Cobby's *Directory* (1800), ESRO Land Tax, Brighton.
3. Ayers, J., *Building The Georgian City* (London: Yale, 1998) explains the building process during the Georgian period in great detail.
4. SWA 21 April 1800, many other references between *c*.1799-1805.
5. *Gentleman's Magazine* Vol. 76 (1806), 163.
6. PRO Bankruptcy Papers B3/523 Bennett.
7. National Archives Bankruptcy C217/68 and 69, Thomas Budgen 1808-1811.
8. National Archives C217/69/2, carriage ledger Budgen 1808-9.
9. *SWA* 26 March 1804. Cairncross, A.K. and Weber, B., 'Fluctuations in building in Great Britain 1785-1849', *Economic History Review*, 2 series IX (1957-7), 283-97.
10. ESRO ACC 6077.
11. ESRO AMS 5575/27/6 day book 1775-76.
12. O'Shea, E.W., 'Mathematical Tiles in Lewes', *Sussex Archaeological Society Newsletter*, No.37 (1982), 290-1.
13. Ellis, J.M., 'Georgian Town Gardens', *History Today* (January, 2000), 38-45; Longstaffe-Gowan, T., *The London Town Garden 1700-1840* (London: Yale, 2001).

14. The calculations in detail are in Farrant (1978), 67-80, which also includes an in-depth explanation of how the manors worked. The previous terrier was surveyed in 1738. ESRO HOW/118/9.
15. Copies of the terrier in book format survive in private ownership and in Brighton Local Studies Library. The map is normally called the Brighton Terrier by Budgen. Various editions have survived.
16. ESRO SAS BRI 83 Brighton 12 June 1785.
17. ESRO Brighton 1814 Rate Book.
18. *B Gazette* 19 January 1826, 'New buildings at Brighton' list compiled by Mr Busby.

10. **The Terraces and Villas of Eastern Brighton, pp.111-22**

1. ESRO Brighton Rate Book 1814.
2. Bishop, J.G. (1890), 13, reproduction of print of 1809, and note that in 1879 the gardens and Neville House nearby were lost to road widening.
3. ESRO Brighton Rate Book 1814.
4. *SWA* 30 January 1804, cliff fall east of Royal Crescent; *BHH*, 3 January 1807 on east side of Brighton, households apprehensive about cliff falls; ESRO SAS N721 Marine House Marine Parade 1812; ESRO SAS N614 New House Marine Parade 1802.
5. *BHH*, 9 Dec.1805 1 Manchester Street. Deeds for 9 Margaret Street, in private ownership when seen assign land to John Bishop carpenter 30 Sept. 1793 – by Tho. Scutt and R.L.Whichelo. N-S 150 foot and e-w 26 feet with carriage road 25 foot wide on east as well as land let by Bishop to Stephen Wood and John Leach on west. Lease from 21 Dec 1791 for 500 years yearly rent £15. Has built on it, bankrupted in 1792 Monkhouse and Hallyar admitted to the land. E Boxall had agreed to buy the third of the houses for £100 from the assignees just mentioned. Land 13.6 from N to S and 26 feet from e to w. Use of road. Residue of the 500 years at apportioned rent. In 1864 after changes of ownership –Thomas Barrowcliffe music teacher and wife. ESRO ACC 2409/563 Conveyance, Margaret St 1803 Marchant 37 foot deep plot.
6. ESRO SAS BRI Brighton-Lewes Manor Court Book for the Sparrow Moiety, 1784 Howell trustees to Stephen Wood, paul piece 7 of six pauls. In 1785, a paul piece 6 of seven pauls in measurement, Richard Tidy licence to lease to S. Wood.
7. ESRO SAS BRI 238 (Manor of Brighton-Rusper), plan of Mr Richard's grounds.
8. According to the *Brighton Herald*, 10 December 1881. The *Brighthelmstone Pacquet* carried an advert for J.D. Richards, proprietor of German Place, on 13 October 1789.
9. ESRO ACC/8642/25/5/3 German Place.
10. ESRO ACC 2049/23,24,33,36,88-90 1815 cites that in 1797 the street was York St in 1815 Camelford. 3 May 1792 deed Mary Ann Richards lease for one year to Tho. Howell builder Lots 4 and 5 of land conveyed to J.D.Richards by T. Kemp on 20/21 Sept 1782.
11. ESRO Hove BRA 1932 Memoranda 4 December 1797 Frances Combs and John Walder.
12. *BHH*, 25 Oct 1806 to be let, 99 yr building leases, Rock House and three lodges in Rock Buildings and three houses in Rock Buildings. *BHH,* 15 Nov 1806; *BHH*, 26 Sept. 1807.
13. ESRO AMS 5278 1789-1844, 4 New Steine. Renting habits: William Roe rented No. 3 in August 1805, 12 in 1806, *Memorandums* 84.
14. ESRO ACC 8642/26/5/10 Plan of the New Steyne. No date, coloured. May be finished plan based sketch. ACC 8642/26/5/15 Garden 73 feet 385. ACC 8642 includes sketch plan of the development.
15. *BHH*, 9 December 1805, unexpired 10-year lease for sale of 6 Marine Parade, suit gents residence also 1 Manchester Street adjoining. *BHH*, 25 April 1807 auction of contents of lodging house, 29 Marine Parade. *SWA* 10 Mar 1800, auction 20 and 21 Marine Parade.

16. *BHH*, 14 Aug 1805 East Laine 5 Furlong and 2 Furlong, Also a list of other land in E Laine.
17. ESRO ACC 7697/12-22, Rock Gardens 1796-1820, Sussex Place 1808-1815.
18. ESRO ACC 2049/32 Edward Street.
19. *BHH*, 6 Sept 1806 auction room and house in St James Street, *BHH*, 3 Jan 1807 2 shops s. side St James Street, *BHH*, 11 Apr 1807, s.side of St James Street 94 years lease, suit fashionable business, faces Dorset Gds.
20. Thomas-Stanford, C., *The Private memorandums of William Roe of Withdean in the County of Sussex* (Brighton, Privately Published, 1928), 37. Roe notes that he rented the house for five weeks on 27 Sept 1793.
21. ESRO ACC 8642/2/26/5/4 ground plan 13 Dorset Gardens.
22. *BHH*, 20 Dec 1806 Dorset Buildings, *BHH*, 1 Nov 1806, *BHH*, 18 Nov 1806, *SWA* 2 Feb 1807 Bankruptcy J. Elam.
23. *BHH*, 6 June 1807.
24. *BHH*, 6 Sept 1806 High St to let, *BHH*, 25 Oct 1806 lodging houses Dorset Gardens. *BHH*, 6 May 1807, 6 Dorset Gardens 2 parlours. *BHH*, 21 Mar 1807 tasteful leasehold 16 Dorset Gardens. 1 Nov. 1806 High St 4 beds. SWA 3 Sept. 1805 High St new built leasehold, 3 beds. *BHH*, 21 Apr. 1807 new house, 3 chambers lease 92 years unexpired, ground rent 2.10 shillings. Cumberland Street Izard main builder ESRO SAS N694 1817.
25. ESRO SAS N669. *The Susan.*
26. Cresy, E., *Report to the General Board of Health on a Preliminary Enquiry into the sewerage, drainage and supply of water and the sanitary condition of the inhabitants of the town of Brighton* (London: Her Majesty's Stationery Office, 1849).
27. *BHH*, 6 March 1820 sale of properties including St James's Street.
28. *BG*, 2 August 1821, eight leasehold tenements on north side of Royal Crescent. Four rooms each and a garden and good supply of water.
29. ESRO AMS 6197/1/6 Rev. Rice correspondence.
30. ESRO ACC 2049/38,41. Plan by Jas. Berry and son, 8 plots, Grafton Street.
31. *BHH*, 6 March 1820 Grafton Street *BG* 1 March 1821.
32. ESRO ACC 2049/658, 1820.
33. *BG*, 1 March 1821.
34. *BG*, 1 March 1821, garden and farmbuildings.
35. *BHH*, 18 April 1807. Richmond Place.
36. WSRO ACC 7600 Egremont Lodge 1736-1825. Owner may have been Sir Thomas Nevill Bart Oxford RO Ruck Keane Papers Vor/XXIV/i/1.
37. WSRO PHA F7/10 Opinion about rates.
38. WSRO PHA 8748.
39. *BHH*, 6 Mar 1820, Egremont Place.

11. The Squares and Villas of West Laine, pp.123-8

1. ESRO AMS 6610/2/1-6, 20 September 1799, lease by T. Kemp to Tho. Hicks stable keeps, Home Furlong, West Laine, 21 years £12 p.a. or option purchase £240.
2. *BHH*, 15 November 1806, 11 April 1807.
3. *SWA* 27 May 1805. Ram's Croft ESRO Adams Ms 102 pp.132-3.
4. ESRO ADA 54 Manor of Erlyes 20 April 1686 half-acre adjacent to the *George Inn* which in due course becomes Hilton's.
5. Cresy, E., *Report to the General Board of Health on a Preliminary Enquiry into the sewerage, drainage and supply of water and the sanitary condition of the inhabitants of the town of Brighton* (London: Her Majesty's Stationery Office, 1849), 11 Great Russell Street. ESRO Hove 824, 825, 435, *BG*, 8 Mar. 1821 Great Russell Street.
6. ESRO A69/649 January 1806. ESRO Howlett and Clarke Artillery Place, ESRO Add

Ms 2268. ESRO SAS/HB428, ESRO SAS HB 428, ESRO ACC 2409/664, 1809, ESRO SASN576, ESRO HAL BRA 568, *BHH* 6 December 1806.

7. ESRO ACC 26/5/11 Cannon Place.
8. BL Add Ms 33658, The Diary of Reverend Skinner, f.37.
9. *BHH*, 5 August 1805.
10. *BHH*, 22 November 1806 'An excellent plan for a superb pile of buildings which is about to be effected. Twenty houses, uniform scale, plan to be sent to principal London coffee house and library here [in Brighton]. West of Belle Vue.' ESRO Acc 2049 11 Artillery Place 24 April 1809. ESRO SAS-ACC5054/2, Regency Squ 1810. ESRO HOW21/1-2 Grenville Squ.
11. ESRO ACC 2409/30 Montpellier Terrace, 1809. ESRO SAS N704-749 Clarence Place. ESRO AMS 6545 Blucher Place. ESRO DB/A1/160 and ACC 7941/14.
12. Brighton Local Studies Library SB3521.1B76, pp. 2-6. This manuscript rate book was to be transferred to ESRO in 2004.
13. ESRO SAS BRI 18, 21 November 1794, 10 August 1818, 21 December 1819.

12. Hilly and North Laines, pp.129-35

1. *BHH*, 20 June 1807.
2. ESRO BRI Manor of Brighton Atlingworth from 24 December 1790-29 May 1803.
3. ESRO Hove 463 King St conveyance 29 December 1788.
4. Brighton Library, Brighton Manor Court Book (Friend moiety) land sold by John Paine to Henry Stiles, house carpenter 18 August 1770. Stiles then raised money on mortgage. On 27 March 1782 Samuel Shergold bought six stables and coach houses from Stiles' creditors. John Paine also sold land to Samuel Paine a bricklayer, to John May a boat builder and John Reeder a carpenter and on this land, Nos.8-11 North Row being built or built before 1774.
5. ESRO SAS N612 1801, Prospect Place.
6. ESRO SAS HA 719 1801, Church Street racing stables on south side.
7. *SWA* 18 February 1805, Furner's Garden. ESRO H&C 32/4-8, Kensington Place.
8. ESRO SAS BRI 29 May 1802, 7 Nov. 1806.
9. ESRO SAS BRI 213-234. ESRO ACC 6065, Candle Factory.
10. ESRO SAS HC 738-74 Bread Street, 1809 and other sheets.
11. ESRO H&C 88/2 Oxford Place from 1807. *BHH*, 14 February 1807 Land in Oxford Place 15 feet wide 42 feet deep.
12. ESRO AMS 6153/16/1-20, York Place, 2-5 as then numbered. ESRO ACC 8642/2/26/5/14 York Place/Trafalgar Street May 1822.
13. ESRO BRI Manor of Brighton Atlingworth, 16 August 1818 sale of land and cow houses. Also the stables belonging to Marlborough House (on the Steine) sold by the Duke to W.G. Hamilton 16 March 1792 and on to Richard Russell (butcher) 29 May 1803 who sold it on for building. This manor court records other butchers buying plots for stock and selling them on at a later date, e.g. Henry Tuppen on 11 December 1809.
14. *Baxter's Directory* 1822.
15. *BHH*, 14 February 1807.
16. *BHH*, 10 June 1805. *BHH*, 21 November 1807. *BHH*, 21 March 1807. *BHH*, 21 Nov 1807. ESRO Add Ms 4106, terrier. ESRO Add Ms 4107. ESRO SAS Bri 22-40, Manor Court Book, Brighton Atlingworth, 26 August 1806-26 August 1808 and sales on to 1818.
17. ESRO ACC 8642/2/26/5/2, ESRO BRI 22-40 Brighton Atlingworth 7 January 1812 and 31 July 1813. ESRO HAL 565 and 566 from 1808. ESRO R/C/4/448 and 449 include Richmond Terrace and Villa.
18. ESRO SAS BRI 27 p. 155, 30 July 1798, 26 August 1806, enfranchised 24 June 1807, 2 August 1819, 3 August 1819, 4 November 1820, 19 September 1820. ESRO Hove

BRA 1544 3-14 Waterloo Place.

19. Hanover Terrace stands in Islingwood Furlong, Hilly Laine. From the 1760s the land was part of the Sparrow share of the manor and the conveyances are in the Sparrow court books ESRO SAS BRI, and see also ESRO SAS E162 which shows that Philip Mighell sold some of the land to William Brooker in 1822 for £1100. Charles Burchett then bought some of the land from Brooker using mortgages, see ESRO SAS E162 for the citation of the sale. The rest was sold to Brooker by Benjamin Scutt in 1810 and ESRO SAS E156 covers that.

20. ESRO SAS BRI 43. ESRO AMS 6356 77. ESRO HAL BRA 1517 29/30 September 1815.

21. ESRO ACC 8642/2 Plan.

22. ESRO SAS BRI Brighton Manor Court Book (Sparrow Moiety) 1 August 1808.

23. ESRO ACC 8642/2/26/5/9.

24. ESRO SAT N670. ESRO SAT N704, N749, N808.

25. Carlton Street: BHH 10 June 1805. BHH 26 Sept 1807. SWA 26 Sept 1807. SWA 7 July 1788 N. Row. SWA 22 Oct 1804. BHH 1 Nov.1806. Preston Manor Stanford ES/AX/38. Chesterfield Street: ESRO SAS BRI 27, sales developed from c.1815.

26. ESRO SAS N 640 14 February 1806, ESRO SAS BRI 27, Land on west side held from Manor of Brighton Atlingworth.

27. Brighton Local Studies library, Manor of Brighton Court Book (Friend Moiety) records the transactions. Hicks obtained a licence to let to Paine in the 1790s.

28. ESRO SAS BRI Brighton Atlingworth Manor Court 2nd Furlong Hilly Laine, and transactions 1809. 22 January 1819, 27 January 1819, 18 May 1819, 17 September 1819.

29. ESRO SAS BRI Brighton Atlingworth Manor Court Books transaction records show a mixture of chair makers, gents, miller, widow etc as lenders and as buyers.

30. ESRO SAS BRI 27 Manor Court Book p.269 plan, p.264 a plan 1820.

31. ESRO SAS BRI 26 10 February 1807, 6 April 1808, 28 September 1808, 30 November 1809, 5 January 1816, 26 July 1820.

32. ESRO SAS BRI 26 Manor Court Book 10 November 1815, Robert Mott 29 June 1815, 8 August 1816, 19 May 1817, 10 July 1817, 6 January 1816, 2 June 1818.

13. Population and Employment, pp.136-52

1. Law, C.M., 'Some notes on the population of England and Wales in the eighteenth century', *Local Historian* 10 (1972). Huzel, J., 'Population change in an East Sussex town; Lewes 1660-1800', *Sussex Industrial History* 3 (Winter 1971/72), 2-4.

2. *Cobby's* and *Baxter's Directories*.

3. Farrant, 1978, 16-24.

4. *Bailey's British Directory*, London, 1784. Brighton section.

5. *The Times*, 25 October 1819, p.3 col.b.

6. Sussex Record Society, *Sussex Apprentices and Masters* 1710-1752 Vol.28 (1924). ESRO/SAS C793 apprenticeship 1762.

7. Thomas Hannington was baptised in 1784 at St Mary Haura in Shoreham (information from Miss I Winthrope. Hannington advertises the shop in North Street from 1800 in the *SWA*. On 1 August 1808 he advertises the opening of no.3 North Street and by 1814 the family had purchased no.4; it is listed in the Town Rate Book for that year.

8. Cobby, ESRO QUS/1/EW1 List of members of masons' lodges. *Baxter's Brighton Directory* 1822.

9. Wilde, P., 'The use of business directories in comparing the industrial structure of towns', *Local Historian* Vol. 12 (1976), 152-6. Duggan, E.P., 'Industrialisation and the study of urban business communities: research problems, sources and techniques', *Local Historian* vol.11 (1975), 457-65.

10. *Cobby's Directory* (1800) North Street.

11. ESRO ACC 8642 plan, North Street. Detached shops e.g. *SWA* 11 Apr. 1796.
12. PRO B3/936 G&T Curme Drapers 7 March – 14 April 1818.
13. PRO B3/3974.
14. *Baxter* 1822, 24.
15. *Baxter* 1822, 1824.
16. Economic and Social Research Council Reference HR 4804. The Royal Exchange Insurance List 1775-87. The Sun Fire Office List.
17. Horsham Museum 357.1 Tripartite Indenture 30 April 1793.
18. Horsham Museum 357.4 undated notice. ESRO/SAS/G34/127, 1793.
19. Horsham Museum 357.1 Agreement.
20. Hill, A.F., *Barclay's Bank, North Street Brighton: a history* (Brighton, 1988), 11-13.
21. Hill, A.F. (1988), 13, 15.
22. ESRO Howlett and Clarke,
23. The practice became Stevens Son and Pope. Thanks to Mr Henry Smith for this.
24. Walker, W., *Attree and Kent: 221 years of Brighton History* (Lewes: East Sussex Record Office, 2001) fact sheet.
25. Dale, A., *Brighton Town and Brighton People* (Chichester: Phillimore, 1976) covers this.
26. ESRO W/A66 f.35. Will of Robert Davis, proved 7 May 1790.
27. ESRO Land Tax: Brighton 1780-1820.
28. ESRO Howlett and Clarke 51/4 from 1809. ESRO Brighton Deeds Terrier 25 November 1929. Conveyance of West Street Brewery. All conveyed to County Borough of Brighton in 1920/29.
29. ESRO Brighton-Lewes Manor Court Book 20 August 1656.
30. Crawford (1788), 26-7.
31. Fencibles were voluntary defence brigades.
32. ESRO SAS BRI 83 Manor of Brighton, 12 June 1789.
33. ESRO LCG/3/EW2 1801 Return.
34. The relocation of the post mill from Belle Vue field was painted. The picture is in Preston Manor, Brighton, and owned by the City of Brighton and Hove.
35. ESRO Brighton Rate Book 1814.
36. ESRO HAL 878.
37. ESRO HAL 879.
38. ESRO HAL 880.

14. Local Government, pp.153-63

1. Borsay, P., *The English Urban Renaissance* 1660-1770 (Oxford: Clarendon, 1989)
2. ESRO AMS 5889 Brighton Overseers Accounts 1744-61.
3. ESRO HOW 34/17-19 includes the remaining vestry books to 1826.
4. ESRO PAR 255/12/1.
5. ESRO DB/B/58/2.
6. Erredge, J.A. (1862), 183, diarist in 1778.
7. Brighton Local Studies Library SB9 B76 Stock ref 34693, Newspaper cuttings.
8. ESRO DB/B/58/22. *BHH* 28 February 1807.
9. *Improvement Act* 1810, schedule 99-108.
10. *The Times*, 19 August 1818, gas lighting. ESRO QDP/30/2 plan of intended waterworks, not Commissioners.
11. ESRO Brighton Rate Book 1814. Brighton Local Studies Library SB 352.1.B76 1791 town rate book.
12. Brighton Reference Library, Jury List.
13. ESRO AMS 6077 Norris Papers Billheads 1, 2, 3, 7.
14. King, S., *Poverty and Welfare in England* 1700-1850: *a regional perspective* (Manchester: University Press, 2000), 18-47.

15. ESRO AMS 5889 Brighton Overseers Accounts 1744-61.
16. *The Times*, 23 August 1816 2e.
17. ESRO Land Tax.
18. ESRO PAR 255/12/1.
19. *SWA* 15 Apr. 1798, Pelham's advertisement.
20. *The Times*, 8 February 1819 2d.
21. Musgrave, C., *The Crown and the Ship and the Queen of Watering Places* (Brighton: Old Ship Inn, 1953), 16.
22. Dale, *Brighton Town and Brighton People*.
23. ESRO PAR 255/12/1 2 February 1791.
24. ESRO PAR 255/12/1 20 February 1797.
25. ESRO AMS 5889 4 May 1744.
26. Burchall, M., *A Calendar of settlement and removal orders from the Sussex Quarter Sessions Rolls 1740-1770* (Brighton, 1973-74).
27. Bishop (1895), 58-60.
28. ESRO PAR 255/12/1.
29. ESRO Howlett and Clarke 30/1-28.
30. ESRO Hove 11 letter 27 May 1761.
31. Crawford (1788), 32. ESRO HOW 34/16 Vestry Minute Book.
32. ESRO PAR 255/12/1.
33. *Baxter's Strangers' Guide and Brighton Directory* (1822), lv.
34. ESRO HB/59/2.
35. *Baxter's* (1822), liii.
36. *The Times*, 3 April 1820. The excise men stopped the coach of an unidentified but influential and wealthy person when they heard of smuggled goods on it. The coachman had hidden barrels of 'Hollands' on the coach and the footman reported it. Both were sacked. The coach's owner was fined £500.

15. Keeping the Peace, pp.164-9

1. Information is drawn mainly from the *Sussex Weekly Advertiser*, which began in 1747.
2. ESRO ACC 3597/3.
3. Riots mentioned by *The Times* on 10, 12 and 18 November 1817, pages 3c, 3e, 3d.
4. ESRO AMS 14 August 1754.
5. ESRO Brighton Magistrates' Clerks record of cases 4 April 1816-12 November 1827 survives.
6. *The Times*, 7 September 1818 3e.
7. Private Collection, photocopy deposited with ESRO, not yet classified.
8. ESRO, QDE Quarter Sessions Records 13 March 1797.
9. ESRO, QDE Quarter Sessions Records selection from 1791-9.
10. ESRO, QDE Quarter sessions 19 July 1799 at Lewes.
11. ESRO, QDE Quarter Sessions 20 June 1791 and 9 October 1793.
12. Teignmouth, Lord and Harper, C.G., *The Smugglers* (London: Palmer, 1923), 210.
13. Quoted in Page, W. (ed.), *Victoria History of the County of Sussex* Vol.2 (1907), 203.

16. Education, pp.170-4

1. Langford, P., *A Polite and Commercial People* (Oxford; University Press, 1992) is one of the clearest books on this issue. Chapters 3 and 4 include middle class and charity schooling in their wider context.
2. ESRO AMS 6153/1/1-36.
3. Caffyn, J., *Sussex Schools in the Eighteenth Century* (Lewes: Sussex Record Society, 1998), 56-8.
4. ESRO/AMS 5912 Minutes of Grimmett's Charity 1801-1977.
5. Caffyn, J., *op. cit.*, 58. Haffenden, G., *The Middle Street School, Brighton* (Brighton: Beal, c.1905).

6. Brighton Local Studies Collection SB374 Union Street Charity Schools. Goff also left money for a school in Herefordshire. He owned 27 houses in Bond Street, Jew Street and King Street. The land was sold to him by Thomas Kemp in 1788.
7. Haffenden, *op. cit.*, 3-7.
8. Haffenden, *op. cit.*, 16.
9. Haffenden, *op. cit.*, 23-32 which also describes the teaching methods in *c*.1817-20.
10. Caffyn, J., *op. cit.*, 64.
11. Caffyn, J., *op. cit.*, 67.
12. Caffyn, J., *op. cit.*, 60.
13. Bishop, J.G. (1880), 325.
14. Caffyn, J., *op. cit.*, 64.
15. BAL 34693 SB9 B76 newspaper cuttings.

17. Religious Buildings and their Congregations, pp.175-82

1. WSRO, Ep I/26/3.
2. ESRO PAR 225.
3. WSRO, Ep I/26/3.
4. Bentham Stevens, F., 'The benefice of Brighton with West Blatchington', *Sussex Notes and Queries*, Vol.VIII (1940), p.71.
5. Dale (1989), 18-19.
6. WSRO EpII/41/12 Brighton and West Blatchington. EpVI/56/12 Brighton Rectory 1727-1799. Dale (1989), 2-6.
7. *Baxter's* (1822), xlv-vii.
8. Thanks to Mrs S. Capo-Bianco for the reference to Wratten, C., *Change Ringing: the history of an English Art* (London: Central Council of Bellringers, no date) 96.
9. *Baxter* (1822), xlv-xlvii.
10. *Baxter* (1822), xlv-xlvii.
11. Dale (1989), 14.
12. *Baxter* (1822), xlviii.
13. WSRO Petworth House Archives Ms 10,600.
14. Dale (1989), 23-5.
15. ESRO SAS N830, N834.
16. *Baxter* (1822), xlix.
17. BL Add Ms 33112 ff.261-8.
18. ESRO/SAS/N727-N738. ESRO Add Ms 3420 c1803.
19. *Baxter* (1822), xlix.
20. Deeds of land for the Royal Pavilion held by Brighton Council.
21. Bishop, J.G. (1892), 333, citing the *SWA* 18 September 1749. Lucas, L.P., 'Some notes on early Quakers', *SAC* LV (1912), 74-6; *Baxter* (1822), li.
22. Brighton Local Studies Library SB287.GRI. Griffin, E.W., *A pilgrim people: the story of Methodism in Brighton, Hove and district* 1807-1957; Bishop, J.G. (1892), 40 says Whitfield preached in 1760 and Dale (1972) says 1760 and 1761.
23. *Baxter* (1822), l.
24. Griffin, 11-13; ESRO, SAS N830, 834; *Baxter* (1822), l.
25. 'Brighton Unitarian Church' (undated leaflet, *c*.2001). ESRO Acc 6121 Union Street Congregational Church 1818-1954. Anon, *Providence Chapel Church Street, Brighton* 1805-1955 (Brighton: The Chapel, no date).
26. Dale, A. (1989), 186-7.
27. Dale, A. (1989), 192; *Baxter* (1822), lii.
28. Spector, D., 'Jewry in Brighton', *Sussex Genealogist and Local Historian* Vol.3 No. 3 (undated), 83.
29. *The Gentleman's Magazine*, Vol 85 (Aug, 1815) 145-6.

Bibliography

Attree, H., *Topography of Brighton and Picture of the Roads*, Brighton, 1809.
Baxter's Stranger in Town and Brighthelmstone Directory, 1824.

BG   *Brighton Guardian*
BHH   *Brighton and Hove Herald*
BL   British Library
Cobby   *Cobby's Brighthelmstone Directory*, 1800
ESRO   East Sussex Record Office
NA   The National Archives (at Kew)
PRO   Public Record Office – now The National Archives
SWA   *Sussex Weekly Advertiser*
WSRO   West Sussex Record Office

Journals

SAC   Sussex Archaeological Collections

Secondary Sources

An Act for Paving Lighting and Cleansing the Streets, Lanes and Places within the town of Brighthelmstone, London: 1773
Aldrich, M. (ed.), *The Craces; Royal Decorators Brighton*, Brighton: The Royal Pavilion and Art Gallery and Museums, 1990
Attree, H., *Topography of Brighton and Picture of the Roads,* Brighton, 1809
Austen, J., *Sanditon*, 1817
Ayers, J., *Building The Georgian City*, London: Yale, 1998
Barton, M., *Tunbridge Wells*, London: Faber and Faber, 1957
Barton, M. and Sitwell, O., *Brighton*, London: Faber and Faber, 1938
Baxter's Stranger in Town and Brighthelmstone Directory, 1824
Bishop, J.G., *A Peep into the Past: Brighton in the Olden Time*, Brighton, 1880
Bishop, J.G., *A Peep into the Past: Brighton in the Olden Time*, Brighton, 2nd edn. 1892
Bishop, J.G., *The Royal Pavilion*, Brighton, 1897
Berry, Sue, 'Pleasure gardens in Georgian and Regency seaside resorts: Brighton 1756-1840', *Garden History*, 28 (2) 2000, 222-300
Berry, Sue, 'Myth and Reality in the representation of resorts. Brighton and the emergence of the "Prince and the fishing village" myth 1770-1824', *SAC* 140 (2002)
Berry, Sue, 'Stanmer House and the Pelham family *c*.1710-1810', *SAC* 142 (2004)
Borsay, P., *The English Urban Renaissance*, Oxford: University Press, 1989
Brewer, J., *The Pleasures of the Imagination; English Culture in the Eighteenth Century*, London:

Harper Collins, 1997

Burchall, M.J., *Brighton Presbyterian Registers* 1700-1837, Sussex: Sussex Family History Group, 1979

Carey, G.S., *A Rural Ramble: To which is annexed a Poetical Tagg, or Brighthelmstone Guide*, London, 1777

Carey, G.S., *The Balnea*, London, 1801

Chalklin, C., *The Provincial Towns of Georgian England* 1740-1820, London: Edward Arnold, 1974

Channon, J., 'Teignmouth as a resort before the First World War', *Maritime South West* No.4 (1987/8), 28-36

Chapman, J., *The Common lands of Portsea Island*, Portsmouth: City Council, 1978

Clark, P., *The English Alehouse: a social history* 1200-1830, London: Longman, 1983

Clark, P. (ed.), *The Cambridge Urban History of Britain* 1540-1840, Cambridge: University Press, 2000

Corbin, A., *The Lure of the Sea*, London: Polity, 1994

Crawford, A., *A description of Brighthelmstone*, Brighton, 1788

Cruickshank, D. and Burton, N., *Life in the Georgian City*, London: Viking, 1990

Dale, A., *Fashionable Brighton*, 2nd edn., Newcastle: Oriel Press, 1967

Dale, A., *The History and Architecture of Brighton*, Wakefield: SR, 1972

Dale, A., *Brighton Town and Brighton People*, Chichester: Phillimore, 1976

Dale, A., *The Theatre Royal Brighton*, Stocksfield: Oriel, 1980

Dale, A., *Brighton's Churches*, London: Routledge, 1989

Daniels, S., *Humphry Repton*, London: Yale, 1999

Dunvan, P., *Lees' History of Brighton*, Lewes, 1795

Ellis, J., *The Georgian Town* 1680-1840, London: Palgrave, 2001

Erredge, J.A., *History of Brighthelmstone*, Brighton, 1862

Farrant, J.H. and S.P., *Brighton before Dr Russell*, Brighton: University of Sussex, 1976

Farrant, J.H. and S.P., *Aspects of Brighton* 1650-1800, Brighton: University of Sussex, 1978

Farrant, J.H. and S.P., 'Brighton, 1580-1820: from Tudor Town to Regency Resort', *Sussex Archaeological Collections*, 118 (1980), 331-50

Farrant, S., 'The early growth of the seaside towns *c*.1750-1840' in The Geography Editorial Committee (eds.), *Sussex Environment Landscape and Society*, Gloucester: Sutton (1983), 208-20

Farrant, S., 'The physical development of the Royal Pavilion Estate and its influence on Brighton (E. Sussex) 1785-1823', *SAC* 120 (1982), 171-84

Fisher, S., *Recreation and the Sea*, Exeter: University Press, 1997

Ford, J. & J., *Images of Brighton*, Richmond: St Helena, 1991

Gilpin, Rev. William, *Observations on the coasts of Hampshire, Sussex and Kent made in the summer of* 1774, London 1804

Grose, F., *The Antiquities of England: Sussex*, published *c*.1784-87

Guillery, P., *The small house in eighteenth century London*, London: Yale, 2004

Hembry, P., *The English Spa* 1560-1815, London: Athlone, 1990

Hudson. A., 'Volunteer soldiers in Sussex during the Revolutionary and Napoleonic Wars 1793-1815', *SAC* 122 (1984), 165-82

Jackson-Stops, G. (ed.), *John Nash – Views of the Royal Pavilion*, Brighton: Pavilion Press, 1991

Jesse, J.H., *George Selwyn and his contemporaries*, London: 1843

Longstaffe-Gowan, T., *The London Town Garden* 1700-1840, London: Yale, 2001

Lubbock, J., *The tyranny of taste c*.1550-1960, London: Yale, 1995

Mahomed, Sake Deen, *Shampooing; or benefits resulting from the use of the Indian Vapour Bath, Brighton*, Brighton, 1822

Miele, C., 'The "First architect in the World" in Brighton: Robert Adam, Marlborough

House and Mrs Fitzherbert', *SAC* 136 (1998) 149-75

Morley, J., *The making of the Royal Pavilion*, London: Sotheby, 1984

Neale, R.S., *Bath; a social history 1680-1840*, London: Routledge Kegan and Paul, 1981

Nichols, J., *Literary anecdotes of the eighteenth century*, 1812

Parry, J.D., *The Coast of Sussex*, 1833

Pimlott, J.A.R., *The Englishman's holiday*, London: Faber & Faber, 1947

Porter, H.C., *The history of the theatres of Brighton*, Brighton, undated *c.*1890

Relhan, A., *A short history of Brighthelmston* ... 1761, reissued 1829

Repton, H., *Designs for the Royal Pavilion*, 1808

Roberts, H.D., *Brighton Parish Register*, Brighton: Corporation, 1932

Roberts, H.D., *History of the Royal Pavilion*, Brighton: Museums and Art Gallery, 1939

Rodger, N.A.M., *The command of the Ocean: a naval history of Britain, 1649-1815*, London: Penguin, 2004

Russell, R., *Dessertatis de Tabe Glandulari et de Usu Aquae Marinae in Morbis Glandularum*, Oxford: 1750

Russell, R., *A Dissertation on the Use of Sea-Water in the Diseases of the Glands*, translated from the Latin ... by an Eminent Physician, 1752

Russell, R., *The Oeconomy of Nature in acute and chronical diseases of the Gland*, Oxford: 1755

Rutherford, J., *A Prince's Passion: the life of the Royal Pavilion*, Brighton: City Council, 2003

Sicklemore, R., *History of Brighton*, Brighton, 1821

Slack, P. and Clark, P., *English Towns in Transition*, Oxford: University Press, 1976

Smollett, T., *The Expedition of Humphrey Clinker*, London: Walker, 1808 edn.

Thick, M., *The Neat House Gardens*, Totnes: Prospect Books, 1998

Thomas-Stanford, C., *The private memorandums of William Roe of Withdean in the County of Sussex*, Brighton: privately published 1928

Whyman, J., *The early Kentish seaside*, Gloucester: Sutton, 1985

Williams, J. [Anthony Pasquin], *The New Brighton Guide*, London, 1796

Worsley, G. and Musson, J., 'The origins of the seaside idyll', *Country Life*, summer 2003 issue: Beach Life Supplement (2003), 14-18

Wright, C., *The Brighton Ambulator*, Brighton, 1818

Index

Abergavennys, 39, 66
accommodation for visitors: 11, 19, 21, 29, 86-96; beds available, 97; pressure on, 97; *see also* boarding houses, inns, lodging houses, lodgings
Ackerson, Thomas, John, 105
Act of Settlement 1601, 159
Acts of Parliament: 1773, 154,169; 1803, 52; 1810, 155
Adam, Robert, 21
Adur, River, 4
agriculture, 150-1
Air Street, 88
Albion Place, 132
alcohol and crime, 166-7
Algiers, 5
Almshouses: Howells 119; Percy and Wagner, 161
Alton (Hampshire), 180
Amelia, Princess, 64
American War of Independence, 69
Anabaptists, 175
Anglo-Dutch Wars, 63
apologies, public, 75, 166
apothecaries, 161
apprentices, 159
Army, 85
artillery, dangers of, 64
Artillery Place, 68, 96, 124, 182
artists, 140
Arundel, 52, 75, 78
Ascham [Asham] (near Lewes), 82
Ashburnham, Mrs Charles, 43
assemblies: 27; decline of, 58
assembly rooms, 26, 28, 59
Atlingworth Street, 121
Attree: Henry, 74; Thomas, 52, 58, 84; William, 142
Attree and Kent, 143
Auctioneers, 29, 89, 98, 112, 143
Austen, Jane, 16, 18
Awsiter, Dr, 25, 27; *see also* baths

Bachelor (Batchelor): John, 71; coaches, 75
Baddeley, Mrs Sophia, 30
Bailey, Mr, 30, 32, 53
Baker, John, 43, 135
Baker's Library, 29
Baley, Abraham, 90, 91
Balls, 27, 36, 37
bankrupt, 89, 100, 141

Banks: 142; bankers' surnames, 142
Baptist Chapel, 181
barley, 5
Barnard: J., 34; Sir Thomas, 180
Barnes, Rev. William, 182
Barony of Lewes, 9
barracks, 67-71, 100
Barry, Edwin, 85
Barrymore, Lord, 167
Barthelemon, 39
Bartholomews, 158
Bartlett, Susanna, 89
Bath, 13, 14, 25, 32, 37, 43, 44, 75, 78, 98, 142
bathers, 63
bathing in the sea, 16-17, 22-3, 26
bathing machines, 11, 16, 21, 22, 23, 36, 38
Baths: 32; Awsiters, 25; Mahomed's, 25; shares in, 28
Batteries: East, 64, 68; Elizabethan, 63; West, 68, 124
Battle of Worcester, 6
Baulcomb, John, 89, 154
Baysford, Mr, 43
beach: access to, 23; erosion of, 4
Beach: George, 157; charity, 177
Beachy Head, 74
Beacon Hill, 151
Beard, Thomas, 151
Beau Nash, 37
Beauclerk, Di, 41
Bedford Square, 103, 126, 127
Bedford Street, 111
Belle Vue, 124, 125, 128
bell ringing, 176-7
Bennett, Bejamin, 100
Best, George (shepherd), 158
Beves, Edward, 181
Bicknell (Prince's solicitor), 54, 56
billiards, 28-9
birth rate, 11
Bishop: Thomas, 5; fisherman, 148
Black Hole, the, 164, 166
Blackburn, 136
Black Lion Inn, 74, 148
Black Lion Street, 1, 7, 8, 75, 86, 158, 161
blacksmiths, 60
Blacksmiths Arms Inn, 87
Blatchington, East, 72
block house, 6, 9, 63, 64